D1030190

A Goodly Heritage

PIERREPONT B. NOYES

A Goodly Heritage

RINEHART & COMPANY, INC. NEW YORK TORONTO

Grateful acknowledgment is made to the following for permission to reprint material controlled by them:

Executors for the Estate of the late H. G. Wells, London, England, for permission to reprint brief extracts from THE FUTURE OF AMERICA, by H. G. Wells; and

The Public Trustee and The Society of Authors, London, England, for permission to reprint a brief extract from MAN AND SUPERMAN, by Bernard Shaw.

Published simultaneously in Canada by
Clarke, Irwin & Company, Ltd., Toronto

© 1958 by Pierrepont B. Noyes
Printed in the United States of America

To all of the men and women who have worked with me—in factories and offices, at Niagara, Sherrill and Kenwood—to build the Oneida Community, Ltd. on the foundations of the old Oneida Community, I dedicate this book with my deepest gratitude.

A Goodly Heritage

CHAPTER I

I WAS BORN in 1870 in that socially radical nineteenth-century experiment called the "Oneida Community," and its protecting arms not only sheltered me but held me incommunicado from outside association and influences until I was ten years old. We Community children lived in a little world bounded on all sides by walls of isolation. We believed that outside those walls were philistine hordes who persisted in religious errors and social formulas under which they sinned and suffered. When I was a child, the word "outside" was a word of taboo.

The story of the Oneida Community begins in the 1830's when my father, John Humphrey Noyes, then a student in the Yale Theological Seminary, made what he always called his "Great Discovery."

From his profound study of the New Testament, he had discovered, or believed he had, that Jesus Christ did not sanction lives of alternate sinning and repentance, but insisted on perfection here on earth. Being a man of strong convictions, my father insisted on preaching his new doctrine at the New Haven Free Church, in spite of threats of expulsion from the Seminary. However, he was graduated and ordained a minister of the Congregational Church.

Later his heresy led to cancellation of his license to preach.

My father's answer was typical. "I took away their license to sin, and they go on sinning; they have taken away my license to preach, but I shall go on preaching." This was no idle threat. During the next fifteen years he went about the country preaching "Perfectionism" and published several small magazines devoted to proving the soundness of his theology.

Granting the premise—that human perfection is possible —the steps in my father's argument, practical application of which grew into the Oneida Community, were relentlessly logical. First and most important: the ownership of personal property bred selfishness, and selfishness could not be tolerated by seekers after the perfect life. Following naturally after this, the ownership of women in marriage, my father said, created the "Family Spirit" which, in turn, elevated selfishness to a virtue. Therefore, his little group in Vermont adopted, first, communism of property and later a modification of the marriage system.

As might have been expected this original experiment in Perfectionism was sufficiently irritating to the citizens of the Vermont village where the Noyes family had long stood high in public esteem, but when rumors regarding John Humphrey Noyes's new social theory and practices were circulated, these citizens rose in righteous wrath and drove the Perfectionists from Putney. Later my father and his faithful followers trekked to central New York. There, other believers—the Burts, the Ackleys, the Nashes, the Hatches—had gathered for a practical experiment in his "Bible Communism," and they promptly invited him to become their leader.

On the Oneida Reserve, a tract of land in central New York opened for settlement when the Oneida tribe was removed to Wisconsin, the Oneida Community was born. This was in the year 1848. Its members (at one time they numbered more than three hundred and fifty) held all property in common, worked without wages for the common support, abolished marriage and, by attacking their problems with Yankee efficiency, lifted themselves from poverty to a comfortable prosperity, to thrive for more than thirty years.

Just as the search for perfection led to common ownership of property, and as common ownership of property led to the system of "complex marriage," so, in the late 1860's, theory and opportunity led to an experiment in eugenics. That was before the word "eugenics" had been coined, and my father called his system "Stirpiculture."

This is where I come into the picture. Of the fifty-four children born in the Community between 1869 and 1880 (of which I was one) the parentage of all but six was planned in advance by a committee. We were not born according to law and were not brought up by our parents. At the age of eighteen months we became members of the Community's "Children's House," where capable men and women devoted all their time to our care. I saw my mother once or twice a week. That was all, and even those visits were dependent upon avoiding excessive exhibitions of the "Mother Spirit." I loved my mother, but I do not remember that, save for brief rebellions, I suffered over this separation from her. With a score or more of playmates, my days were too full of work and study and sport to leave much room for emotional regrets. I was a very objective boy.

Memory tells me that our guardians were wise men and women. If there was no petting, there was also no harsh discipline and little regimentation. Although education was a major Oneida Community enthusiasm, our school periods were short. Work was another enthusiasm, which probably accounts for the fact that even as little children we were expected to spend an hour every day after lunch working at allotted tasks. Then at five o'clock came Children's Meeting. There "Papa" Kelly, the head of the "Children's House," read the Bible to us, and at least in theory, prepared us to be good Perfectionists. At other times we were left largely to ourselves. We played games, organized athletic contests, and roamed widely over the Community's huge domain, always charged to keep within certain rather liberal boundaries. We were outdoor children.

[The "mothers" of the Children's House saw to it that we were properly dressed, served us with simple but attractive food, tried to teach us manners, cared for us in sickness and fed us sulphur and molasses every spring to eliminate winter poisons. The "fathers" built equipment for our sports, enforced the rules they had made, taught us religion and Perfectionism at Evening Meetings, and punished erring ones.] Living under them all, mothers, fathers and teachers, I had, so memory tells me, a healthy and happy childhood.

And then, in 1880, came the shock. My father had grown old. A generation of young men and women who lacked the religious enthusiasm of the early Perfectionists had arrived at maturity; internal dissention was rife, and external pressure increasing. During 1879 the Community decided to abandon their radical social system, hoping thereby to salvage Bible communism and their religion, Perfectionism.

One year's experience, however, proved that communism of property was impractical when subjected to the strains of separate family interests. On January 1, 1881, the Community businesses were transferred to a joint stock company and the shares divided among the old members. The Oneida Community was at an end and the new corporation, The Oneida Community, Ltd., began its life.

The division of the stock of the new Company among

the members of the old Oneida Community was carried out in a spirit of fairness, and it was only after weeks of homely discussions of schemes to ease unfortunate impingements of the new social order on the lives of women and children—in certain cases of men—that the terms were settled. Investigators and writers have since expressed surprise at the serious emphasis placed on the elimination as far as possible of personal hardships in connection with the capital-stock transfer.

Briefly every man and woman over sixteen years of age was offered 5½ shares of new stock for each year spent in the Community since their sixteenth birthday, plus one half the value of any property they brought in when they joined. Every child under sixteen would receive one hundred dollars per year in cash until sixteen, and two hundred dollars "to help in their education" at that time.

Believing that there might be old members whose age, unworldliness or scanty allotment of stock might make them fearful of their future, it was provided by a so-called "guarantee," that such could elect a pension in place of stock. In addition to two hundred dollars cash per year, there was provision for sickness and unexpected expenses. Only two members chose the guarantee—one elderly man and one woman. These two, within my memory, lived out comfortable lives in the old Community Mansion House. One of these was Mr. Warne, our childhood schoolteacher. The woman was a Mrs. Sweet. I find, in the Board Minutes of twenty years later, a voted appropriation for the medical and nursing care of Mrs. Sweet.

The breakup of the Community, followed by the marrying of most of its members and a plunge into joint-stock economy, brought my generation, for the first time, face to face with realities of the outside world. The discovery that we eu-

genic children were marked by that outside world as illegiti-
mate, came to us as a great shock. We were bewildered and
apprehensive, and our fears were magnified by the fact that
many of our elders seemed equally bewildered and apprehensive.

As an "escape," I first tried to be tough like "outside"
boys. Then, at the age of thirteen, I decided that work was
the only possible way out of the social and economic pit my
birth had apparently dug for me, so during school vacations
I welcomed long hours at hard physical labor. For nearly two
years my ambition centered on becoming a first-class journey-
man carpenter. Luckily, events shaped themselves so that my
fifteenth year was spent with my father, John Humphrey
Noyes, in his new home at Niagara Falls, Canada. He had
been the head of the Community during all its thirty-two
years of communal existence. Now, he was nearly seventy-
five years old. I found him mentally active and I was impressed by the fact that, in spite of the apparent failure of his
life work and an avalanche of hostile criticism, he seemed as
sure as ever that he had done right.

I say "luckily" because the recovery of my belief in my
father's righteousness and the honesty of the Community
experiment put an end to shame over my birth just at the time
when experience and adolescence were extinguishing my
timidity.

It was not only the attacks by old members of the Community on their former leader during the breakup but the
twitting of "outside boys" with whom I now played that had
raised doubts in my mind as to the righteousness of my father
and the rightness of my birth in the Oneida Community. Of
course there may have been some less spiritual elements in
my emergence. Perhaps, recognizing that my technical il-

legitimacy could not be helped, I decided to bury the past in a successful future for, quite unexpectedly, I became possessed by a towering ambition to try my mettle in a struggle with the hostile world. And with that ambition there came, in 1886, a new respect for education. While this was stimulated at first by the conviction that education would be a valuable weapon in life's struggle, memory suggests that I had, in addition, visioned the pleasurable possibilities of mental activity. Whatever the cause, "going to college" became for me, at the age of sixteen, an obsession.

With the ending of the old communal life, my mother, with her three children—my half brother, Ormond, seven years older than I, my younger sister, Stella, and myself—had moved a mile away from the old Mansion House to the straggling village then known as Turkey Street, now the handsome and prosperous little city of Sherrill. Her total income from her shares in the new stock company was $350.00, which included the hundred-dollar-a-year allowance for her two younger children, granted by the terms of the Community settlement. Even by the standards of nearly eighty years ago, we were poor, and an education such as I dreamed of seemed an impossibility. But my mother was a remarkable and indomitable woman. Undaunted, so far as I remember, she took up the then-popular business of selling books, door to door—*The Life of Henry Ward Beecher* and *Samantha at Saratoga* are two titles I remember—and her labors included not only selling but also delivering those heavy tomes to her customers up and down the valley. Ormond's wages from his work in the Trap Shop, and mine from acting as carpenters' helper during vacations, helped a little, but college seemed out of the question.

However, when the time came and I had received the

final two-hundred-dollar payment from the Company, at six-teen, Uncle Abram—Abram Burt of old Community days—came to the rescue, and the impossible was achieved.

This "Uncle Abram"—who was not my uncle, was not, in fact, any blood kin to me—deserves my grateful and affectionate remembrance. He was the father of my half brother, Ormond, but he was as fatherly to me and, I believe, as fond of me as of his own son. Ormond was a handsome and rather frail boy and enough older than I so that I never knew him very well. He died, at the age of twenty-one, of what would probably be diagnosed today as a stomach ulcer, but even after his death, Uncle Abram continued to father our family. What his help and sympathy must have meant to my mother, I can only imagine. For myself, I loved Uncle Abram like a father and accepted his authority, although his strict New England "spare the rod and spoil the child" theory of upbringing occasionally tempered my affection. He made rules, and when I broke them, the whippings he gave me were both exemplary and realistic.

The whipping I remember best was well deserved and certainly effective. As boys will, we had a habit of competing for the skate-mark nearest an open hole in the ice. This brought me home wet so frequently that my mother, in despair, appealed to Uncle Abram. His word to me was, "Pierrepont, don't get wet again." This kept me dry for a considerable time. In the end, however, I broke through the ice once more and went home very wet. This occurred while we were still living in the Mansion House, before our move to Turkey Street, and although I tried to get into dry clothes without being seen, someone saw me, told my mother and she told Uncle Abram. When he arrived on the scene, the tone of his voice—"When you're dressed, come to my room" —left no doubt as to what I could expect.

When I entered, two of the familiar willow whips stood in the corner. Uncle Abram reached for one of them—and applied it. When that was broken, he took up the other. My mother, who was, by Uncle Abram's standards, no disciplinarian, burst into tears and tried to plead for me. Uncle Abram said, with finality, "Don't interfere, Harriet." The second whip did its duty.

If this incident seems to show Uncle Abram in an unflattering light, I should like to add that for those occasional punishments—always richly deserved—I bore him no resentment. I had disobeyed, been caught, got punished; that was all there was to it. I was still fond of Uncle Abram and knew he was fond of me, and when, later, I wanted so desperately to go to preparatory school and college, the hundred dollars a year that Uncle Abram contributed from his own slender means was proof where no proof was needed. With that help I was able to enter Colgate Academy, in Hamilton, New York, in the fall of 1886, en route, I hoped for college.

The odor of burning leaves, caught when nature is yellow and brown and equinoctial rain clouds hang low over a bedraggled world, always carries me back to that time when, as a boy of sixteen, I stood on the porch of my boarding club in Hamilton, emotionally shaken by alternating waves of happiness and depression; happy that I was established as a third-class boy at the Academy, depressed by traces of first-term homesickness.

CHAPTER II

LIFE IN THE DEMOCRACY of a preparatory school put a final end to my fear of the great world beyond our Oneida hills and, in a measure, reduced my respect for the superior equipment of those worldlings with whom I hoped later to compete. Not that I lost interest in that world or those worldlings; on the contrary, the future, the adventure of life, took on new color, and expectation soared.

There was still in my consciousness a recognition of the gulf that separated me socially from "outside" boys. Much of the time this recognition was dormant, only an ultimate, driven far down out of sight in my subconscious by the absorbing activities of school life and the friendliness of my classmates. On one or two occasions, however, the skeleton was dragged from its closet: once, I remember, by an exasperated student whom I had beaten in a physical quarrel; at another time, by a religious busybody, president of the "Greek-letter" society to which I belonged, who was apparently disturbed by the fact that boys born according to churchly and legal formula should accept me at par.

His excuse for the attack was my absence from certain Sunday services. As a matter of fact, I attended the morning church service regularly (this was obligatory) but often neglected prayer meetings and the Y.M.C.A. I can still remember the trepidation with which I entered the society's meeting hall in answer to his summons. I faced a reverend senior.

D—— was a theological student with the zeal of a fledgling evangelist.

He began suavely enough, but when I defended my Sunday habits, he gave way to his spiritual irritation. "You know, Noyes, you, of all the boys, can't afford to be talked about. You need to convince us all that you are really religious."

I was puzzled. That subconscious skeleton became suspicious. I asked, "What do you mean?"

"I mean just what I say. Remember your birth in the Oneida Community."

At that point, the skeleton emerged and with it a spirit of defiance. My class-three respect for a senior evaporated in the heat of resentment. I burst out indignantly, "What has birth got to do with going to prayer meeting?"

The worthy president—I can see him now, sitting in the chair of state—leaned back and looked at me for what seemed a long time; looked solemnly and pityingly. When he spoke, his tone was offensive. "I don't need to tell you. You know, yourself, Noyes, that you have much to live down."

I have a clear recollection of what I said and that I said it as insultingly as I knew how. "My birth is none of your business!" With that I stalked out, slamming the door behind me.

This episode was exceptional. I have recalled it to explain a certain hardening of my soul at the age of sixteen, which must have been responsible for some of the mental and spiritual idiosyncrasies with which I emerged into adult life. If some of them proved valuable, others—I did not think so then, but I do now—proved unfortunate. My early conception of a hostile world, my conviction that I could expect no help from anyone and hence that whatever I got I must get for myself was, I still believe, an excellent start for a young man. In my case, it added a touch of hardness and a spirit of enterprise to a somewhat excessive inheritance of self-confidence.

On the other hand, everyone else being in "the opposition," I nursed a positive disrespect for their opinions. This disrespect for intellectual and spiritual authority, a disrespect which has followed me through life, must be credited, or debited, to those early scars. If credited with creating a certain intellectual independence, it must be debited with the loss of much valuable aid from men of greater wisdom and broader experience than myself.

On the whole, I got along well in Colgate Academy and made many friends. Some of them now, seventy years later, are still my good friends. Fortunately, I was a fair athlete and could score in that field. Once, in a baseball game with a neighboring school, I started as catcher, but, when the pitcher failed to deliver, I pitched the game out and we won. I need hardly tell anyone who has attended a prep school what that did for my relations with the student body.

However, by the end of that first year in the Academy, I became impatient. I believed it possible to shorten my preparatory course and, against the advice of fraternity seniors, I decided to attempt, during the summer vacation, what was known as "jumping a class." My mother approved. She rationalized the plan as ultimate economy and, as she always did under like circumstances, found a way to make up for the money I had earned during previous vacations. So, through the summer of 1887 I studied long hours. I remember learning Greek, from the alphabet to that passage in Xenophon's *Anabasis* where the phalanx charged, crying, "Ζεὺς Σωτὴρ καὶ νίκη." ("Zeus, the father, and victory!") I remember also reading three of Cicero's orations, studying quadratic equations and beginning French.

By September, I felt sure I could pass the necessary examinations for entrance to the senior class. But I was faced with a dilemma. During the summer of 1887, what I may call the family unity of the old Community members, developed by many years of living together with common spiritual ambitions, came to the surface in a very practical way. A group of the older men—Mr. James Herrick, Mr. John Lord, Mr. Henry Allen, Mr. William Hinds—decided that, since so many of the younger generation were planning to go to college, they ought to be able to get their preparation at home; to be exact, right in the old Mansion House where most of them still lived.

These men raised sufficient funds among themselves to accomplish their object. For schoolrooms they fitted up the lower story of the "New House" (built in 1877). They engaged as Principal, Frederick Loomis, a graduate of Colgate University and added a lady teacher for the primary grades. Before the end of August, classes had been organized for children ranging from six years old to students pursuing college preparatory work. My cousin George and I were expected to constitute the senior class of this new academy.

Thus came my dilemma. I had worked hard to "skip a year" and make the senior class at Colgate Academy. Both pride and love of accomplishment urged persistence in this effort to prove, by passing the senior examinations, that those Hamilton unbelievers in my ability to "make up" a year were wrong. And yet, in the new school at home would be gathered nearly all the companions of my childhood. That gathering looked very attractive. In the end, however, pride con-

7703

quered. I passed the Hamilton examinations and entered the senior class at Colgate Academy. That hot summer of "boning" Latin, Greek and mathematics had brought its reward. Within a month I was pledged to one of the leading Greek-letter college fraternities and found myself an accepted and respected citizen of the academic world which had so fascinated me one year before.

From nearly every standpoint, I had done the right thing; from every standpoint but one. Emotionally, there was a fly in the ointment. The new school at home and reports of the doings of my old companions intruded upon my academic satisfactions. The newly integrated class of former Community children was reveling in a fraternal reunion and, by November, my desire to be with them had deepened into a form of homesickness.

It was not homesickness insofar as that word implies sickness. It was the pull of family affection that has followed me through life and has, on several later occasions, resulted in somewhat unaccountable decisions. As children in the Community, we undoubtedly had partialities but, beyond these special friendships, as a group we "liked each other." During all my childhood—say until my tenth year when the struggle that broke up the Community was in progress—we "liked" our elders and were under the impression that all of them, men and women, "liked" each other.

The old religious discipline had been abandoned, but there still existed among young and old a unity that was like a family unity; a sense of responsibility for the welfare of the whole group and a spirit of co-operation in joint enterprises that was the fruit of thirty years of Community life.

This impulse—the desire to take my place in the group once more, to do what it was doing, to have a part in the new project—was strong enough to solve my dilemma. On November tenth I packed my belongings and exchanged Colgate for Kenwood Academy, a boarding club for life with my mother in the old Mansion House.

It was not, of course, all plain sailing at home. Professor Loomis never quite forgave me for my original desertion, and his unforgiveness brought me plenty of trouble when I returned to the fold. My cousin George was reviewing Homer's *Iliad* and Virgil's *Aeneid* at the rate of one hundred and twenty-five lines a day. I had barely commenced those difficult poems and was still finding twenty-five or thirty lines a tough day's assignment. But the worthy professor refused to "temper the wind to the shorn lamb." It was one hundred twenty-five lines, or drop out of George's class. Pride saved me. I went through the first books of the *Aeneid* and *Iliad* at the required speed and, metaphorically, thumbed my nose at my tormentor.

That was not my only clash with our professor. In the spring, he tried to outlaw my baseball activities. During the two preceding summers I had organized baseball teams which played nines from the city of Oneida and neighboring towns. Professor Loomis objected; said that I neglected my studies and led other boys to neglect theirs. At one time he threatened to deny me a graduating diploma. We locked horns, and I told him that I did not want a diploma, since I intended to take college-entrance examinations for free-tuition scholarship, anyhow. Of course he gave me the diploma. Otherwise, he would have had a graduating class of one.

During that summer I added materially to my unpopularity with the older generation, more especially the Community's elder statesmen who ran the business. They were finding the problem of making money under the wage system of the world a more difficult task than under the old communal system where no wages were paid. My somewhat bumptious opinion that most of them were "old fogies" tainted the thinking of my class of young people.

As a matter of fact, looking back now, I can see that those business managers were honest, hard-working men, rather above the average in intelligence but handicapped by lack of training in the rough and tumble of late nineteenth-century competition. Their promotional efforts suffered also from lifelong habits of economy. There must have been, however, bright spots of commercial efficiency among the executives, since by 1888 they had for seven years paid an average annual dividend of 6 per cent and kept the Company financially sound.

I think that I was especially annoying to the Company's President. He was a worthy man but unversed in the ways of modern business and singularly inept in his official relations with men—and boys. During the summer of which I write, my struggle with him over baseball came to a head. By this time, certain neighborhood boys from the West Road and over the hill in the Cowasselon Valley had been drafted into our team. These "outside" players proved the straw that broke the camel's back. When our venerable President refused us permission to play on the Company's property, I carried my troubles to a neighbor who, in the old days, had been hostile to the Oneida Community. He was delighted to let us play in one of his pastures, and—this is the ridiculous part of the affair—we lost the game because our pitcher was, metaphorically speaking, shanghaied. Our outraged President had offered a silver dollar to every Community ball-player who kept away from that game and, although our pitcher had deserted only because his parents forbade him to play, he got the dollar. It was some time before the team forgave him for accepting it.

Theta Pi was the grandiose name of a society we created in imitation of college fraternities, and to this day we still think and speak of that time as the "Theta Pi Year." It was not this society alone, however, or even the school itself that made the year romantic. Our sentimental memories today surround the reintegration of a group of twenty or more boys and girls, brought up from infancy almost as brothers and sisters in one great family, later separated by the breakup of the Community and now brought together again by a common interest and filled with enjoyment by old-time attractions.

After nine-o'clock study hours, we foregathered in the halls or danced impromptu dances in the big recitation room or timidly courted in dusky corners. We raided the kitchen for food. At intervals there were formal dances, beginning at eight and ending officially at ten thirty. Courting undoubtedly added a tint to the coloring of those days. It was not, however, the most important factor in our happiness. Our courting was casual. It was glamorous but not sufficiently glamorous to compete, except intermittently, with the explosions of youthful activity generated by reunion and the normal ebullience of our ages. Courting never, in my memory, reached far into the area of the physical.

We had one rather perilous adventure. That was in the winter of the "Great Blizzard." After school in the afternoon it was the custom to take "gang-walks," and during cold weather those walks often took us down the railroad.

One day found perhaps eighteen or twenty boys and girls a mile from home, tramping through the snow along the O. & W. Railroad track, when that celebrated snowstorm broke upon us with such fury that we could not see twenty feet before or behind us. As a matter of safety one boy dropped a hundred yards behind the group to give warning of any approaching train. Another boy went ahead for the same purpose. We were very thankful when, before the arrival of any train, we were able to leave the railroad for a cross-country path.

The urge to "do something" and the pleasure of doing things we had never done before as a group left no space for boredom in the winter of 1887–88. Memory tells me that the hours outside of school and study periods were overfull of eager enterprise. Serious-mindedly, we organized musicals, debates and a kind of mixed entertainment which might consist of recitations, short dramatic sketches, choral singing or what not, which we called "publics." Sometimes, however, these organized entertainments were not very serious in character. I remember a well-advertised debate in the great hall, for which my cousin George was mainly responsible. He proposed the question and wrote out forensic material for the debaters. The question was: "Resolved, that animalculae, ruminating in a vacuum, devour second intentions." Our professor was baffled. Frederick Loomis, B.A., managed a nervous laugh when the announcement was made. He had great respect for George's erudition and evidently wanted to make sure that George had not unearthed a scientific problem which had escaped his teacher, before acknowledging ignorance of "second intentions."

It was during this year also that we older boys concocted a second and really secret society for a secret purpose, under the name of C.E.L. Being questioned, we took great pleasure in mystifying the girls by explaining that the initials stood for "*Compagibus ex Lapsometha.*" When they asked Professor

Loomis, who was familiar with both Latin and Greek, what
those words meant, he laughed uproariously. His answer was,
"They mean nothing. The first word is Latin, the third, Greek,
and *ex* is common to both languages."

As a matter of fact, C.E.L. stood for "Coöperative Es-
corts Limited." A certain girl of our class, thoroughly estima-
ble but for some reason not particularly attractive to the boys,
lived half a mile from the Mansion House and, after some of
the many social evenings there, found herself without an escort. Obviously, something had to be done. She must not be
allowed to go home alone, but no one boy was willing to be
a permanent sacrifice to the cause. Hence, the C.E.L. was
organized and its members agreed to take turns seeing her
home. A schedule was drawn up and, regularly, one after
another of the boys did his duty. So convincing was our performance, as my wife told me many years later, that the
other girls were not only baffled but slightly annoyed by
the whole proceeding: What had made A. so suddenly popular with the boys?

Our system was not without its difficulties, however; so
much so that presently the C.E.L. became practically a de-
bating society. We were given a clubroom upstairs in the
Playhouse, and there our hotly argued debates often lasted
until midnight. The most exciting of these debates, naturally,
had to do with breaks in the Escorting Schedule. For instance, when A., understandably confused and annoyed because her favorite young man retired in favor of our substitute, ran away from Bert Dunn and went home alone, a
furious debate tried to decide whether Bert's unsuccessful
effort had actually served his turn or he must try again the
next time. Another somewhat similar question arose when,
after a dance, a favored young man escorted A. home out of

turn. Question: Did this action relieve the regular, scheduled escort for that evening, or did it push the whole list along one place?

Perhaps I cannot better characterize the ebullience of my eighteen-year-old summer than by telling of one of Dick Wayland-Smith's and my foolish escapades. We were visiting the Noyes family at Niagara. With neighborhood boys, we went swimming in an eddy of the Niagara River perhaps a mile below the Falls, and when someone mentioned that a certain man had swum across the river and back at that point, we decided, Dick and I, that if he could do it, we could. Thereupon, we swam across the river in the gorge below the Falls. Then, without landing and walking upstream on the American side of the river, as the other man had done before swimming back, we merely touched the farther shore and then turned around and swam back, to climb out of the water at last, a mile downstream, on the last possible point above the place where the whirlpool rapids begin their mad rush. We were not frightened simply because we did not know enough about the river to realize our danger.

That was a summer when youthful energy and enterprise were not to be denied. We organized a tennis club and played matches with boys from the city of Oneida. We got together a baseball team to play against teams from neighboring towns. We swam, we hiked and we picnicked, and my first recollection of romance is associated with one of those picnics. We had hired an ancient bus and, packed within it, a score or more of boys and girls were on their way to The Cascades, nine miles up our valley. At the foot of a long, steep hill we all alighted, as was the country custom, to ease the horses' labors by walking up steep hills.

I have said that "courting" added a tint to the coloring

of those early days. This would be misleading were I not to add that it still lacked any serious intention. None of us was ready to tie himself down or to look forward practically to the time when we must take up the serious business of life. Still, I was not the only boy in the class whose feeling for a certain girl was progressing beyond the point disrespectfully referred to as "puppy love."

In my own case, I had discovered—or, more accurately, rediscovered—a little girl who, in the old Children's House days, had been too young and too feminine to attract or be attracted by an uncouth boy of nine or ten. Now, she dawned upon my consciousness as something beautiful and desirable. In the Victorian 'eighties, the courting of a sixteen-year-old girl by an eighteen-year-old boy was proverbially timid and self-conscious, but my instinct to "show off" the new sophistication acquired in a worldly college environment led me to daring advances in the presence of others. How bashful or awkward they may have been in private, I have luckily forgotten. In any case, her acceptance of those advances may perhaps be credited to the glamour surrounding a boarding-school boy. Until the day of that picnic, my courtship of Corinna had been desultory and not taken seriously by the other boys and girls or, I am sure, by Corinna, herself. It was when we two deliberately lagged behind while the others hurried up the hill to the picnic that a romance was born which has lasted nearly seventy years.

I have tried to recover the aura of that year, to relive it, to analyze its color into those separate colors that have made its memory golden. We were men and women—young men and women—and our childish affections had been transmuted into adult friendships. These friendships played an important part later in our decision to organize our lives so that ambition, energy and eagerness for life's adventure, so compelling in youth, need not be aimed exclusively at amassing individual wealth. While the subconscious urge underlying this effort may be attributed to our upbringing in the Oneida Community, the practical steps taken later to realize those ambitions were, I believe, partly motivated by an enthusiasm for a project which would let us live and work and play together for the rest of our lives.

CHAPTER III

SUMMER PASSED all too quickly. On September seventeenth I entered Madison University—now Colgate University—joined the Delta Upsilon fraternity, and felt fairly embarked on my voyage to a land of promise called education. That is exactly what education seemed to me in 1888, a land which promised intellectual pleasure and practical efficiency. I elected Latin, Greek and higher mathematics, just for the love of them. I missed the calculus prize only by a plus sign carelessly written in place of a minus. The members of our mathematics class were offered a forty-dollar prize, to go to the winner of a special examination—solution of five mathematical problems. I loved mathematics and financially needed to win this prize. One question started with a "differentiation of sine X." In my haste I wrote a plus sign when I knew as well as I knew A B C that the sign should be minus. It was my only mistake, but it queered the answer to one of the five problems, without which the prize, which would have meant so much to Mother and me, was lost. I decided then and there that carelessness could beat me in my plans for life as well as exams.

My marks suffered from my inability to resist the lure of college pranks and class activities. The youthful exuberance of our first spring term led a group of freshmen to devote one entire night to vandalistic enterprise. We took apart a heavy lumber wagon, hoisted it piece by piece through a skylight, and put it together on the peaked roof of East College. We carried most of the classroom benches up the hill to some woods. We were guilty of many other silly—some outrageous—breaches of law and order, and later paid for our fun by visits to the President's home. There we signed bonds for future good behavior, whose violation, we were informed, meant automatic expulsion from college.

When certain members of the class ahead of mine had visited the President the year before to explain a similarly overenthusiastic exhibition of spring fever, Dr. Dodge met their recalcitrance with a statement typical of the man. He was a grand character and singularly wise in his dealings with youth. On that occasion he had spoken regretfully of their lawless escapade (I can imagine the quiet dignity of his language) and had presented the well-known paper for their signatures.

One of the boys asked, "If we refuse to sign, what then?" The Doctor's answer required no interpretation.

"I may say to you, young gentlemen, that our ambition is not for a big college; it is for a good college."

They all signed.

As freshmen, we stole the toastmaster scheduled for a sophomore banquet, and in our sophomore year the freshmen stole ours. This later escapade had a humorous ending. Having scoured the countryside, boiling with sophomoric rage and swearing vengeance, and having failed to find the missing man, we were obliged to select a substitute speaker. Then, just as the speechmaking was about to begin, our lost chairman appeared in the hall.

It turned out that while he was being taken over the hills to a neighboring town in a cab, John Herman Randall, our kidnaped toastmaster—later pastor of one of New York City's leading churches—talked the freshman riding beside

him into a funk. With the persuasive eloquence that later
carried this sophomore to heights in his calling, he pictured
the predicament of men guilty of kidnaping. He sympathized
with them; he turned the heat on until his captors called a
halt and held a whispered conversation. Contritely they carried him back to the banquet.

Then there were underclass "cane rushes." That was before Colgate's cane rushes had been organized, and the fighting was rough. As a freshman I received a black eye admin-
istered by a sophomore sitting on my stomach (against the
rules), whose excuse was that another excitable freshman, a
Turk, had slugged him.

As sophomores, the struggle was to prevent a huge freshman from carrying his class cane down to the post office and
back to the hill. We had a small class, smaller still in fighters,
and the freshmen's strategy allotted two or three men to
each of us. I remember winding up in the dark of the campus,
lying on one freshman with two others on top of me. I also
remember taking a futile revenge on the man below me. He
was wearing a light suit, and my nose was bleeding profusely.
I decorated him within my possible range of action. His linen
suit must have looked like Joseph's coat of many colors.

I recall one real tragedy. I played on the varsity baseball
team through both my freshman and sophomore years; and
that was an unusual team, due largely to our marvelous bat-
tery, Kirk Thompson and Charles Dillingham. I was not an
especially good batter, but I went nearly through two seasons
in left field without an error.

We played in a New York State varsity league and won
every game excepting our last game with Union College. I,
personally, lost that game. I lost it twice, and before a home
crowd. First, I dropped an easy fly. Then, in the ninth inn-

ing, with our score six to their seven, I came to bat—two out and a man on third! Any kind of a hit would have tied the game. To this day I can remember exactly where I knocked the ball—an easy grounder between first and second base. It requires little imagination to know how I felt after that game. Life was not worth living. I locked myself in my room and remained there for hours, refusing consolation offered me through the locked door by Bert Wheat, my upperclass room-mate.

When, during my sophomore year, the name of the University was changed from Madison to Colgate, a grand celebration was staged, the climax being an oratorical feast in Tripp's Opera House. Old alumni from every state in the Union visited their Alma Mater. In 1889, Madison University was essentially a preparatory school for Baptist preachers; hence a majority of the guests who packed the ancient auditorium were ministers, mostly D.D.'s.

At the last moment, the boy who was to speak for my class went sick thinking about his speech, and I was the only sophomore the committee could find who was willing to substitute for him. For years afterwards, whenever I met alumni men of classes '91, '92, or '93, I was kidded about a certain *faux pas* made in that speech. It seems that I quoted, " 'The very stones will cry out,' " prefacing the quotation with, "Someone has said." The "stones" quotation being from the Bible, my audience of ministers must have raised their eyebrows.

During summer vacations I worked for the Carpentry Department. A day's work in the 1880's was ten hours, and only by putting in an extra quarter hour each noon could we get off at four thirty on Saturday.

Memory has preserved two facts about those summers.

The first tells of certain Sundays—the first Sundays after I had exchanged sedentary college life for laborious "outside work," as my friend, Frank Hyde, called our repair jobs. All day long I lay around on the lawn with no ambition to do anything. Every muscle ached.

The second concerns Frank Hyde himself; the very Frank Hyde with whom I worked as a boy. He was the same now, four years later, except that he had conceived an immense respect for my college education. As we worked together, he was continually trying, by questions, to exhibit my superior knowledge. Once he asked, "Pip, what does this mean: *'Ingens hiterabimus equod?'*" It was evidently mutilated Latin, and where Frank got the quotation I cannot imagine. The vividness and persistence of this particular memory arises from the fact that, while I was nonplused by the quotation, Corinna, without my four years of Latin, suggested, "Isn't that from Virgil?" Then she pointed out in the *Aeneid*, "*Cras ingens iterabimus æquor.*"

She has always been like that. A wide reader with a marvelous memory, she has made my attainments in the realm of literature and history seem minor. As a writer and speaker (and a cross-word puzzler), I have leaned on her memory and erudition.

Which leads me to add that while, in the summer of 1890, the partiality begun at that Cascades picnic had progressed, it had not resulted in any formal engagement. Corinna had become what the young people of today would call my "girl friend." I may have "proposed"—I have forgotten. I certainly proposed many times before I finally captured my wife.

The sophomore year, 1889–90, marked the end of my play days. While the tragedy of 1881, the breakup of the

Community, had left what I may call a tinge of seriousness in my thinking, academy and college had stimulated naïve ambitions and abounding activity, both of which were, on the whole, still boyish in character. Before the end of that year, however, I was attacked by the much ridiculed virus of Sophomoric Wisdom. In my case this took the direction of serious questioning as to the relation between education and life.

My early plans for a college education envisioned mostly (not altogether) a preparation for successful competition with the men of the world. Fortunately, Colgate University and Dr. Dodge, its spiritually cultured President, radiated a belief that education should mean much more; that those brief years should prepare one for lifelong self-education, and, peering into the future, I could see the possibility of a life immensely richer and more satisfactory than one embodying only practical success.

So it came about that by the end of my sophomore year I had very definite ideas as to the studies I wished to pursue: history, sociology, political science—but history first, because in history the human adventure could be seen running on and on until its clear-cut lines were lost in the social and political confusion of my own time.

I was somewhat mystified by that social confusion. This was, perhaps, natural for one whose early years had been lived in a communal society where the economic side of human relations was, it seemed to me as I looked back, amazingly simple. In the Oneida Community men and women worked cheerfully at their tasks, whether important or menial. As I remembered the "grown folks" of my childhood, those who washed dishes and those who managed the Community's businesses seemed equally happy, equally respected and, as far as I could see, took equal interest in their particular jobs. I think that, in 1889, I was especially impressed, perhaps puzzled, by the savage impingement of a Western strike, then raging with murderous violence, in both social and political life.

I decided that only with the aid of history could the causes of this confusion be understood, and youth's naïve conviction that all human problems can be solved if understood had not then been chastened by experience. Further, I now suspect that then I overestimated the amount of light that history, preoccupied as it is with kings and battles and dramatic events, can throw on real human problems.

Studying college catalogs, however, I was attracted by a course in history and political science offered by Harvard University. I knew that historical data, to be serviceable, must be organized, and that, if I were to learn what I wanted to know, my teacher of history must be able to interpret events as being basically a struggle of the mass of human beings with their aspirations and passions, rather than the achievements of brilliant men and conquering nations. What more certain than that historical interpretation could be found at its best in this oldest of American universities?

It was not until midsummer that my plans took definite shape. From the first, my mother joined enthusiastically in the Harvard enterprise, but Uncle Abram's financial assistance was necessary and it required much argument to persuade him that I needed something which Colgate could not furnish. I remember his asking with a mildly truculent note in his voice, "Can't you get a good college education in Hamilton?"

Recalling my state of mind and the character of Colgate teaching in 1890 (it is quite different now), I feel sure that I replied in substance, "Colgate courses are made for Baptist preachers. I want something different." My educational ambitions were still decidedly pagan.

／ In the end, Uncle Abram yielded. Late in August, I journeyed to Cambridge, with my mother's blessing and the romance of a new educational future in my heart. I can still remember the naïve congratulatory happiness that descended upon me when I first entered the campus and wandered among the red-brick and ivy-covered custodians of culture called Harvard University.

I found the Dean's office but not the Dean. An unsympathetic secretary informed me in short, terse sentences that in transferring from a small college to Harvard I would have to drop back a year. He pushed a blank form at me saying, "Sign this and your application will be considered," and added, "It will be useless to trouble the Dean." I can still see the picture: a sadly disappointed youth facing a hardhearted secretary, whose hardness, to be sure, merely reflected Harvard's traditional academic superiority.

I wandered gloomily about the campus. I wanted those Harvard courses, and I could not afford to drop back a year. In the end I decided to stay in Cambridge until given an opportunity to tell the Dean of my situation and ambitions.

When I finally saw the Dean, Dr. Clement L. Smith, I found him sympathetic. Perhaps he was attracted by my evident search for education rather than college degrees, for he offered me a special arrangement. This called for examinations in September on all subjects for which I was prepared; then, if I tutored the junior subjects during the following year and in the fall of 1891 passed these, plus all the earlier courses I had omitted, he would enter me in the senior class where this greatly desired course was scheduled. This was a concession. It meant, however, that I must take examinations covering practically all of my educational career, except those subjects which had been passed that summer.

It looked like a tough proposition, but I went home determined to make the grade, although only three weeks remained before the first batch of examinations. How I studied! In September I returned to Cambridge, but not with the light heart of my first visit.

I engaged a room near the Harvard campus. There, between examinations, I continued my studies, working always late into the night. For two weeks I spent forenoon and afternoon in Harvard examination rooms, struggling through five Latin exams, four Greek, five mathematics, French, German, Roman history, and I have forgotten what else.

Two of those examinations have stuck in my memory. With only three weeks' preparation in German, from a standing start at the alphabet, I knew that I could pass only if the examination called mostly for translation. What luck! The exam was all translation, and I passed.

Then Greek history; I had never studied formal Greek history at Colgate. The scheme I hit upon was a bold one and, although it proved successful, I shall never know how I managed to pass. I left the subject until the evening before examination; then I took Smith's *History of Greece* to my room and spent the night reading it from cover to cover, 312 pages. I suspect that I went without breakfast, for I seem to remember rushing through the last pages in a race to reach the examination room on time. I passed Greek history.

Those were two hectic weeks, and afterward my study at home during the winter of 1890–91 was equally hectic. I became a miser of time. Through long evenings and often well into the night, I sat in the old Mansion House library pouring over Ladd's *Physiological Psychology*, Hume's *Treatise on the Human Understanding*, or somebody's *Political Economy*—all junior studies which must be passed the following September. It was exciting. Education had become my Primrose Path.

Recalling those evenings in the library brings back a memory amusing and just a little pathetic. In the early days Mr. Chester Underwood was one of my teachers. Although elderly, he had never lost his enthusiasm for education nor his interest in young people. He had shown a special interest in my progress through prep school and college. Often through the winter evenings of 1890–91 Mr. Underwood sat near me, reading by the same kerosene lamp that served me. He was not one to intrude, but I came to know that, sitting there reading or just quietly thinking, he hoped that later when others had left the room I would discuss my studies with him. This I frequently did. He had an interesting mind and proved a veritable encyclopedia of information on many subjects.

Mr. Underwood had made a hobby of phrenology. In his youth he had studied the science under Fowler and during Community days had acquired a very considerable reputation for reading people's character by feeling the bumps on their heads. There came an evening when, looking over my shoulder, he noticed, on the pages of Ladd's *Physiological Psychology*, diagrams of the human brain. That was enough. At the first opportunity Fowler's pupil introduced the subject of phrenology and asked to see the diagrams.

Unfortunately, Ladd discouraged the idea of any very detailed "differentiation of cerebral functions." It was equally unfortunate that my academic pride and love of argument led to a discussion with Mr. Underwood, in the course of which I overlooked the feelings of a man who cherished the science of phrenology as the romance of his intellectual life. Ruthlessly I did my best to demolish the theory of bumps. Several times he relapsed into a rather pathetic silence. I hope that in the end I came down off my high horse of sophomoric wisdom and conceded something to his pet theory, but I only remember Mr. Underwood's shaking his head and saying, more to himself than to me, "I am sorry." Whether his sorrow was for me or for himself, he did not indicate. I hope he was sorry for me.

Suddenly, in the spring of 1891, all my educational plans went by the board. My mother's illness put an end to them. Warning symptoms had appeared in the previous September, but, having suffered no serious ailment through all her previous life, she treated the matter lightly. Perhaps I should have been more suspicious. My aunts worried, but it never entered my head that her illness could have a serious ending.

Through the winter months she grew steadily worse until, in April, warned by those aunts, I took her to a specialist in Syracuse for expert diagnosis and help. Three days later the doctor took me aside and gave me a terrible shock. He told me that my mother's condition was hopeless.

I begged him to save her. He said, "Not a chance!" I shall never forget my journey home from Syracuse that afternoon on the old Canajoharie Local. My world was falling about my ears. I could not bear it. Life without my mother! I could not believe it and I would not believe it. Next day I went back to Syracuse to tell the physician that he *must* save her.

That was more than sixty years ago, but recollection of those hectic days still brings me a heartache. In the end I had to accept the inevitable. One thing seemed certain: my educational plans must be abandoned. My mother objected, but I was resolute; I would devote myself to her care and watch for possibilities, however unscientific, for saving her.

During the rest of the school term I taught Latin and mathematics as assistant to Professor Loomis, and after school hours acted as Mr. Herrick's secretary. He was then treasurer of the company. My work consisted mainly of copying his letters and such others as I wrote for him. I remember well the old-fashioned iron press that squeezed the letters between damp cloths in a tissue-paper copybook.

With an eye on the future, I registered in an Oneida law office. Such registration, under the sloppy regulations current in 1891, would give me credits towards admission to the bar. I had decided to be a lawyer. My ambition, which at the age of twenty easily soared, anticipated nothing less than a justiceship in the Supreme Court of the United States. When my various duties and the care of my mother permitted, I still haunted the library, but Ladd and Hume were exchanged for Blackstone and Coke and somebody's work on contracts.

On the second day of September, 1891, my mother passed away. Brought to the Community by her father as a girl of nine, she had been a faithful member of the group, believing in its fundamental tenets to the end of her life. When the Community turned into a joint-stock company, she found herself with a somewhat meagre income and three children—Ormond, seventeen; myself, ten; and Stella, three. She had worked and always made a good home for us children. She had prayed. When she knew she could not recover, I remember that she said, "I leave you in God's hands." No one ever had a better mother.

CHAPTER IV

DURING THIS PERIOD I frequently discussed the future with my half brother Holton. After the death of our father, in 1885, this brother had become my most intimate friend and companion, and during my mother's sickness we lived together in a small room at the top of the Mansion House. His sympathy and affection comforted me through those months of suffering.

Holton was then working in the Trap Shop. We both decided to apply for positions in the Company's silverware factory at Niagara Falls. Our applications were pigeonholed. At the time we felt that we were badly treated, but, looking back, I cannot blame the elderly executives of the Company for scenting trouble from the employment of two "fresh" young men. (That was our characterization, "fresh," by a young assistant superintendent at Niagara Falls, when we later forced our way into that organization.)

Late in November we decided to take the bull by the horns. Holton and I went to Niagara and, on the ground, insisted that we be given employment. Mr. George Hamilton, the Superintendent, proved friendly in spite of our reputation. Holton was given a job as press-setter in the Chain Department, and I was employed in the office. We lived together in the old Stone Cottage across the river in Canada, where my father, with a small loyal group of family and friends, spent his last days. The house was empty save for the presence of Mr. Henry Seymour, an old Community member, who acted as caretaker and spent the winter months inventing new steel traps and warming evil-smelling muck on the kitchen stove for use in his hothouse operations.

In summer, Henry Seymour bred new vegetables. It was his experimentation that developed the first yellow sweet corn, which he named Golden Bantam. Atlee Burpee bought this from him.

Mr. Seymour was one type of the men who joined my father's Perfectionistic experiment in the 1840's. He was intensely religious, intellectually ambitious, agricultural in training, and sensitive to everything that was beautiful in nature and people. Back in 1847 he had attended that "Convention" in Lairdsville, New York, where John Humphrey Noyes preached and "wrestled with unbelief" for three days. Mr. Seymour left Lairdsville convinced. When, a little later, Jonathan Burt, with a little band of local believers, gathered at Oneida Creek to make the Burt home and sawmill the foundation stones for what later became the Oneida Community, Mr. Seymour and his sister Chloe joined them.

As a boy and later in my teens, I was impressed with the simplicity and earnestness of those early joiners, who came mostly from the farms and villages of New England and New York State. Thirty years of community living had left them simple and earnest. In 1892, Mr. Seymour still played the flute (badly) and sang old songs. I remember hearing him sing while he hoed potatoes:

> "Whist——tle and hoe,
> Sing as you go,
> Shorten the row
> With the songs you know."

Holton and I worked in the factory ten hours a day and kept house for ourselves. We simplified our housekeeping by eating at a table drawn so near the kitchen stove that we could attend to the cooking and turn back to the table with finished products without leaving our seats. Our menu was reduced to a few items easily prepared, primarily beefsteak. The Stone Cottage pantry being heavily stocked with silver and china, we adopted the plan of stacking up used dishes after each meal and leaving them for the laundry woman to wash when she came on Thursday, or for our sister, Miriam, who lived over the River and visited us often.

Holton's half-information about housekeeping resulted in one unpleasant episode. He told of a "stockpot" to be kept always on the back of the stove, into which cooks threw the bones and surplus meat left from each meal. I have forgotten what he said cooks did with the result, but we established a stockpot and thereafter congratulated ourselves on its convenience.

We had no occasion to examine the contents of the pot for a week or ten days. Then one evening we raised the lid. The stench that arose from that pot nearly drove us from the kitchen. In the end we pushed a long pole through the bail of the kettle and with one of us at each end, carried the nauseous concoction to the orchard and buried it, pot and all.

Looking back on those days from these later years, we have both found romance in our struggle for advancement. We served the Company to the limit of our abilities. Mr. George Hamilton was, I am sure, personally pleased with our work, but he became alarmed at the hostility toward me shown by a young man, K——, a member of his staff. Mr.

Hamilton had asked that I work out some kind of cost system. He told the different foremen to co-operate with me, and
most of them were very decent about it, in spite of the fact
that old hands are never enthusiastic about innovations. My
greatest trouble came when I tried to get assistance from
K——, and his attempt to keep facts and figures from me
aroused my suspicions.

This young man, with a partner, M——, had a prosperous outside business known as K & M, and the check-hooks
they sold were manufactured in the departments of our factory which he superintended. I tried to apply my new cost
system to his check-hooks. K—— did his best to block me,
but I obtained a reasonably accurate guess at the costs, partly
by appealing to Mr. Hamilton and partly by going behind
K——'s back. When I showed Mr. Hamilton my final figures,
and pointed out that we were selling the check-hooks to
K & M for 30 per cent less than it cost the Company to manufacture them, he thanked me, but issued a note of warning.
"K—— will try to make you all the trouble he can. You must
be tactful."

I had already noted the "trouble." A friendly foreman
had whispered that K—— was spreading stories about me.
Another told me that K—— was trying to get all the room-
foremen to refuse the data I asked for, and this informant
reminded me that K—— was the son of the Assistant Works
Superintendent.

The crisis came when, as noted before, I showed Mr.
Hamilton complete and accurate estimates, and persuaded
him to raise K & M's prices on check-hooks. A few days later
he called me into his office and carefully closed the door.
He seemed quite disturbed. Mr. Hamilton was essentially
a man of peace. "I hope," he said, "you will irritate K—— as

little as possible. You know he is a violent fellow. He told me yesterday that you were 'hounding' him and that he intended to give you a thrashing."

Perhaps I was at an age when the threat of a thrashing seemed more interesting than dangerous. In any case it turned out to be as I suspected, a threat only, and the affair settled down into a deadlock. K—— did his best to undermine my position in the factory, and I proceeded to force through realistic cost estimates on other articles made for him.

I think that most of the foremen felt more friendly to me than to K——, but he was a bully and a bluffer and his father, as noted, was assistant superintendent. The affair reached a point where many were afraid to have K—— see them talking with me; men high up in the organization who wanted to give me some information, though it might have nothing to do with K——, would beckon me into a private office and lock the door.

Having expatiated on the difficulties encountered at the Niagara Falls factory, I was about to add that the situation became uncomfortable, but, searching my memory, I find no trace of discomfort or discouragement. I think that, on the whole, Holton and I did both enjoy our life and our activities at Niagara. We cherished hopes. Mr. Hamilton showed me increasing friendliness and confidence. He sought my company and employed me on confidential work. I knew that I was accumulating enemies among both the dishonest and the lazy-minded members of the staff, but this did not worry me. If Mr. Hamilton and the home management approved, I felt sure we would emerge.

Then something happened that turned all our positives into negatives. I went to Oneida for a week's vacation and while I was gone, Mr. John Sears, a member of the ruling party, spent several evenings with Holton at the Stone Cottage trying to convert him to Spiritualism. He, himself, was an ardent Spiritualist. Today's generation may have forgotten that after the so-called revelations of the Fox sisters, in 1851, and their ingenious invention of what they called the Spiritual Telegraph, for direct communication with the Other Plane, Spiritualism spread like an epidemic through the country. Books were written on the subject, journals were published for the army of true believers, certain mediums became famous as healers through the instrumentality of dead-and-gone physicians. Indeed, it was said that half the homes in America had their own family mediums.

My father had always discouraged Spiritualism, as such. Although he certainly believed in the reality of communication with the spiritual world through prayer and meditation, I think he must have regarded the extraordinary manifestations of the popular mediums with a good deal of suspicion, since he warned that, even supposing that such spirits existed on another plane and that such communication was possible, no human being, either medium or believer, could distinguish between bad spirits and good spirits, and he urged the safety of sticking to the Biblical saints chosen by Christ to perpetuate His message.

My father interpreted his own inspiration as coming through a study of the writings of St. Paul, and his relation to the Heavenly Powers through this agency he called, in his vivid way, "the link and chain." Parenthetically I may say that, although it is doubtful if any of us children understood this rather abstruse theory, we were certainly familiar with its name, and the "link and chain" was a part of our religious vocabulary. However, in those early days—only a little more than a decade after the Civil War—I seem to remember that in my mind, at least, by a quite natural confusion of ideas, I thought of it as "the Lincoln Chain."

However, this new Spiritualism went beyond mere politics and became an enthusiasm whose contagion spread through the membership of the new Company. An elderly member who, in Community days, had soft-pedaled his Spiritualistic leanings in order to keep his "place by the throne," now established himself as a sort of high priest of the new religion and drew into his circle many old Community people. This was, psychologically, quite understandable; having been spiritually shepherded all their lives, those old members were unhappy without a spiritual leader. This new prophet claimed to have got into communication with my father at a seance, during which the medium announced to the assembled seancers that "Mr. Noyes says his mantle has fallen upon Mr. Pitt."

Doubters pointed out that in Community days my father had given this man a public criticism for substituting unknown and, as he said, spurious spirit advisers for his own spiritual inspiration. But now, apparently, from the other side of the veil, J.H.N. had recanted. Wherever the truth lay, this Spiritualist group became, in 1888, a political party, and by 1889, old members, owning collectively a majority of the Company's stock, had flocked to Mr. Pitt's standard, which enabled his party to elect five of the nine directors for the next six years.

This new management, together with a working majority on the Board of Directors, soon made itself felt in the operation of the Company. The old Community ideal of "doing business as unto the Lord," which they interpreted as the greatest good to the greatest number, the renouncement of

private ambitions and the most scrupulous honesty in all
dealings, was now temporarily in abeyance.

To go back a little: after the Community was given up
and until his death in 1885, my father had personally selected
seven of the Company's nine directors. This arrangement
eliminated Company politics, and his advice on the larger
questions of policy governed the business. The arrangement
preserved a reasonable prosperity—and 6 per cent dividends.
As a matter of history, political peace outlived my father
more than a year, or until his latest appointee, Mr. George
Campbell, had lost his usefulness and influence. It was the
Company election of 1888 that loosed political ambitions, until then held in check by the leadership of Father Noyes.

When, in that year, the Oneida Community, Limited,
stockholders tried to agree on Mr. Campbell's successor in the
old Community way, the great split began. A majority favored William A. Hinds as the new President, while a substantial minority, swelled by those older Community members who had accepted Spiritualism as a substitute for the
Bible communism of their late leader, nominated John R.
Lord. It is a matter of record that a certain stockholder, himself elected by the aid of Mr. Hinds's votes, turned his coat
at the last minute and voted his stock and his proxies for Mr.
Lord. John R. Lord became the new President and the Spiritualist party was born.

While most of the Oneida Community, Ltd., Spiritualists
were interested primarily in ethical accomplishments, one
of the most prominent of their leaders became so involved in
private financial speculation that his fortunes depended upon
continued control of the Company, and certain worldly-
wise coadjutors took advantage of this fact to acquire
a balance of power and influence in the management. Be-

ginning in 1888, Oneida Community, Limited, politics degenerated into a combination not unknown in business history—a combination of spiritual propagandism with secular ruthlessness.

And now, Mr. Sears had hoped, in my absence from Niagara, to convert my brother! Sears had lived most of his life in the Oneida Community and had been a good member. He was an excellent machinist and had been intensely loyal to the religion of the Community until the death of my father. Later, he became loyal to the new Spiritualist leader, and equally uncompromising in his attitude towards opponents. With John Sears there was no halfway: people were either "with us" or "against us."

Spiritualism, together with its obvious application to our own advancement in the business, must have been the burden of Mr. Sears's diatribe to Holton, for when I returned from Oneida I found my brother convinced that we had no chance for advancement unless we became Spiritualists. His story alarmed me, especially Holton's report of the answer made by this representative of the management to his suggestion that the Spiritualists were driving away all the young men.

In describing the affair, Holton's imitation of Mr. Sears's tone suggested to me the crisp finality of iron cuttings or the metallic ring of those alloy steels with which he had always worked. Another man might have temporized—"Why should it drive them away," or something of the sort. Not so, for this sturdy partisan with the nearsighted eyes and mathematical mind. He said flatly, "We don't need young men."

As a result of the Sears visits, Holton and I discussed our situation from every angle. Our future with the Oneida Community, Limited, did not seem promising. My first reaction was, "We'll leave the Company. We'll go out on our own and make a success of our own." And yet—this was home.

There came back to me a dream I had encouraged during the long months of my mother's sickness, a dream of remaking the Oneida institution. I would defeat both the right wing, which was turning our fine old Company into a mere machine for making money, and the Spiritualists' left wing which "did not need any young men," quite evidently, because they knew that the young men were sure to object to running a business by seances.

That was the old dream—to preserve this wonderful home for the elderly people who had spent their lives there and for our own generation who had come to love it. And now, I was planning to leave it to its inevitable decline.

It seems to me now quite possible that our months of menial work without much prospect of advancement had created in Holton and myself a desire for adventure which needed only the spark of managerial hostility to start a blaze of new ambitions. Whatever the effective cause, in the end, we decided to leave the Company.

CHAPTER V

IT WAS EARLY in the "gay Nineties" and April Fools' Day to boot, when Holton and I shook the home-town dust from our feet and set out for the Big City. We knew that many of those elderly worthies who controlled and managed the home industries were not sorry to see us go—and anyhow, as I said before, we had ambitions. Perhaps our going should not be laid too heavily upon the shoulders of our elders. From boyhood days, the world beyond our blue hills had called to us loudly. Out there lay adventure and—youthful self-confidence added—success.

If I am uncertain as to the relative importance of the urges which led us to say goodbye to Niagara and Oneida, no such obscurity dims the memory-picture of our ferryboat ride across the North River from Weehawken, after a grimy all-day trip on that heroic thunderbolt of our childhood days, the Ontario & Western Express.

About us, in every direction, busy little boats were sliding silently through the darkness, their lights drawing straight lines towards seemingly important destinations. Athletic tugs whistled and chugged and maneuvered, while ferryboats, pouring light from a hundred windows, picked their way cautiously amid the visible and invisible denizens of the river. Far away, a Sound steamer or an ocean liner added its impressive basso to the raucous cacophony of the smaller fry.

But more than all, the City—New York, shadowy, inscrutable, reflecting in the clouds the brilliance of its night life—was drawing every moment nearer. Here, in the river, we seemed surrounded by thrilling, flaming activity, but there, under those glowing clouds, lay the fairyland of opportunity. Any nostalgia we may have felt—and I think we had been touched with homesickness on the train journey —was smothered in a great joy of anticipation. We were ardent and simple youths in 1892.

Perhaps the measure of our simplicity is to be found in our plan of action. Having sold our bicycles and a few shares of inherited Company stock and combined the proceeds with the savings from our work at Niagara Falls, we were boldly heading for Wall Street. With scant capital and high hopes, we had planned a raid on the country's largest gambling machine.

Vanity leads me to offer whatever palliation I can for our temerity. When, in 1891, my mother's sickness forced me to give up college and I filled in my time with schoolteaching, office work, and on the side, the study of law, I also studied (equally on the side) the stock market. I remember that my mother was immensely entertained by the pile of analytical charts and graphs I constructed, each illustrating the financial history of a railway or an industrial corporation; and those same charts persuaded Uncle Abram to loan me two hundred dollars with which to "play a cinch." I took the two hundred and the charts to New York City (all night, I remember, in an O. & W. day coach; round trip $7.50). I bought Atchison (I think it was), on a margin, sold it a few days later, and returned home with fifty or sixty dollars more than the original two hundred in my pocket.

This earlier success must at least partially account for our landing in New York that night with a bagful of charts and graphs and hearts full of hope. Perhaps we would have ventured out anyway. Our prospects at home were not bright, especially in my own case. I was rated, by the powers that were at Oneida, an uncomfortable youngster with a swelled head acquired in college, superimposed upon a background of disrespect for authority. If, however, we had ventured out with ambition only to find new jobs, our state of mind as we approached New York City would probably have been less exuberant. We were fortune hunters.

Our Wall Street adventure followed with ghastly fidelity the pattern traced by the experience of millions of hopeful speculators. Each day from ten to three we sat in a bucket shop, called euphemistically a "brokers' office," watching the tape and trading, mostly in ten-share lots. Our capital was limited.

When not watching the tape, we looked across Broadway at the imposing front of the old Consolidated Exchange where we knew our orders to buy or sell were being executed. When things were going well with us, this edifice seemed the golden hope of young America. It defied the big Exchange, where only one-hundred-share lots were wanted. On dark days, however, when every tick of the ticker told us of further losses, I disliked even its architecture.

I still remember the senior partner of the brokerage firm. He was well groomed and jovial and might have been the "Get Rich Quick Wallingford" of fictional fame. I also remember several of our fellow victims. There was a youngish man with a clipped mustache and a wooden personality, who affected nonchalance in spite of steady losses. He told of these in a bored tone and then bought more of the same stock.

We worked hunches, tips and "systems." We made profits for several weeks at a time and then, caught on the wrong side of the market, we lost it all, and more.

There came a time when Holton and I could see approaching the end of our financial resources. We were living in one room and boarding with Holton's mother, Mrs. Johnson, who, we had come to suspect, was very dependent on the twelve dollars per week we paid her. Hers was a very comfortable flat on St. Nicholas Avenue, between 118th and 119th Streets. The foreign invasion of Harlem had not yet begun, and St. Nicholas Avenue was eminently respectable. Neighboring apartments were occupied by prosperous tradespeople and professional men. I remember taking a neighbor's daughter, a "well-brought-up" and intelligent girl, to the weekly band concert on the rocky heights of Mt. Morris Park.

After the breakup of the Community, Mrs. J. had married a rather distinguished-looking old man who talked much of his work selling insurance, but seldom showed evidence of a sale. Every morning he was up early and bustled out with silk hat, Prince Albert coat, flowing mustachios, and a great show of energy. Mr. J.'s silk hat and voluble energy fooled us for a time, but the truth would out. When either of us returned unexpectedly to the flat for a forgotten paper or other article, we found that Mr. J. had doubled back from somewhere around the corner. Gone were the beaver, the frock coat, and the dignity of a veteran insurance agent. From his shoulders there hung a voluminous calico apron and he was washing dishes.

So the need of income loomed large, for the sake of the family as well as ourselves. We held a directors' meeting. In fact there came a time when we held daily sessions; when even our weekly relaxation at Dean R. Robus's billiard par-

lor on 116th Street degenerated into financial discussions.
Every session became more serious than the one that went
before. Always, however, we passed a motion unanimously,
vehemently, even truculently, that we would not go back to
Oneida—never! I remember that Holton declared he would
drive a horsecar (horsecars still jangled up Broadway) before he would go back.

As the days went by, it was forced upon us with increasing clarity that presently we would be forced to find some
paying employment. Still clinging to hope, however, our first
plan involved a half-surrender only. Since I was the firm's
stock-market "analyst," we decided that Holton should tackle
some job while I continued my "studies" and cautiously employed what little capital we had left in a final attempt to
extract blood from the Wall Street stone.

During this period our speculative enterprise was kept
alive by mirages. Often, just as we were on the point of
falling, financially fainting, in the desert of speculative losses,
a fortunate turn in the market would bring back the old allur-
ing picture of easy money. Those were the same mirages that
have kept the bright lights burning in brokers' offices since
stocks were first invented; the same that, before the day of
stocks, sent youths on all sorts of desperate enterprises which
promised wealth without the drudgery of productive labor.

On the other hand, I am not sure that mirages deserve
all of the opprobrium cast upon them. Have they not kept
many an exhausted wanderer in the desert plodding along
after he would have lain down to die were it not for the
illusory hope held out by a vision in the sky? Certainly, in my
own case, the occasional mirage that rose before my eyes
in lower Broadway kept me from surrender until experience
had stiffened my emotional resolve not to go back home—

stiffened it with an alloy of confidence that I could earn a living in New York by other means than speculating in the stock market.

It happened that Mr. George Miller—my Community-born first cousin, but a generation older than I—who was New York agent for Oneida Community products with an office and wareroom on Murray Street, took an interest in us. When we let him peek into our financial charnel house, he advised us to give up the Wall Street idea and (as a practical suggestion), urged that we try our hands at selling silverware to small stores and restaurants. He offered to sell us merchandise at wholesale prices.

I suspect that one of those mirages was then showing itself above the ticker in Chisholm's office, since in spite of Mr. Miller's advice, we stuck to our halfway scheme. I continued my attendance at the brokers' office while Holton sold spoons.

It was only a first step, however. If Holton's selling proved financially insufficient, the step was in the right direction and, when our financial stringency became unbearable, we took another step in the same direction. I still watched the ticker during the forenoon, but in the afternoon took to the highways and byways with silverware samples. This was the beginning of the end. Within a month our Wall Street venture was over, and we were both working full time, trying to sell silverware.

Only those who have attempted to sell something to storekeepers on the island of Manhattan, or in that sprawling haunt of the cave dwellers called Brooklyn, can know what real competition is. We found shopkeepers and restaurant owners unwilling even to look at our samples. I called upon every possible user of silverware in every block. They made short work of my calls as soon as they discovered that I had come in to sell, not to buy something. It looked bad.

In that crisis of our affairs it was one of my antisocial traits that saved us. I happen to be the sort of person who is profoundly irritated by being beaten, and my irritation takes the form of an egotistical and truculent determination to break through the stone wall of opposition. I studied my failures. I tried ever-new techniques until I found the Third Avenue buyers' weak spot; for even men living in the shadow of the elevated railroad had Achilles' heels.

It came about in this way: Late one afternoon I took refuge from the cold winter wind in a recessed doorway and reviewed my experiences. I had been working up Third Avenue, crossing and recrossing the icy street. As soon as the proprietor of a restaurant learned that I had something to sell, he said "no" emphatically, and vanished into the unapproachable kitchen regions of his establishment. They all seemed to regard peddlers as a swarm of annoying insects. They brushed me away as they would a mosquito and appeared exasperated by any sign of the well-known persistency shown by such insects.

"They just hate peddlers," I said to myself. "After all, they are busy men and grudge the time wasted by the typical peddler's persistency. There are too many peddlers. These restaurant keepers have their regular sources of supply for silverware, and they are unwilling to waste their time listening to salesmanship which experience tells them has nothing valuable to offer *except* salesmanship."

Then a bright idea came to me. "Why not trade on this hatred of peddlers' persistency?" I elaborated the thought.

Directly opposite the doorway in which I crouched, was a substantial-looking restaurant. I prepared my layout and entered. An anaemic waiter looked at me uninterestedly, when I asked for the proprietor. "He's busy," was all the play I got.

I assumed an attitude as imposing as a youth of twenty-one could command. I spoke decidedly, "This is important. I must see Mr. Bortel."

Grudgingly, the waiter disappeared behind a screen and in due time there appeared a very large man draped in a white apron, which suggested that I had dragged him away from the important ceremony of cutting up the day's meat ration. His "no" was unusually emphatic.

Instantly I showed exaggerated symptoms of diffidence and indicated immediate retirement. I said, "I'll leave my card and call some other day."

The effect was magical. I looked to this busy man like an easy mark. He held out his hand. "Good! Give me your card."

He actually smiled as I opened my bag to get the card. In the top of that bag I had placed a package of spoons and, with the sudden rapidity of a magician, I produced this package instead of the card. Before Mr. Bortel had time to resent my importunity, I was orating at full speed ahead, holding the spoons under his nose.

"How is that for eighty-four cents a dozen? White metal all the way through . . ." etc., etc., etc.

I watched the expression on his face, while resentment rose and fell and thoughtfulness replaced hostility.

He considered. "Eighty-four cents?"

"Yes, and they are genuine white metal, solid all the way through. They'll always look the same. They can't wear out . . ." and other arguments, ad libitum.

He fingered the spoons. "Do you guarantee that they're solid white metal?"

At this point I dropped my oratorical tone and spoke judicially rather than eagerly. "The spoons and forks are solid white metal. Of course the knife blades are of steel, but the handles are well plated with pure silver."

As I remember it, Mr. Bortel again mused, "Eighty-four cents!" Then he disappeared behind the screen.

That must have been another of those nerve-racking moments of which I later experienced many in my work as a salesman. Would he come back or was that the end?

He came back. "You may send me three dozen teaspoons, two dozen tables, two dozen forks and knives."

I remember the exact quantities because Mr. Bortel later had that same order ready for me each month when I called. As a matter of history, we became great friends and he recommended my goods to several of his restaurant acquaintances. Several years later, after I had sold my Noyes Bros. business and was back with the Oneida Community, Limited, I called on Mr. Bortel for old-times' sake. He seemed delighted to see me; said, "Mr. Wayland-Smith told me what you are doing. I buy my silverware from him now. I'm glad you're making good, but I miss you." I remember that—"I miss you."

That was much later, of course. At the moment Mr. Bortel's surrender, although a pleasing break in the Avenue's indifference, was only one order. However, within a week I had pierced the Avenue's enmity towards peddlers and I found a way—not the same way—to pierce the defense of the smaller jewelers in the district.

I would not like to suggest that life became a bed of roses after I discovered the key to overcoming the negatives of certain classes of buyers. It was always grim business. I zigzagged back and forth across icy avenues and streets all day long, often without getting a single order until late in the afternoon.

Very soon, however, I was able to adopt a rule that I would not go to bed any night until I had made a profit of at least three dollars; a resolution which often compelled me to spend the evening, sometimes until a very late hour, working Sixth Avenue, where the proprietors of all-night restaurants could be seen only at night. It took me four weeks to work Third Avenue—my best avenue—from Cooper Union to Fordham. Seventh Avenue required only a week. After that, I tackled the purlieus. On the old Bowery of the 90's I drank awful beer and ate worse food to interest Beefsteak John in tin-plated spoons. Then I tried my luck on East Broadway and the East River fish-market districts. I aimed to cover every street in New York which sheltered a restaurant.

There were disagreeable incidents. I especially remember one experience on Carmine Street. The proprietor of a little "quick and dirty," a thick-chested, red-faced fellow, was cleaning the mirror behind his oyster counter. I must have been a little more persistent than he thought proper, for suddenly he grabbed an oyster knife and leaped over the counter, roaring, "I told you to get out!" I disliked his looks and, although I knew that an oyster knife was blunt, I did a hundred yards faster, I think, than I ever did them before, with the Irishman in close pursuit.

If the cold and wet and the icy streets and the endless assaults on hostile prospects color many of my memories of that winter a shabby gray, the evenings were bright spots. Always Holton and I figured the day's profits down to the last cent. That was fun. We were paying expenses and adding a little to our capital. Yes, I remember that occasionally, on evenings when our additions and subtractions revealed an unusual profit, we decided unanimously that we owed ourselves a little extra relaxation. Then we voted a special session at the billiard parlor.

Which reminds me of the queer people we met at our favorite 116th Street billiard parlor. They all seemed acquainted with each other. They were also friendly with us, and Holton's later billiard skill was acquired through their good-natured advice and coaching. When we discovered that this 116th Street resort was a rendezvous for the city's confidence men and gold-brick artists in their leisure hours, a touch of romance was added to our weekly nights out. We also discovered that our light-fingered friends drew a sharp line between business and recreation. By a tacit understanding, it was "time out" for the "fraternity" at Dean R. Robus's.

I have tried to recall our quondam friends at the billiard parlor, but my memory brings back only the fellow who took great pains teaching us massé shots. He had a mustache and looked like a college professor; I remember that. It occurs to me (a ridiculous idea, of course) that he may have been the very same man who nearly succeeded in swindling my Grandfather Worden, a dozen years before.

This Grandfather, who rejoiced in the wonderful name of Marquis de Lafayette Worden, was one of the original members of the Oneida Community. He had left it in 1876, but he was still friendly to the Community and occasionally visited at Oneida. Grandfather was a simple soul. On one of his visits he told of an adventure which befell him when passing through New York City. A "nice-looking man," he said, made his acquaintance on the ferryboat and told him of a charitable work he was engaged upon. He offered to give Grandfather a suit of clothes if he would perform some sim-

ple service for him. Just as the pair was about to enter a
building on a back street, where Grandfather would doubt-
less have been robbed, a policeman who, evidently, had been
following them, arrested the man. He advised Grandfather
to seek the seclusion (he meant the safety) of his hotel. If
this was not the same man, I have no doubt that Grandfather's "confidence man" looked as respectable as the habitué
of Dean R. Robus's billiard parlor who taught Holton and
me massé shots and caroms.

I was on the point of saying that billiards represented
our only recreation during the winter of 1892–93, but that
would not be quite true. While the burst of theatregoing
which marked our first weeks in New York was only a
memory, we did, at rare intervals, treat ourselves to a show.
More often on a Sunday night we would climb to the highest
gallery of the old Madison Square Garden and, sitting in
twenty-five-cent seats, listen to Anton Seidl's magnificent
orchestra discourse Wagnerian music.

I tried to like it. If music interprets the spirit of the times,
Wagner, in 1893 was, for the rank and file, a generation ahead
of his time; and I have always been rank and file, musically.
Holton, however, was a genuine musician and music lover.

CHAPTER VI

By January, 1893, prosperity led Noyes Bros., "Wholesalers of Silverware and Novelties, 56–58 Warren Street, New York City," to branch out. I traveled upstate New York and portions of Pennsylvania, going as far west as Pittsburgh, while Holton handled the office work and shipping. My sister Gertrude recently resurrected one of my letters written at that time, in which I state that I could easily make twenty-five dollars profit every day I was out selling. Twenty-five dollars was more money in those days than it is now.

For many years thereafter Pittsburgh was my favorite city, for the very good reason that in Pittsburgh I wrote my first *big* order. I can almost recall the name of the bakery-supply house that gave me the order. Up to that time my orders had called for dozens. A gross of any item was a rarity; whereas that Pittsburgh order specified case lots: two cases of teaspoons (20 gross), a case of tablespoons (5 gross), a case of forks (5 gross), a case of knives (5 gross). I remember spending Sunday in a $1.50 room (meals included) at a dirty hotel overlooking the Allegheny River and feeling like a prince in his palace; more than fifty dollars profit! Good credit, too!

As a matter of fact, I entered Pittsburgh in a very happy frame of mind, and would have enjoyed that dismal hotel without the big order. Stopping over at Niagara Falls, where Corinna was then working in the Company's office, I had persuaded her to renew our former engagement. Her first con-

59

sent, the previous year, was dictated—I now think—by sympathy for my bereavement in the death of my mother. Later she had broken that engagement by letter. She told me afterwards that I had kept all the other boys away from her from the time she was fifteen years old and, when moving to the Falls, she decided to have a whirl. I have always regarded that renewal of our engagement as the greatest selling success of my life.

From that time on, Noyes Bros.' sales were limited only by our capital. I had learned the selling game and liked it— at least, I liked the results. Although limitation irked me, Holton and I decided to play safe, and we sold only the best-paying jewelry and hardware customers, concentrating most of our efforts on the restaurants, which always paid cash on delivery.

By June, increasing prosperity and the inevitable diversity of human aptitudes brought us face to face with a personal problem. I had proved a more natural salesman than Holton. He disliked "peddling," and the pressure of our profit-making urge had gradually turned him into a packer and shipper, or deliverer, of the goods I sold. This did not suit us. We were brothers, affectionate brothers, and our conception of a brotherly partnership called for equality. So we looked around for some business more fitted to Holton's talent.

In the end we bought a restaurant on Ninth Avenue near 23rd Street. This new enterprise became such a family enthusiasm that our sister Gertrude gave up a position as a teacher at the Columbia Teachers' College to help in the restaurant, and my sixteen-year-old sister, Stella, having unconscionably left the preparatory school where I was trying to get her educated, proved a surprisingly efficient manager for the Noyes Bros. office at 56–58 Warren Street.

The restaurant seemed to all of us a rather thrilling adventure. Stella and I opened its doors every morning (Holton and Gertrude having worked late the evening before), and while I "managed," Stella took in the cash.

We got along very well save for one hectic morning when the chef failed to appear. With the aid and advice of Little Johnny, our handy man, who had worked with the chef, I undertook to cook breakfast for customers who swarmed in at the regular breakfast hour. All went well until an order came down the shaft for an omelette soufflé. I had never heard of a soufflé, and Johnny's mind went blank, with the result that, after much discussion and with many misgivings, I sent up an order of scrambled eggs. Whether the customer made a scene in the room above or Stella exercised her sixteen-year-old charms to calm him, I do not remember.

Holton always arrived at the restaurant by eight thirty. After breakfast he gave me a list of things to buy at the West Washington market, and thither I proceeded by streetcar, while Johnny pushed his cart to the market and later pushed it back loaded with my purchases.

I pause to record my opinion of the "farmers" who, in 1893, brought their vegetables, eggs and fowls to the West Washington market. They were the toughest citizens I had ever met up to that time. At first they "did" me, good and proper, but soon I learned to buy nothing until I had scoffed at the prices offered by at least a half a dozen vendors. Once I remember being very near to a ruckus with a hairy yokel who insisted that I had insulted him.

From the market I went to Warren Street and thereafter

spent the day selling silverware. During the summer it was
my custom to return to the restaurant early in the evening.
At the 23rd Street Pier I handed out dodgers advertising the
Berkeley Restaurant to passengers returning on the Coney
Island boats, and after that, distributed advertising matter
along old London Terrace which, in 1893, was a very dignified residential neighborhood.

At one point in our restaurant career we had doubled the
original receipts, and if we could have held our patronage, it
would have been a success. I "shopped" the nearby eating
houses, especially those on Eighth Avenue. I found that, because they were just a little outside New York's white-light
district, they thrived on the patronage of men who dined
with other men's wives, and I found also that such patrons
must have liquor. Some obscure inhibition, probably a relic
of our early training, prevented our getting a liquor license.

During that fall our silverware business continued to
grow. I was able to figure a good profit as the result of any
forenoon's work, in place of the three dollars per day of the
year before. I have referred to "Noyes Bros., 56–58 Warren
St." This address sounds rather imposing—unduly imposing
—but we really had an office. The space was small and on a
second floor, rented from a wholesale paper merchant. There
we had a desk, a telephone and room enough for a small stock
of silverware. Mr. Miller's wareroom was on the next street
where we could fill in more items at a moment's notice.

Holton had become engaged to another of the Community Children's House girls and, if his engagement was
later than mine, it encountered fewer vicissitudes. Josephine,
his fiancée, was a fine girl, brave and loyal. She longed to
share in his arduous days, with the result that early in No-

vember he made a quick trip to Oneida and brought his bride back to New York. She was a good soldier. Holton let the chef go and Josephine, with the aid of my sister Gertrude, took over the kitchen. They worked long hours, hoping to make the enterprise pay.

Conditions were against them. In spite of hard work and economy, the restaurant insisted on running behind. By the end of December we all agreed that the time had come to sell out, and we were fortunate enough to find a purchaser at a reasonable price. Then the problem of the future descended upon us.

Holton still believed that he could make a success in the restaurant business, while I preferred to go on with our silverware business, so that the firm of Noyes Bros. came to an end. Our partnership settlement left the silverware business with me, along with the debts contracted during stock-trading days, and, as was only fair, most of the cash went to Holton. This enabled him to purchase a small luncheon restaurant on Pearl Street, at a location now near the center of Foley Square. With the aid of his wife, his mother, and the venerable Mr. Johnson, he made this restaurant pay.

My own prospects for 1894 were favorably affected by world conditions. The business panic of 1893 had reduced Mr. Miller's commissions so seriously that he was obliged to let his outside salesman go. His selling contract with the Oneida Community, Ltd. included New England, Philadelphia, Baltimore and Washington, and he now made arrangements with me to cover this outside territory on a split-commission basis.

Moreover, another man's misfortune brought me what I needed most—additional capital. When, in December, the majority party at home demoted Mr. Herrick from the position of Chicago Sales Manager, for political reasons—he was a rabid Noyesite and one of the fiercest opponents of the Spiritualist regime—he joined Mr. Miller in New York. He had a very substantial amount of capital and this he made available, on an income-sharing basis, for my Noyes Bros. sales.

Now I could expand. Even more important was the chance Mr. Miller's agency would give me to gain experience in dealing with larger customers—the Oneida Community, Ltd.'s jobbers of silverware, steel traps and chains. My field would be wider. Life promised fulfillment of the adventure I had hoped for as a boy.

On New Year's Day, 1894, I was exultant, elated by past success and even more by future prospects. With Mr. Herrick's new financial backing, the favorable traveling program arranged with Mr. Miller and my experience as a salesman, I saw myself invading a new and larger area of operations. Noyes Bros. had been increasingly successful during 1893; but now I felt that my feet were firmly on the road to a bigger success, to wealth.

My ego was further inflated by a development which at the moment seemed only a recognition of maturity, but which turned out to be one of the many fortunate happenings that have, quite outside my own planning, reshaped my life. On January 18, 1894, I was elected a Director of the Oneida Community, Ltd. This directorship was not included in my New Year's plans or expectations, but came as an accident—unless you believe that fate has plans of its own.

During January, 1894, Uncle Abram, desiring to spend the winter in California, proposed that I take his place as one of the four *helpless minority* directors. I have forgotten whether or not I suggested the nomination. I may have done so, for I was at the time ardently courting (mostly long-distance courting) my future wife who lived at Oneida, and as a director I could visit her once a month at the Company's expense. Incidentally, I had found long-distance courting unsatisfactory, subject to painful ups and downs, but I had great confidence in personal salesmanship.

Under my arrangement with Mr. Miller, I now called on the Oneida Community wholesale customers and large department stores and I enjoyed it immensely. I do not remember either timidity or embarrassment. And yet, after watching for many years the education of young salesmen, I am suspicious of memories that suggest a very quick adjustment to the new technique called for by this larger salesmanship. Instruction and experience are invaluable aids in dealing with buyers even today, when most of them treat salesmen as though their interests were mutual. In 1894 the generation of buyers were hard-fisted, hard-faced bullies, or they posed as such. Some were authentic. All were paid, or thought they were paid, to intimidate salesmen. I had no instructor.

One of the first of Mr. Miller's customers upon whom I called was a large hardware jobber in New York City. The buyer, Mr. Howard, noting that I was young and new on the job, decided to dramatize his toughness. I quoted our season's price on traps. Mr. Howard exploded.

"Why, young man, you evidently don't know your own firm's prices and terms. You had better go back and get posted. Get your prices right before you come in again."

When I stuck to my guns and insisted that I had given him our best prices, he turned half round in his swivel chair, indicating an end of the interview. He remarked to the room in general, "Ridiculous!" Bereft of any weapon except insistence that my prices were right, and a congenital dislike of being beaten, I stayed with this buyer until he gave me an order.

Another man, the buyer for a large New York commission house, treated me in much the same cavalier manner, but I forgave him because in the end he furnished me ammunition for attacking the management at home. I remember that he rose from his chair and declaimed with righteous indignation ringing in his voice, "They haven't told you the arrangement with me! Probably they don't want you to know it. Perhaps it is best that you don't. I shall write to your manager."

I stayed with this man until he told me of his "arrangement." When he showed me a letter from our home office, my commercial instincts were outraged. He had insisted on an extra 5 per cent and had got it. I deliberately humbled myself until he came down from his high horse and showed me all the past correspondence. There I discovered that he had each year, by threats, persuaded our weak-kneed management to give him an additional 2½ per cent until, in that year of grace, 1894, he made bold to demand 5 per cent on top of the other "extras."

At the next Directors' Meeting I asked that the manager of the Trap Department be invited to attend. In his presence I told the assembled directors of these concessions and insisted that such weakness involved not only the whittling away of profits but, even worse, the demoralization of our other trade relations. I quoted important jobbing customers who had said to me, "How can we sell your traps, when small wholesalers, scattered over the country, clients of this commission man, can buy traps a lot cheaper than we do? We will be forced to push Peck, Stowe & Wilcox traps." (A rival brand.) The directors backed me.

That was New York City. When I visited Philadelphia,

the list of customers seemed like a roster of ancient and honorable names, made romantic for me by ledger pages from the days when I served as a glorified office boy for Treasurer Herrick. "And now," I said to myself, "I shall be responsible for keeping those names [Supplee Hardware Company, Seltzer Klahr, Shields Bros., Biddle Hardware Company, and others] in our ledgers."

I was prepared for more grief, but Philadelphia proved a surprise. The buyers received me cordially, largely I think, because they were personally fond of Mr. Miller. One man said, "Mr. Miller ought not to be selling goods; he is too fine a gentleman."

When visiting Boston, I avoided Cambridge. Memory suggests that Cambridge seemed a symbol of disappointment, and I was in no frame of mind to fraternize with disappointment. One odd relic of my youthful enthusiasms followed me to Boston. It must have been a sentimental regard for the Boston of Harvard, Emerson and William Dean Howells that led me each noon to the public library on Copley Square where I drew a book I had been reading at home and read it in that cultural Back Bay atmosphere for as long a time as the noon recess could be stretched. Was Boston different in the 'nineties, or was my romantic feeling a hangover from those two weeks in Cambridge? Perhaps a little of both.

My travels in 1894 brought me in contact with the typical drummer of the "Drumming 90's." I sat with him—many of him—in railway smoking compartments and hotel lobbies. Always he discussed the hotels on his route and swapped stories with other salesmen, regarding orders received from firms they both knew. He would ask, "Do you call on so and so?" and Drummer No. 2 would reply nonchalantly, "Sure.

I got a two-thousand-dollar order from them last week. Rotten! It should have been twice that." Often the first speaker would try to get even by telling of the commissions he was making. It made my own work seem small and ineffectual until, after the others had gone, a friendly salesman remarked, "Don't believe all you hear. Cut those stories of sales and commissions in two, and *then* they'll be twice too large."

I was a busy boy in 1894. After calling on the Oneida Community, Ltd.'s jobbers, I wandered through the smaller cities, selling silverware for Noyes Bros. That was my arrangement with Mr. Miller.

In those days my preoccupation with material success was so complete that I find myself puzzled by memories indicating that the educational ambitions with which I left Colgate had survived. I remember a determination to fill the blank spaces in my knowledge of world history—with the result that Gibbon's *Decline and Fall,* Draper's *Intellectual Development of Europe,* the *Rise of the Dutch Republic,* or some other book, covering a period about which I had only fragmentary knowledge, could always be found in my traveling bag.

The Company's minority directors had for years received scant courtesy from the majority, and found their only satisfaction in hectoring that majority. There was plenty of ammunition lying around for political sniping. Several political appointees were notoriously incompetent, and several political allies were busy cashing in on their alliance. My arrangement with Mr. Miller having brought me in touch with the Company's principal customers, I learned more during that year about the management's delinquencies than the managers themselves knew. As a director, my hectoring was so detailed and factual that both directors and managers were obliged to take notice. Every Directors' Meeting became a field day for the minority.

It was not long, however, before I became genuinely alarmed for the future of the Oneida Community, Ltd. I thought of all the elderly ex-Perfectionists whose income depended upon the Company's profits, and before the year was over my criticisms were aimed more at reform than at annoying our opponents. It was not alone incompetence and profiteering that worried me. I saw what had not penetrated the consciousness of the average Oneida stockholder; that business conditions in the 'nineties had radically changed from the days when honesty and industry were the chief essentials for successful enterprise; that men able to run a business profitably in the 'sixties or 'seventies, were just out of luck, struggling with the competition of the 'eighties and 'nineties when mass production was taking the place of the little factory on the mill stream.

Memories of that year when I served as a minority director bring me both regret and satisfaction. It pains me just a little to recall the zest with which I badgered men whom I had revered in childhood and most of whom, when I came to know them better, proved worthy of that reverence. It shames me that I took pleasure in annoying them. I remind myself that they were elderly men and that defense against the attacks of an aggressive youth with damaging facts in his arsenal must have been a tough proposition, if not "unfair competition." And more, I am bound to say for those ex-Perfectionists that they treated me fairly. They might have disregarded my criticisms as the carping of a political enemy, but they did not. They took them seriously.

Against such self-accusation I place the fact that my criticisms started a ferment of general criticism of the management and revitalized the fighting spirit of the minority. In 1894, the Oneida Community, Ltd. was sinking into a morass of elderly incompetence, where leeching political allies were already sucking its blood. At the moment I was just a gadfly. It comforts me to remember that in later years more than one member of the 1894 majority expressed thankfulness that I interfered when I did.

So much for the obvious but, as it turned out, the least important aspects of my life in 1894. I have said that on New Year's Day I was exultant. This exultation was short lived. Before the year ended I was neither exultant nor elated. The yeast of a new outlook on life was fermenting in my soul and progressively making my planned and hoped-for future less attractive. I was in full cry for the riches that "moth and rust doth corrupt," and my optimistic nature had already transformed prospect into accomplishment when I discovered that the color of a glorious financial future was changing to a shabby gray.

Searching among the memories of that year, however, I do not find that my new outlook on life led to new planning or any change in my old plans. I worked harder and ranged wider in my struggle to build a fortune. I was still ambitious for business success, but that success no longer thrilled me.

I am still somewhat puzzled that a youth of twenty-three years should have developed a distaste for "getting rich," but that is certainly what happened to me. Apparently the emergence of success raised a question as to what I could do with wealth, and the answer left me cold. This reaction was, in all probability, subject to ups and downs, as the year went forward. Periods of unusual success must have revived the old thrills, but on the whole I suspect that the deflation was progressive. Of one thing am I certain: that when new year 1895 came, my subconscious—what the Honorable Frederick Frankland, a noted mathematician and social scientist, called my subliminal self—was prepared for change. I am equally certain that my political struggle for a more capable management of the Oneida Company's affairs had not consciously suggested for myself any return to Oneida.

I could wish to sort out the considerations or incidents that led to the submergence of my previous ambitions, but all that suggest themselves seem insufficient. I am still in doubt. More than sixty years have passed since then, and I still find it difficult to evaluate even the importance of those influences that I can recall.

In the past I have been satisfied with an explanation which I now suspect is too simple. It was associated with a well-remembered incident. I was walking along Central Park West (then the Park Avenue of New York), beneath the towering façades of fashionable apartment houses and hotels, when a revulsion of feeling seized me. "This," I said to myself, "represents the normal goal of a successful career: an apartment here, living among other men who have devoted their lives to money-making and have cached the things worth while, to be enjoyed—sometime." My imagination, as often happens, insisted on something pictorial. "When at last they open the bag, what do they find? . . . Not a damn thing in it!"

I remember the rather crude metaphor of a paper bag with which I clinched my thought, because I repeated it to Dr. Noyes, my half brother, thirty years older than I. I can still hear the Doctor's wheezy chuckle. He said something like, "You'll get over that feeling."

My wife suggests that those monthly visits to Oneida in 1894 aroused fugitive visions of a happier life surrounded by my companions of the "Children's House." But such thoughts must have been vague as well as fugitive. I feel sure that the dream of building a business on the old Oneida foundation did not enter my mind as a practical enterprise until the political victory, January, 1895, unexpectedly opened the door to a future encouraged by that fading of old ambitions.

Seeking further for other causes than a psychological revulsion that may have influenced my change of heart, I do, however, recall that I returned from later Directors' Meetings genuinely alarmed for the future of the Oneida Community, Ltd. and fearful for the fate of those elderly ex-Perfectionists whose income depended upon the Company's profits. Still, I cannot directly connect this anxiety with my change of outlook earlier in the year.

It remains only to inquire whether any person influenced my conversion. Was it the effect of talks with my Cousin George? During the first half of that year, George and I lived with Dr. Noyes in a flat on West 114th Street, in a room whose windows opened at the exact point where elevated trains, easing around a curve, made the most outrageous noise. We ate dinner, I recall, at nearby restaurants. Memory selects curious facts—that for our evening meal we usually settled on a restaurant where excellent fried oysters could be had for thirty-five cents; a complete meal for fifty cents. My cousin, George Noyes, was, through a long life, the most conscientious and consistent Christian I ever knew. He was also an ardent disciple of John Humphrey Noyes and never wavered in his belief that my father pointed the way to a more Christlike social system. And yet, I do not recollect his ever calling in question my materialistic ambitions.

Was it Dr. Noyes who influenced me? He was very much the social philosopher and natural skeptic. Having lived to the age of forty in the Community, established by his father, John Humphrey Noyes, he was now reveling in the intellectual freedom granted him by the breakup of that Community. I remember that he criticized his father's "Bible communism" and the antisocial aspects of "outside" capitalism impartially and with equal good nature.

Although he had strayed from his father's religion, I suspect that deep down in his consciousness the socialistic virus was still active. I lived with this half brother until June, 1894, and yet I do not remember his ever seeking to influence the direction of my ambitions. As a matter of fact, he shared my enterprise from the side lines and rubbed his hands gleefully over my successes.

Some of the most vivid memories of the months when I lived with Doctor Noyes tell of evenings spent listening to philosophical discussions between him and Mr. Frankland, who had been brought from England to America by the New York Life Insurance Company to work out a mathematical basis for old-age annuities. He had been a greater admirer of the Oneida Community. In New Zealand, where he had lived for a number of years, he showed this admiration and demonstrated his communistic leanings by organizing social groups which he named "Oneida" and "Wallingford." He was vocal in his appreciation of the principles of the Oneida Community, and yet, as in the case of Dr. Noyes, I do not remember that he ever criticized my enthusiasm for a money-making career.

Incidentally, I enjoyed my evenings with those two men, although both were absorbed in developing metaphysical theories which, while they stimulated my intellectual faculties, did not seem of practical value. Such idealities as the "subliminal self" continually bobbed up in their discussions. At one time they worked for an entire month on diagrams which aimed to picture the fourth dimension of space. The Doctor became so fascinated with Frankland's equational explanations of metaphysical principles that, at his request, I attempted to induct him into the mysteries of higher mathematics. It was too late; he was too old.

I remember his half-humorous anxiety over a potted plant left in his care by an insistently religious relative, a lady who went out as a missionary and later died in China. He called it the "Sacred Plant." He watered it faithfully and each evening called our attention to the gain or loss of a leaf. In spite of his attentions, the plant faded away until little was left but a bare stem. The Doctor wagged his head solemnly. "The fact is," he told us, "that plant has a religious background; it cannot stand the secular atmosphere of this flat."

Just one other anecdote to characterize this lovable half brother. His six-year-old, motherless son, who then lived with him, was very mischievous, and the Doctor, in spite of elaborate theories regarding the bringing up of children, proved weak in his dealing with young Raymond. I remember an evening when the boy, sitting on the back of his father's chair, amused himself by sticking strips of gummed paper onto his father's bald head. Then he pulled the strips off. The Doctor's pained, "No! No! Ray, don't do that," led only to loud laughter from the little rascal, and a repetition of the process.

I have left to the last the fact that those monthly visits to Oneida resulted in what I have always accounted my most outstanding selling success; I persuaded Corinna to marry me right away. However, I had to answer a certain practical question asked by every sensible girl when considering matrimony, *i.e.*, can you afford it? I persuaded Corinna that, while I still had debts and no money, I had a large amount invested in "experience," and on the twenty-sixth of June, 1894, we were married in the Mansion House Hall. Then and there I made sure of the best wife any man ever had.

Our plan, after the wedding, was to spend a week at some mountain resort in the Catskills, but after going as far as the town of Catskill, common sense asserted itself, and we decided to go straight to New York, saving our slender means for furnishing our new home. Our address, 123 Bradhurst Avenue, was so far uptown that we could hear the cheering at the Polo Grounds, but it was within a five minute walk of the 145th Street Elevated and, unbelievable as it seems today, the rent of that brand-new five-room flat was only twenty-two dollars a month. Even with the addition of our cherished wedding presents, it was nothing elegant, but it was pleasingly comfortable, and very shortly we were settled and ready to receive our friends.

Gerard Wayland-Smith, who always had a genius for nicknames, promptly christened the place Lonesomehurst, but it never seemed lonesome to us. There were several families of former Community people living in New York at that time, and never a week passed without a call by some of our old friends. Even more often, all three Wayland-Smith boys— Dick, Gerard and Louis—would drop in for an evening of cards, or, after a long day of walking from store to store selling silverware, I was only too glad to spend a quiet evening at home with my wife and my sister Stella, who was living with us. Occasionally we saw a play or light opera from seats in the upper balcony. These were special treats, however, since we were counting the pennies, not anxiously, as I never doubted my *ultimate* success, but wisely, with the result that by December we had saved enough to go home for Christmas. (Fare, from Weehawken to Community, the O & W station near the Mansion, $3.75.)

The necessity for more and more capital in the business led me to draw out only one hundred dollars per month for family expenses, but we kept within our income and at the end of six months had seventeen dollars savings to show. As a matter of fact, the economy of those days remains one of my wife's romantic memories. In her household regime she had the word "economy" underscored, which accounted for our living within our means. She often walked many blocks to save a five-cent carfare.

Unquestionably I told my wife of the new psychology that was fermenting in my brain, but our discussions must have been theoretical, since we both concentrated our attention on the success of Noyes Bros., Wholesalers of Silverware and Novelties. Corinna is an uncompromising idealist— a real Perfectionist. She has encouraged every scrap of idealism to be found in me, but I do not remember that in 1894 she threw any cold water on my ambition to get rich.

On the whole, for an explanation of the cloud which suddenly obscured the lodestar of personal wealth, I am obliged to fall back on the conditioning, during my childhood in the Oneida Community, of my "subliminal self." Perhaps my 1894 fortune-promising visions dissolved when subjected to the catalytic left in my subconscious mind by Bible communism.

The old idol, wealth, had shown its feet of clay, but my search for a new idol, if search I made, was sketchy. At the moment, it had no standing among the pragmatic problems of daily life. I was still pursuing success along a trail—half ambitious, half vengeful—that my conditioning at Niagara had mapped out for me. It is a fair gamble that my new ideals would have evaporated, would have gone the way of most youthful ideals, if circumstances had not, at the critical moment, opened a door through which I saw the possibility of practically applying them.

That directorship which I had accepted as a temporary appointment during the absence of Uncle Abram, was certainly a freak of fate. Because of this new responsibility, it happened that as early as March, 1894, I visited Niagara Falls, primarily to complain of defects in the goods, but incidentally to obtain information regarding the arrangement with K. & M. by means of which they were siphoning off large profits from the Silverware Department. This trip was evidently unauthorized. The minutes state: "Resolved, that $25.00 be allowed for P. B. Noyes's expenses traveling to the Falls," but adds, "In future, such trips should be a matter of consultation with the Tableware Department." If the expense account was voted grudgingly, my report was taken seriously, for further along in the minutes occurs this statement: "Samples of O.C.L. silverware were shown with white spots. It was thought that our goods should be more carefully inspected."

A vivid memory of that visit to Niagara comes back to me. The young man who was going to thrash me three years before had, after Mr. Hamilton's death, invented a more profitable, if technically less criminal, method of mulcting the Oneida Community, Limited. And now his father, the superintendent, refused me access to the Company's books. I insisted that, as a director, I had a right to examine the books and threatened to employ a lawyer. In the end the elder Mr. K—— succumbed. When the interdict had been removed, Mrs. Barron, who happened to be head bookkeeper at the Falls, aided me in getting the statistics I desired.

The echoes of that trip to Niagara Falls can be found in the April Directors' Meeting Minutes. I read, "Complaints were made that K. & M. have been offering to the O.C.L.'s best accounts prices lower than the Company's lowest price." It was resolved, "That K. & M. be notified that they must not sell or quote prices to trade in the East, worked by Mr. Miller."

But K. & M. persisted in their customer-stealing. They quoted our best customers 2 per cent cash discount, instead of the Company's traditional 1 per cent, and by this means transferred to themselves many of the Company's best accounts, with a profit to themselves of 6 per cent. The futility of my complaints peeps out from the minutes of the November meeting. The Secretary notes in passing, "There was a discussion as to changing our discount from 1% to 2%, but it was not thought expedient to make any change at present."

I must have harped on the unbusinesslike special prices given commission houses, since I find this in the August minutes, "Resolved, that the Hardware superintendent be requested to withdraw all special prices allowed to commission houses."

And then in November I returned from the Directors' Meeting truculently out of patience with the directors and managers at Oneida and convinced that their derelictions had provided enough ammunition to make their defeat a fair gamble. I reported this conviction in New York. Dr. Noyes, Mr. Miller and Mr. Herrick were all violently antagonistic to

the Spiritualists, albeit their hostility—I always thought—
was aimed more at Mr. Pitt's usurpation of John Humphrey
Noyes's spiritual leadership than at his political power. They
agreed that I should return to Oneida, there to conduct a political campaign.

CHAPTER VII

So, UNEXPECTEDLY, I found myself on a train headed for Oneida only three days after returning from a Directors' Meeting there. Sitting by the window of a nineteenth-century Pullman I fell to studying practical plans for the political campaign Mr. Miller, Mr. Herrick and I had agreed upon; a campaign aimed at displacing the "incompetents" who for six long years had managed—or mismanaged—the Company. Mr. Miller and Mr. Herrick had been strong for my going and had promised to handle my Noyes Bros. business as well as they could in my absence.

All at once, a very disturbing idea came into my mind: "I am going to Oneida—to attack many of the friends of my childhood." From that came pictures of childhood in the Community with these friends. I saw sunny afternoons where groups of men and women gathered in shady places on the great north lawn. From some, laughter and lively talk could be heard; from others, a man's voice, evidently reading out loud to the group. Farther away, behind a grove of pines came the sound of croquet balls hitting against each other.

These memories were disconcerting. But with them recurred the feeling that had followed me home from each monthly visit to Oneida, a feeling that the divided and elderly management might put an end to the old institution. Its common stock was already selling at a price far below par. That day on the train I promised myself a sincere attempt to reverse the control of the Oneida Community, Ltd.; to make

80

possible a revision of its management on a more modern and youthful basis. I decided that only thus could the business, and with it the Oneida family, be made secure.

As a result, I spent a month electioneering with the aid of Mr. Hinds, the Kinsley brothers, and other opponents of the Spiritualists. Our activity must early have raised a doubt in the minds of the majority directors as to the result of the coming election. An item in the December record suggests this doubt, but it also illustrates the fundamental fairness of Oneida-Community-conditioned minds. A letter was read from K. & M. urging another year's renewal of their one-sided contract. The Board's Secretary noted, "Action postponed until the formation of the new Board."

K. & M. finally became alarmed. One day, the more diplomatic and less objectionable member of the firm turned up at Oneida, where he made himself extremely agreeable to everyone. Our worthy President, a man gifted with more good nature than perspicacity, urged me to discuss with M—— the contract I had attacked continually for a year. I consented to talk with this emissary from K. & M., but quite naturally was noncommittal. He must have overrated his salesmanship or underrated my intelligence, for he reported to his partner at Niagara Falls that he had "fixed everything all right, whichever party wins the election."

Our canvass for votes was very complete. We visited or corresponded with every holder of Oneida Community stock. Taking advantage of a business trip to Portland, Maine, I drove, with my wife, from Kennebunk to Kennebunkport to labor with a Mr. Pillsbury who owned 125 shares and who had, in the past, given his proxy to the Spiritualists.

That is an interesting memory, that call on Mr. Pillsbury. He was the Mr. Pillsbury who interested me as a child when visiting the Community. Corinna and I located the house in which this peculiar old man lived alone, but found him not at home. A neighbor suggested the village grocery store. Mr. Pillsbury was a shy man and our entrance into the store, which was evidently his favorite hangout, sent him scurrying for concealment behind the stove. I pursued. After some dodging back and forth, I caught up with him, introduced myself, and sprayed him with the highest quality of 1894 salesmanship. He was noncommittal. His few words offered no points for argument and left us no clue as to his ultimate decision. As a matter of record, we never received his proxy.

Then there was an important business man in Oneida, who had a very considerable block of stock which had been voted, in previous elections, for the Spiritualists. It was one of my triumphs that he decided to support a "business management." This incident will suggest the earnestness—I had almost said bitterness—of that campaign. On election day, Mr. Kinsley, my father-in-law, went to the village of Oneida and parked his horse and buggy in a local livery stable.

During the forenoon he saw an opposition member hobnobbing with our pet proxy, Mr. Remick. He followed the two men and found them seated in a beer saloon. When he entered Remick arose and, pointing to Mr. Kinsley, exclaimed, "No, sir—spirits can't can corn—not by a damned sight they can't! There's the man that's got my proxy, and he's going to keep it!" The canning of fruits and vegetables was then one of the leading enterprises of the Oneida Community, Limited.

Those were exciting days. I could relate many tales of successes, reverses, negotiations, promises, desertions and other episodes, all of which made the election of 1895 a disagreeable memory for most of the peace-loving residents of the Mansion House. I have, however, indicated sufficiently the intensity with which the struggle was conducted by both sides.

To understand the turmoil caused in the Mansion House by this political campaign, I should explain, first, that in 1894 —fourteen years after the change from a Community to a Joint Stock Company—a majority of the Company's stock was owned by residents of the Mansion House and second, that the old Community habit of informing the members of important or even interesting happenings in the conduct of the business had been revived by reports at evening meetings called for that purpose. Not only questions but discussion by men and women alike were encouraged at those meetings. I remember my mother telling me she considered that being a stockholder brought with it a serious responsibility, and I believe the other old members felt the same.

On the day of the election, balloting was not finished until a late hour, and, by mutual agreement, the counting of the votes was postponed until morning. Strange to say, both parties went to bed believing that they had lost the election.

One of the legends of the "Great Election," a legend which the ensuing sixty years of political peace have made only a humorous memory, is my midnight awakening to the fact that we had won. I slept that night in the Kinsleys' house at the Four Corners. It was an old-fashioned farmhouse, and the second-story bedroom, occupied by my wife and myself, was heated by a stovepipe which admitted warmth from the room below. Lying awake, I mentally reviewed the votes and the voters. A month of proxy-chasing had fixed in my mind the ownership of every share of stock and on which side it had probably been voted. Suddenly I recalled that a block of stock which had not been voted at all was figured by us as entirely negative, while it should have been reckoned one half in our favor. That changed a small minus into a sixteen-share plus—a defeat into a victory!

I arose and called down the stovepipe hole to my father-in-law. "We've won the election!" He told me afterwards that he thought I was having a nightmare, but I promptly descended and convinced him that I was right. We had won, by a sixteen-share margin, an election wherein nearly twenty-four thousand shares were voted. On that day, or perhaps I should say on that night, in January, 1895, the new Oneida Community, Ltd. was born.

It was ten o'clock on the morning of January 13, 1895, when the inspectors of election officially announced the result. A majority of the Mansion House residents were pleased, and at eleven o'clock five directors, even more pleased, went into a huddle in Mr. Hinds's room. It was a large room on the third floor in a section called "the Mansard," a room which many a game of high-low-jack had made familiar to the older directors, and many a chess game to chess players for miles around. Mr. Hinds was the President of the Madison County Chess Association.

He was a short man, but he had a personality which made one forget his lack of stature. His face-enveloping beard was trimmed, but only after it had attained in all directions the generous proportions so popular in mid-Victorian America. His eyes, peering out from drooping eyelids, registered intelligence—perhaps an analyst, uninfluenced by affection, would call it shrewdness. Altogether, Mr. Hinds might well have passed for one of those village elders who, in earlier days, kept the Puritan lid clamped firmly down on undue levity, and whose pictures now adorn family albums and New England histories. He had, however, a lively sense of humor which one would never suspect until some episode or a funny story convulsed his visible features.

Mr. Hinds was truly religious. When a mere boy, in the 1840's, he had become an enthusiastic Perfectionist and, so the story goes, my father bought off his legal apprenticeship so that he might join the group of converts then emigrating from their Northern Vermont homes to join the Community at Oneida. He had, however, a passion for political strategy; also, underneath his serious preoccupations, a lively sporting instinct which did at times threaten, or at least obscure, his spiritual-mindedness.

One incident which occurred in our boyhood days will illustrate this. His son, Elliot, had a wild broncho in which he placed great confidence and which he entered in a running race at the annual Oneida fair. When his father objected, Elliot was defiant. It was steel meet steel, and all the answer Mr. Hinds could get from his son was, "I'm going to, though."

Father Hinds tried to compromise. "I don't like your getting mixed up with the racing business, but if you're bound to do it I certainly don't want you to ride the horse."

Elliot was no compromiser. He simply repeated, "I'm going to, though."

On the morning of the race, while Elliot was grooming the broncho, his father appeared at the barn. Realizing that he could not shake his son's determination to race, he said (Elliot told me the story), "You know I don't like to have you go into this race, but if you are going to do it anyway"— he produced from under his coat a pair of spurs—"perhaps these will help you." Elliot and the broncho, with Father's spurs, won the race before the next contender was barely around the corner.

It was the same colorful and reckless Elliot who, as an aviator on the French front in the First World War, insisted on "ferrying" an unfamiliar plane from Columba de Bel to Toul, when the rest of the company transported theirs by truck. He was killed.

Our political caucus had been postponed until eleven o'clock, awaiting the arrival of Doctor Noyes who had been elected one of the new directors. He came from Niagara Falls where he had been visiting his mother, the "Mother Noyes" of Community days. She still, at the age of eighty-seven, made fish-scale flowers, played solitaire and washed dishes three times a day in the old Stone Cottage where my father spent his last years. By common consent the Doctor was to be our new President.

I say common consent; it was primarily Mr. Hinds's consent and an example of his political shrewdness. He, himself, yearned to be President, as a testimonial of forgiveness for his machinations in 1879 and 1880 which had helped to break up the Oneida Community. As a matter of fact, Mr. Hinds was a lifelong believer in Perfectionism, but, in those later days of the Community, so-called "disaffection" had led him into insurgent maneuvers, and now, in January, 1895, the logic of events promised him the presidency of the new company.

I knew of his ambitions and urged the candidacy upon him until, in the middle of our campaign, his political sagacity told him what we all knew, that he had too many enemies among the Noyes loyalists to be elected. One evening he took me aside and voluntarily abdicated in favor of Doctor Noyes. I remember well that conversation. We were

on our way to the Mansion House dining room when he led
me into the darkness of the old laundry. He said, "Doctor
Noyes must be our candidate. I have too many enemies. He
has few and—well, after all, he is his father's son."

To return to that first caucus on the morning after the
"Great Election." Mr. Hinds was still tacitly accepted as
leader of the party and, as such, automatically became chairman of the meeting. I remember that his irrepressible chuckle,
interlarded with jibes at the chagrin of the opposition, delayed the business of the meeting for some time. Finally the
wrinkles at the corners of his eye relaxed. He became serious.

"Our selection of officers has already been made and
needs no discussion. But one important and difficult question confronts me. We won this election largely by exposing
the mismanagement at Niagara Falls and elsewhere. We
promised to remedy this; but who is there to do the job?
Whom shall we appoint as superintendent? What do you suggest?"

Being evidently a rhetorical question, his query remained unanswered. He continued. "I confess I don't know
what to do. Silverware is a comparatively new business with
us, and there aren't many on our side of the fence competent
to handle the whole thing."

Mr. Kinsley, whose twinkling eyes had not lost the
sparkle that came with my sudden announcement that we had
won the election, prompted his lifelong friend. "You've someone in mind, William. Who is it?"

But William Hinds was not ready to be smoked out. He
shook his head and his shrewd eyes roamed from one to
another. "I am in a dilemma. Nearly all the men I can think
of lack something for this position. Amos, for instance, knows
how to make silverware; he is a reliable young man, but he

is not available because he has had no experience selling silverware. We must have someone who can manage both manufacturing and selling."

Mr. Kinsley, smiling and nodding knowingly at others in the group, persisted, "Don't beat around the bush, William. Who is it?"

Mr. Hinds evidently decided to take the bull by the horns. "I'll tell you my dilemma. Pierre [they all called me Pierre in those days] has served in the factory and has proved his commercial ability as well. He could fill the position. On the other hand, I ask you, what would our stockholders say if we put a young man of twenty-four years in charge of half the Company's business?"

If I remember rightly, there followed a considerable period of silence, broken finally by Mr. George Kellogg, the fifth majority director. He had never been an important executive and would have been the first to acknowledge his inability to handle large industrial or commercial responsibilities, but he was a forthright man and one of few words. He spoke impulsively and there was a note of impatience in his voice. "Why not appoint Pierre?"

So far Doctor Noyes had said nothing. He was slowly nodding his head and now he spoke hesitatingly.

"I am greatly interested in our opportunity to get this new Oneida Community—the Oneida Community, Ltd.—back on a business basis and insure a prosperity which will make it a harbor of safety for the old members of the Community. My hesitation is somewhat natural because I have watched Pierre, from a standing start, with gruelling labor, overcoming the difficulty of selling merchandise in the toughest market—New York City. His prospects now seem to be very bright. However, if he's willing to make the sacrifice

I'm willing—and, of course, it will make the task delegated to us by yesterday's election much easier." After a pause he added, "I still want to be sure Pierre is making a choice he will never regret. I've been proud of his success, and I personally can set no limit to that success he will be exchanging for his loyalty to his old home and old friends."

Logically it was my turn, and I was thinking hard. During the political campaign I had pondered this problem of Niagara management and had discussed it with Mr. Hinds. I mentioned two of the older men. He refused both very positively and gave me his reasons. Running over in my mind other possibilities, I had thought of Mr. Miller. He knew silverware business, but his age and his temperament made unlikely the vigor I knew must be expended on our businesses if they were to be successful.

I thought of Stephen Leonard, but he had had no experience in selling; besides, we needed him to revive the trap business. Paul Herrick was too young. My brother, John Humphrey, would not accept such responsibility. Grosvenor Allen was still working for the Pope Company, and I did not then know what I learned later about his ability. I found myself in the same dilemma as Mr. Hinds. I suspect that in the heat of the campaign, I had deliberately closed my eyes to this problem, salving my conscience by an optimistic feeling that we would find some one to take charge at Niagara and that with my location in New York I could help the new manager. This definite suggestion that I take the job myself was a shock.

When, later, the meeting actually decided to offer me the position, I stalled. As nearly as I can remember I said, "I appreciate the honor, but it would involve a violent change in my plans. Let me think it over."

When the meeting ended, I sought my wife. We had

then no room in the Mansion House, so we foregathered in the Nursery Kitchen. There, surrounded by the furnishings of our childhood—the ironing table, the clothes-drying rack, the kitchen stove, and the old iron sink where a hand pump delivered the only available soft water—I told her of the revolutionary proposition made to me by the directors. She is sure that her answer was "accept"—without reserve. She remembers saying, "Your New York career with all its possibilities has seemed to me alien—alien to you." That is the particular word she remembers—*alien*.

She added as she arose and left the room, "Of course, the decision must be yours."

In a previous chapter I described my search for the cause of that sudden lack of interest in wealth which had assailed me early in the previous year; but memory does not suggest that with that subsidence of financial ambition there came any thought of going back to Oneida. I am sure that I then tried to recover my old ambition. I think that I accused myself of sentimentality. But now, looking from the Nursery Kitchen across that friendly old Quadrangle, I saw two men who had been an essential part of my child world and a woman who had nursed me through a sickness. These were my people. This was my home. I did not follow my wife to the dining room. Instead I remember that I went through the house and crossed the front lawn. I needed to be alone.

I presume that I stood there only a few minutes. As I looked at the (to me) beautiful old Mansion House, there welled up from my inner consciousness a feeling that must have lain there unexpressed during all those three years in New York—a realization that I had *deserted*.

Here had lived a group of people—and many still lived —who had learned to live together, on the whole, in peace

and happiness and consideration for each other. A story of
the past came back to me; a story told by a Community
woman who was showing a stranger through the Mansion
House. She was asked, "What is the fragrance I smell here in
this house?" The answer she gave was typical of the Community. She said simply, "It may be the odor of crushed
selfishness."

As I knew from childhood, the membership of the Oneida
Community had acquired many of the elements of human
accord that idealists always hope for and theorists write
books about. We Community children were taught that
"quarreling"—not to mention fighting—was a sin. In general
the older members lived by the rules of Perfectionism which
meant self-abnegation. Competition, rivalry, fighting to beat
the other fellow was unthinkable. Now, however, with but
little of the aggressiveness and business sagacity that would
have fitted them for the struggle in what my Father once
called "the grab-all world," the earlier generation had been
left to compete in the *new era* of mass production. It seemed
likely that what remained of the Oneida Community would
ultimately go the way of other attempts at co-operative living.

If it failed and passed out of existence, there would never
be another like it. Miles Robertson, now President of this
Company, who as a young man joined it much later from
the "outside," once commented, "No one could go out in a
field and build alone an institution like this. It had to come
by evolution." I was one of the products of that evolution,
and perhaps, the resolution I now made was a result of that
evolution—I decided to return to Oneida.

When the full Board of Directors met and the decision
to appoint me superintendent of the three Niagara departments was announced, the Spiritualists, now in their turn

minority directors, had what we used to call a "conniption fit." They argued and they stormed. "A boy of twenty-four! . . . How can you propose . . ." etc., etc. Although the minority could not defeat my appointment, they undertook to block the plan by refusing to vote me any salary. Unfortunately, the bylaws did not permit me to vote on my own salary. Without my vote the membership stood four against four.

The meeting adjourned in a deadlock. Doctor Noyes, having adopted the majority plan, was outraged that the minority should hold it up and insisted that he was the one to tell them so. Ordinarily the Doctor avoided personal clashes, but on this occasion he went "out of his class." He demanded admission to a private caucus of the recalcitrant directors and read the riot act to them. He told them that the stockholders had delegated responsibility for Company management to the majority, and that their blocking of an appointment which the new management considered necessary was entirely out of character.

Incidentally, there was a typically Community passage of arms between the Doctor and one of the minority directors. The qualities sought for responsible positions in the Company by those disciples of John Humphrey Noyes would seem odd to any other Board of Directors, and the Doctor's statement would sound irrelevant. He told the meeting, "I think that Pierrepont has in him more of his father than any of his other children." Mr. Allen, a man who, in later years, became one of my most ardent supporters, countered, "Do you really think so, Doctor? I have always thought that he had a good deal of the Cook in him."

Without a word of explanation, a reader will hardly realize the crushing nature of this reply. It happened that my mother's mother was a descendant of the Cook family, whose menfolks had been successful lawyers and politicians; two of them became mayors of large cities. Their extreme worldliness was proverbial in the old Community, and when, in accordance with the Community system of "mutual criticism," my mother was criticised, the most damaging accusation against her was that she "showed signs of the Cook spirit." Twenty years later, I had inherited the stigma, at least in the eyes of one old member. Worldliness, ambition and an instinct for commercial success still seemed to him undesirable qualities in any Community enterprise.

The Doctor's onslaught and the fundamental reasonableness I have noted before in old Community members resulted in the breaking down of opposition. In the session next day, Mr. Freeman refrained from voting, and a yearly salary of fifteen hundred dollars was voted me by a four to three ballot. The turn in my road was complete. All that remained was to report to Mr. Miller and make a satisfactory settlement of our relations.

A week after my appointment as superintendent of the O.C. factories at Niagara Falls I climbed the dirty stairway leading to the second floor of 59 Murray Street where Mr. Miller presided over the New York Office of the Oneida Community, Limited. In the workroom, cases were piled to the ceiling and shipping packages littered the floor. Moran, the shipping clerk, was crowding shavings into a box. As I passed him he said, "Hello," but I thought I detected in his tone a note of reproach not present in the unimaginative syllables with which he was accustomed to greet me.

The familiar untidiness and peculiar odor of that workroom wakened in me an unexpected feeling of homesickness, to which Moran's coolness added a touch of remorse.

It had not occurred to me before that I was deserting Mr. Miller. I had written him of my decision to go back to the Company, but now I must face the practical consequences of that decision. I was very fond of Mr. Miller. He had been kind to me when I was struggling for a foothold in New York City, and what especially disturbed me now was a recollection that during the last few months he had plainly shown his gratitude for my assistance.

Mr. Miller's office was in the rear of the workroom. He must have seen me through the glass partition for, when I opened the door, he was hurrying toward it. He clasped my hand in both of his, and his glowing smile, together with his first words, put an end to my feeling of remorse. He said simply, "You are doing right, Pierre."

Mr. Herrick, just behind him, seized my other hand in a firm grip. He was one of those hearty, friendly men, who normally would have told me with warm, if formal, words how glad he was to see me. Today, however, his mind appeared concentrated on the new development which had evidently been thoroughly discussed by these two men. Mr. Miller having set the pace, Mr. Herrick wasted no time on words of welcome. His reaction to my right-about-face was typical of the Herrick realistic religiosity. He spoke solemnly. "Your father's hand is in this. You think you decided the issue yourself"—if Mr. Herrick's eyes were not gazing upward, his voice had in it a from-the-heavens quality when he added—"your father inspired you."

We three sat down and proceeded with a most enthusiastic talk about the future. I remember feeling a little embarrassed by the atmosphere of sacrificial righteousness with which they surrounded my decision to throw away the results of three years' successful struggle and go back to the Company. I also remember trying to give it a slightly more materialistic coloring. I suggested, "It will be an interesting adventure. It certainly offers me a wider field of operation." They were not impressed by this nor by any other intimations that the new work promised very considerable compensation for the abandonment of my fortune-hunting career. I can see now that my weak attempt to dilute the sacrificial nature of my decision was disregarded by men who knew me better than I knew myself. They would have none of it. Mr. Miller was an idealist and Mr. Herrick, a man who had made religion and John Humphrey Noyes' apostleship the romance of his life. They united in the belief that he was still, from the heavens, watching over the fortunes of his former Perfectionists and his son.

He and Mr. Herrick wanted to hear the whole story. They made me analyze my motives for the decision I had made. I told them that, while distaste for a life devoted solely to hunting riches undoubtedly turned me in the new direction, the prospect of getting back with the companions of my childhood also attracted me strongly. In the end, however, I gave those good friends satisfaction by telling of a third motive which my own self-analysis had uncovered.

I called this an instinct to "cover my father's rear." I remember saying, "It just shows that blood is thicker than water. Father never fully approved of me and suspected that I did not accept him 100 per cent. Of all his sons and nephews, I am probably the last he would have selected as his successor. And yet, I can say truthfully that one of the urges which led to my decision was a fear for the future of the Oneida Community, Limited, and a desire to ensure that all his loyal followers in that Perfectionistic experiment be comfortable and cared for as long as they live."

Later—and it was considerably later—we turned to the practical problems involved in the liquidation of my New York business and especially of my semi-partnership with them. To make a long story short, I later found a purchaser for my Noyes Brothers business, and Mr. Miller took back into his stock other goods I had purchased from him.

When the question of his own future plans came up, Mr. Miller beamed on me with what I suspected was an exaggerated cheerfulness. He assured me, "Don't worry about us. Business is so much better that we can well afford to hire an outside salesman again." Mr. Herrick seconded the motion. I found a secret satisfaction in the thought that, as superintendent of the silverware department, their New York Agency would be under my charge, and I registered a resolve to give Mr. Miller a brand of co-operation such as the previous administration had never given him.

CHAPTER VIII

THE ELECTION of January, 1895, as I have said, resulted in my appointment as Superintendent of the Company's Niagara Falls factories. This, of course, meant that we must abandon Lonesomehurst and move to Niagara Falls, where, fortunately, the old Stone Cottage was waiting for us on its terrace overlooking the Falls from the Canadian side. Our factory and offices were on the American side of the river, within fifteen minutes' walk of my new home, which meant that four times daily I had the great stimulus of seeing mighty Niagara and breathing the ozone-laden air while crossing the bridge.

Often during that first strenuous year at Niagara Falls, after our day's work was done or on a Sunday afternoon, my cousin George and I used to sit on the Stone Cottage veranda and talk of our new adventure. George had joined me at Niagara as secretary and first assistant—salary fifteen dollars per week, voted by an economy-minded Board of Directors. It was the same veranda from which, as boys, we had viewed the mighty cataract. Standing there ten years before, we had shared my father's never-waning awe as we watched its green flood plunge into a yawning chasm from which jets of spray rocketed upward until lost in that same silvery cloud which guided the red men and, later, American explorers to this "wonder of the world." From that veranda the grandeur of Niagara was still to be seen, but now, in 1895, we seldom took time to look at or listen to the falls.

97

Instead, our eyes sought a group of sooty factory buildings which, on the American side of the Niagara gorge, stood
so close to its brink that they might have been grimy continu-
ations of the gray cliffs. Over there lay our future, and end-
lessly we talked of knives and forks and spoons, or of dog
chains, halter chains and open-ring cow ties, for of such was
compounded the substance of our hopes.

George had been heart and soul for my new social ideals,
but at the end of a month I think he found himself, as I found
myself, submerged by the practical details of management.
Not that our ideals evaporated—I am sure they did not—
but our plans for building an ideal institution were temporarily crowded into the background by the more immediate
and pressing task of building a business which would support
such an institution.

It was not alone youthful ambition or ideals that urged
us on. At all times we were keenly aware that our elders—
friends and foes alike—were watching apprehensively this
experiment in youthful management. We felt like the proverbial goldfish. We were performing in plain view of a
friendly and, I think, hopeful audience of stockholders at
Oneida, and a less friendly sprinkling of political opponents
scattered around us at the Falls. We did not need the Doctor's warning, "You boys will have to make good the first
year," to tell us that we were on trial and might not be given
a second chance.

During those days we never spared ourselves. The range
of things to be done was so wide and the necessity for speed
so great that youthful vitality proved our most valuable asset.
Several problems, inherited from the previous administration,
were necessarily sandwiched between my efforts to master

the science of factory management and sleeping-car trips to
the East, West and South, aimed at cultivating acquaintance
with the company's customers.

The most immediately pressing of these demands upon
my time was one created by what Mr. Lord called "E——'s
over-cleverness." Mr. E——, although he was a disciple of
John Humphrey Noyes, never joined the Community. After
the breakup he entered the Noyes colony at Niagara, built
himself a home and was appointed sales manager for Oneida
Community, Ltd. in Canada. He had a "special arrangement."
He traveled at the Company's expense and, whenever it
seemed to him profitable, sold *our* goods to *our* customers for
the account of his own private "Niagara Falls Supply Company." Unscrambling this arrangement consumed much valuable time and further enlarged my bump of patience.

Importing steel to Canada for the making of chain-links,
Mr. E—— had hit upon the clever idea of getting the Pittsburgh steel mill to cut out the links and retain the scrap and
bill those links in such a way that we paid duty on the links
only at the same rate as had been paid on the raw steel. Presently the Canadian Government discovered the subterfuge
and, a short time before I took over, sent Oneida Community,
Ltd. a bill for three thousand dollars undervaluation, with
an added six thousand as penalty.

During my first weeks at Niagara I made three trips to
Ottawa. Negotiations with the Canadian Government were
not as formal sixty years ago as they are now, and the final
settlement of this claim was negotiated with the Minister
of Customs around a billiard table. I frankly admitted our
guilt. With equal frankness I described my situation: a young
man with his first large responsibility handicapped by some-

one else's error. The Minister compromised on payment of the undervaluation of three thousand dollars and forgave the six-thousand-dollar penalty.

Next came Mr. Lord's "special arrangement" with K. & M. It involved so many ramifications and had enabled them to channel so large a proportion of the Company's silverware sales through their organization, that it took me several months to disentangle our relations. Mr. Lord, the Company's former President, whom our January victory had tumbled out of the Presidency, fumed over the negotiations. K——was truculent, and his partner, M——, suavely argumentative.

I remember a day when Doctor Noyes, John Lord and I were sitting on the veranda of the Stone Cottage at Niagara Falls, where Corinna and I had established ourselves in an apartment fashioned out of the second-floor rooms. Mr. Lord was growing peevish.

"I don't know why you think you have got to quarrel with K. & M. They're the biggest customers our Company's got."

Mr. Lord was an easygoing, good-natured man, but his temperament always seemed that of a salesman rather than a president. As a matter of fact, he had been a salesman until, in 1889, the fortuity of Company politics unexpectedly elevated him to the presidency.

At the moment I had no time to argue with him about K. & M.; I said flatly, "They're crooked."

He interrupted, "Why do you say that? That's prejudice."

Overlooking the interruption, I added, "And they're dangerous."

That word increased Mr. Lord's irritation. He burst out

with "Dangerous! No! No!" Then he calmed himself and took a new tack. "Come now, Pierre, I don't feel unfriendly to you just because you beat us. I'm trying to give you some good advice and——"

Again I broke in. "It's the arrangement you, yourself, made with them that's dangerous. With their special prices, they endanger our relations with all the rest of the trade."

"But they sell goods, don't they? They bought over seventy thousand dollars' worth from the O.C.L. last year."

"They sold most of the seventy thousand dollars' worth to our customers, whom we would have sold if they hadn't quoted lower prices."

Mr. Lord always dodged negative arguments. "Oh, pshaw, Pierre, they have a splendid selling organization. Now, you're a young man, just starting. I'd like to see you make a success. I really would. You can't afford to lose the K. & M. sales."

I bored in. "Mr. Lord, they're crooked. You know that. K—— is crooked." I fired this shot, realizing that it would still further irritate him, and it did.

He flushed. "What's the use of making a statement like that?"

I faced him. "Let me see, Mr. Lord. You were present, if I remember rightly, when K—— owned up to a total of some six hundred dollars worth of goods absolutely stolen from the factory, and you arranged to have his father pay the company back."

Mr. Lord stumbled. "Yes, but—well, that was several years ago; and, anyway, M—— is honest and a good businessman. You can count on him."

Mr. Lord's friendly attitude was not altogether make-believe. He still owned a large amount of O.C.L. stock, and,

while it was all hypothecated to support his real-estate specu-
lations, the future prosperity of the Company meant much to
him. I can believe that he honestly feared that if we lost K. &
M.'s account it would reduce departmental profits.

He attacked the problem from another angle. "You know,
Pierre, you have a very small selling organization; Mr. Miller
in New York and, now that we have let Mr. Levison go, no
one at all in the West, excepting Alfred Clark. He has traps,
chains and fruit to sell, as well as silverware. He covers a
territory that reaches from Winnipeg, Canada, to New Or-
leans, and from Denver in the West to Pittsburgh. He can't
help you much."

My answer was dictated by the insolent confidence of
youth. "I'll help myself. I'll sell the goods."

After Mr. Lord left, my cousin George asked, "Do you
think he has a financial interest in K. & M.?"

"No." I spoke positively. "Mr. Lord is honest. It's just
that he can't get over the seventy thousand dollars in sales."

Throughout the interview Dr. Noyes had remained silent
but, looking from one to the other as Mr. Lord and I exchanged punches, he had beamed approval. In fact, there
was a humorous twinkle in his half-closed eyes that said to
me, "Go to it, Pierre." Now he turned to George. "Besides
the sales, Mr. Lord has been very friendly with K—— and
M——. You know him. He hates to see them thrown out."

I have related this conversation with Mr. Lord in some
detail because it reveals one of the difficult problems that
confronted me when I took charge at Niagara Falls. The special arrangement with K. & M. had already disturbed our
relations with the trade, and I believed it should be discon-
tinued at any cost. I was well aware that the sales lost through
liquidating this account could only be replaced with diffi-

culty. I knew, also, that they *must* be replaced if I were to succeed, but instinct told me that my first job was the scraping off of leeches. At the age of twenty-four I was obsessed, as twenty-four often is, with an overweening self-confidence.

Within three months I had disposed of K. & M. and later was obliged to ask for the resignation of a certain man who, under the old regime, was in charge of Company sales at Niagara. He was honest in an everyone-has-to-look-out-for-himself sort of way, but the year before, with K——'s "pull" operating threateningly, he had surrendered and accompanied him on a trip to New York, during which K—— transferred many Oneida Community customers to his own account. The K. & M. problem, at least, was solved.

In the factory my selection of helpers proved fortunate. Amos Reeve served ably as a first assistant and adviser, and there had emerged from the ranks a man who, during those critical days, earned my lifelong gratitude. This man—his name was Fred Filby—became our Works Superintendent. He was resourceful and tireless. He organized the staff, labored ceaselessly for the betterment of manufacturing processes and, more than all, he spread his own spirit of enthusiasm and loyalty through all the working force. With the aid of Reeve and Filby, I was able to concentrate under my personal supervision most of the manufacturing activities. These two made it possible for me to interest myself practically in wages, manufacturing processes, purchasing problems and costs, and that without too greatly limiting the time I must necessarily devote to the pressing problem of more sales.

My first traveling took me to New York City and from there into New England. I helped Mr. Miller select a salesman to call on the trade I had visited in 1894, and introduced this new man to many of my former customers. Then I went West.

The sales possibilities of Chicago seemed enormous; it was a commercial beehive, and more particularly a hothouse for daring enterprise; its spirit youthful and ambitious, more so than any of the Eastern cities. On my first trip, I stayed in Chicago nearly two weeks, calling on the company's old customers and hunting new prospects. In Chicago, my Noyes Bros. experience of trying to make commercial bricks with very little helpful straw served me in good stead.

Strangely enough, the first big fish I caught was Mr. Levison, the same Levison whom my political nagging had forced the previous administration to drop as the company's Chicago representative. At least, we thought at the time that they dropped him, but I now suspect that he, himself, resigned. If he was dropped, he certainly landed on his feet. In 1895, I found him embarked on an enterprise already bringing in larger returns than his commissions as our agent had brought him, and promising a fortune.

I found that Mr. Levison was now offering the great public, through advertising (mostly in the *Christian Herald*) a set of half a dozen orange spoons with gilded bowls in which were stamped the likeness of various buildings of the recent World's Fair. These spoons, according to his advertisements, were "left over from the World's Fair" and were offered "as long as the stock lasts, at the ridiculous price of 99 cents per set, cash with order." He had plunged dangerously, but the scheme was making good. Each morning's mail brought a golden shower.

When I called on him to get information regarding the company's customers, I was surprised to find him helpful. I

remember particularly a pointer he gave me regarding
Sears, Roebuck and Co. This firm was then running a
small mail-order catalogue, following the methods which had
built Montgomery Ward's huge business. Our home-office
records showed that we had sold Sears Roebuck small quantities of traps, but had recently reduced their credit limit,
because of the firm's "inadequate capital."

Mr. Levison told me, "You can sell Sears Roebuck all
they'll buy now." He became dramatically confidential, "I
happen to know that a man named Rosenwald has joined the
firm and put in a lot of money, so now they have plenty of
capital." Mr. Levison was not the man to leave my recognition of his magnanimity to chance. He raised it to the level
of "coals of fire." "I know, Pierrepont, that you were mainly
responsible for my discharge from the Company's employment. Mr. Lord told me."

If I remember rightly, I covered my embarrassment by
a somewhat flippant reply. "Didn't I do you a favor?"

"No thanks to you." Mr. Levison sat up very straight in
his chair. "I, myself, found a way to get along without the
Oneida Community." Then he unbent. "You'll find, however,
that I am not one to hold a grudge." This was spoken so
affably that I was filled with admiration for the man's broad-
mindedness.

However, the next time I called on him I made a discovery that explained, at least partially, his friendly attitude
and somewhat modified my admiration. He told me, "This
souvenir spoon scheme is succeeding beyond my wildest
dreams. I've been buying the spoons from your company, but
the credit limit Mr. Lord gave me doesn't at all cover my
requirements. If you'll arrange to make me all the spoons I

need—and that will be a lot of spoons—and if you'll allow me adequate credit, I'll give you the business. Otherwise I must find another source of supply."

"Aha," I said to myself. "He needs me as much as I need him," and I must have added, still to myself, "And the Lord knows how badly I need him."

With equal thankfulness, and, I fear, equal insincerity, we "got together." I owe it to Mr. Levison, however, to add that I became quite fond of him during the two years of our association, and I think he liked me. He was, on the whole, what the boys now call "a good egg." He treated me with absolute fairness, and his orange spoons were responsible, during many months, for full-time work in our factory— often overtime.

Having studied his plan, and especially his morning mail, I agreed to persuade our directors to offer him liberal credit terms, if I were permitted to be present at least once a month when he opened his mail and could have access, at all times, to his sales records. Then I took the whole plan to Oneida.

Our Credit Department today would be shocked at the amount of credit I persuaded the 1895 directors to grant Mr. Levison. I assumed entire responsibility for the gamble, and agreed to keep in close touch with his business, both orders and cash in bank. It was understood that I would cut down his credit whenever returns from his advertising showed signs of slackening.

As usual, I profited by the Doctor's backing. He said to the Directors, "Give Pierre a chance. He knows what he is about."

As a matter of history, in the years 1895 and 1896 we manufactured for Mr. Levison what then seemed an enormous quantity of orange spoons. The margin of profit, too, was excellent. In the end, he overstayed his game and failed, but not before he had paid us nearly two hundred thousand dollars for the spoons. If I remember rightly, we had to charge off less than three thousand, which represented only a small percentage of the profit we had made on the deal.

Levison turned out to be a very decent citizen. It was either on that first interview or perhaps later, when we got better acquainted, that he made the unexpected and quaint suggestion to "treat well the old men you have beaten—Mr. Lord, Mr. Freeman and Mr. Allen. I got quite fond of them."

I told him that he needn't worry; that, outside of business, they were for me not only friends but almost foster parents. It was those same men, together with other men and women of the Community and still others no longer there who had surrounded my childhood with happiness and my youth with security. Those Perfectionists, men and women, although their experiment had proved a failure, certainly set a pattern for right living. Kenwood, with many of their descendants still living and the ideals they left behind, is a happy home. There is no place like it in the country.

Levison's orange-spoon deal was the first of many similar deals which, during the next few years of catch-as-catch-can selling, kept our factory running to full capacity. Whenever we were threatened with a shortage of work, I used to pack my bag and sally forth, and I rarely came home until I had found some business to fill the gap.

The fact is that my most colorful memories of that period concern themselves with sniping expeditions after factory fillers, like the Levison orange spoons. Not that I neglected the regular trade, but whenever one of those life-saving special schemes began to fade, I devoted myself to finding another to take its place.

At this point it occurs to me that youthful adventures in management and salesmanship have engaged more than their share of my attention. The original purpose of this writing was to inform my children and grandchildren, and the children and grandchildren of the men and women who stood with me through those early struggles, as to our ideals and ambitions in the 1890's, and the plans we then made to realize those ambitions in a new society at Oneida.

When I left college in 1891, my first struggles were struggles to escape poverty—to support myself. As I have said, it was only later when my early success had disposed of this primary incentive, that I discovered how little appetite I had for the orthodox pursuit of wealth. I must add, however, that I was not seized with any disgust for the secular scramble which is said to turn sensitive and artistic souls away from the "madding crowd." I loved that struggle; I was still fascinated by the adventure of business. Mr. Allen was probably right about the "Cook Spirit."

Still, looking back, I am inclined to suspect that, but for my fortuitous substitution for Uncle Abram as a minority director of the Oneida Community in 1894, my somewhat sophomoric ideals might have evaporated. I had accepted the appointment as a director principally to have a chance to visit Oneida once a month at the Company's expense, where I could personally carry on a courtship which had not been making satisfactory progress by mail. Corinna, now my wife, was then still living at Oneida. It was only when, in January, 1895, I found myself back in the old Company, and surrounded by the friends of my boyhood, that the vague dissatisfactions of the previous year suddenly crystallized into a definite dream for the future.

The dream I dreamed in 1895 had its locus at the old

home and, for its personnel, my companions of the Children's House, surrounded by the still very sizable group of members of the old Community and their children. Our new religion was to be an exhilarating struggle in the world of business to obtain a common prosperity for all members of the group. Within this group I proposed social equality. Moneywise, I accepted inequality, but always modified by a semi-Perfectionistic principle which I called "a reasonable equality of income"; meaning that inequalities should never be large enough to force different standards of living. I disbelieved in absolute equality of rewards because I disbelieved in the possibility of maintaining efficiency, initiative or self-denial in the relaxing atmosphere of equalitarianism.

All of which suggests the fact, and memory vaguely corroborates it, that in January, 1895, I, myself, and my youthful coadjutors were thinking and planning mainly for our home group. We envisaged, at first, only the social and financial relations of "our folks."

To be sure, we were interested in the welfare of our employees, but only as the Community had always been interested in the people who worked for them. The Community had paid good wages, as wages were reckoned in those days, and we expected to continue this policy, but, looking back from this distance of time and from the distance we have traveled in our conception of what is now called "industrial relations," I must admit that in 1895 our aims were narrow. Our blueprints of the future were extremely simple. They provided that, in our own group, the inevitable disparities in executive ability should not create the kind of income disparities that separate friends. Our vision had gone little further. It was at Niagara, during 1896, that I discovered how narrow my ideals were. There, I lived in close touch with our employees, and this brought me recognition of the poignant human problems with which their lives were surrounded.

One experience comes back to me and suggests the many less dramatic happenings that opened my eyes to the crudeness of my original planning. One of our workmen had been badly injured. I called at his home and what I saw there greatly disturbed me. There was no complaining. In fact, his wife and his old father seemed very grateful for my interest. The house was small—not more than three rooms beside the kitchen. An old grandfather occupied one of the rooms, the injured workman another room, and the four children with their mother, the third. As might be expected in such a crowded house, the disorder was great.

Later I told George that this fine young workman was living in a "rat's nest" and I told him further, emphatically, that we were going to build a manufacturing institution wherein no employee should be obliged to live that way. Remembering this man's cheerful face as I had known him before, working at his polishing wheel, what especially shocked me now was his brave attempt still to look cheerfully at me, lying on his mean little cot in the midst of dirt and disorder.

Perhaps I should have anticipated that experience since, having been poor, myself, I had gone to work at the age of thirteen as a carpenter's helper and had visited other carpenters' homes. But either I had forgotten or at that age did not understand what I saw there, or carpenters' homes were different from those of factory workers. Here, on his bed in this squalid house, was a capable and loyal man who had always appeared cheerful when, on my trips through the factory, we chatted together. I had thought of him as going with equal cheerfulness to a comfortable home when he left his polishing wheel—and this was the home he went to!

That picture came back to me repeatedly during the years of our struggle and it always revived my determination to succeed and my equal determination to abolish poverty among the employees of Oneida Community, Ltd.

I have always looked upon the 1895 political struggle as the first bend in the road along which youthful ambition was hurrying me. Now I am inclined to regard my visit to a workman's home as a second and more important bend in the same road. I told my associates that, in our new Oneida Community, Ltd., no man who worked for us should ever again live in such a home. The first bend largely represented acceptance of the opportunity to go back to an environment and a philosophy to which boyhood in the Community had evidently conditioned me. The second was an intellectual and, I may say, a spiritual "conversion." It expanded the possibilities in a life of business struggle and adventure; added a new value and purpose to that struggle.

There was another side to the lives of our employees which I discovered during those early years, one which impressed me greatly and started a whole new line of thought. I saw in their relations with each other a simple but very practical spirit of helpfulness. Without any fuss or any theory, they just naturally went to each other's aid in case of trouble. Was the mother of a family sick and the children ailing? Other women, themselves hard-working wives and mothers, helped care for them, turn and turn about, until the crisis was past.

Thereafter, the living conditions of our workmen, those partners upon whom we must basically rely for success, loomed large in our discussions, and, because of this, a larger

conception of our new Oneida Community, Ltd. took form. I
am equally certain that before the end of the nineteenth
century, our entire generation of young businessmen had
embraced the idea of a group responsibility, encompassing
every man and woman who worked for its success. This responsibility called for an equitable distribution of the profits
of success among all who worked for it. From that day to
this, such distribution has been a fundamental principle of
our association.

In this chapter I have intimated that my sociological
ambitions were temporarily parked at Niagara while I strove
to build a profitable business, but that is only partly true.
Each month when I attended the Directors' Meeting at
Oneida, the smoldering fires of earlier ambitions blazed into
flame. There I found the young people of my generation
full of enthusiasm for the building of a new Oneida Community, Ltd., and many of our elders lifting their eyes to
new possibilities.

Believing, as youth always believes, that creating the
new is a job for youth, I devoted time and intrigue (I use
the word intrigue without its evil implications) to pushing
my generation of young men into the managing positions.
Always, too, I got in touch with others who had left Oneida
and urged them to return.

John, my older brother, had worked in the silk department for several years. Now, with the approval of Mrs.
Joslyn, the superintendent, he was placed in charge of sales.
Holton, having returned to Oneida when I did, was learning
the canning business. Mr. Hinds, superintendent of that department, had often expressed a wish to retire from active
responsibility, and the directors' minutes record that he promised to bring Holton along as fast as possible.

My greatest worry and most difficult problem was the Trap Department. The double superintendency created by the previous administration for political purposes, was far from satisfactory and yet (also for political reasons) the Doctor and I hesitated, at the end of our first year, to unseat the incumbents. They were worthy men, but incapable of competing in the new world of business. Stephen Leonard was my choice for the position of Trap Superintendent. He was then twenty-two years old, had served his apprenticeship in the factory, and was also our only college-trained engineer—a B.S. from Cornell. We could not push him forward too fast, but we did discourage his application for work at Niagara and urged the managers of the Trap Department to delegate as much as possible to him.

B. L. Dunn, the "Bert" of Children's House days, and the man who later, as Advertising Manager, did much to make Community Silver a commercial success, was still in college. As a matter of fact, I fancy that he created a new record for college attendance; he was a college boy for ten years, and left behind him a trail of five Alma Maters. The three Wayland-Smith boys were still helping their father, who had left the Community and obtained a profitable New York City agency for one of the steel companies. Grosvenor Allen, who later became one of my right-hand men and who was largely instrumental in creating those designs which have made Community Plate famous, was still in Yale. It was not until 1898 that he joined us. Don, the "Dorr" of Children's House days, was working in the Machine Shop. Rutherford had entered upon a business career in New York City. Of the younger men, Paul Herrick was learning the silk business, Karl Hatch played clarinet with a traveling orchestra, Herbert Freeman was in the Niagara factory, Ethelbert Pitt lived at Niagara with his father, Elliot Hinds was just leaving Cornell, and Clifton Inslee sold bicycles.

This sounds like Homer's catalogue of ships. I have called the roll of Children's House boys because those were the timbers with which I then hoped to build a new Oneida Community, Limited, and enlisting as many of them as possible in the enterprise seemed a vital part of that program.

Perhaps those monthly visits to Oneida profited most from my intimate association with my brother, Dr. Theodore Noyes. He had adopted my social dream. He insisted that political peace was a most necessary preliminary. Together, therefore, we plotted appeasement of political life in the company's affairs. The Doctor was a man who might well be called, in the simple language of Biblical reverence, a Wise Man. He had, however, little stomach for personal conflict with his fellows, so that whenever a clash threatened, or when it came to putting into effect ungentle policies (often the policies were his own suggestion) I, although thirty years younger, had to do the job.

For example, during the political confusion of those first troublous months of our management, a certain combative member of our party insisted that we discharge several of our political opponents, and, when the Doctor said "no," he became violent. The Doctor sent for me. I remember well that interview. He was sitting in the same room where his father—my father—sat when I saw him as a child, and he was stroking his beard with the same unconscious preoccupation that father registered when he rubbed his thumb along the oft-renewed leather patch in his vest.

As always, the Doctor seemed unruffled, but I detected worry when he told of his talk with the recalcitrant member. "X—— says that he'll start a third party if we don't discharge

Y—— and Z——. You'll never have peace, Pierre; you'll never have any basis for the kind of institution you plan, if we start with revenge and old-fashioned, political strong-arm methods. What would you do with him, Pierre?"

"If you leave it to me," I said, "I'll tell X—— to go jump in the creek."

"Yes! Yes!" the Doctor beamed. "But tell him tactfully!"

So it fell to my lot to interview this man who was more than twice my age and to "tell him tactfully" to jump in the creek.

Incidentally—and this was by no means incidental in the Doctor's philosophy—he afterwards urged, nodding his head significantly, "Find X—— a good job."

I told our disturber to start his third party, that we didn't care; but—I found him a good job.

CHAPTER IX

WHEN, IN JANUARY, 1896, the stockholders assembled at Oneida for their annual meeting, progress toward political peace was in evidence. Credit for this must be given, first, to the policy of pacification initiated by Dr. Noyes; second, to the persistence of that habit of "agreement" cultivated by our elders in Community days, and, third, to the excellent showing made by my three Niagara departments. They had contributed to the annual "closing of the general ledger" nearly twice the profits turned in by those same departments in the previous year.

Politically, our will-to-peace had registered with the reasonable members of the opposition. In spite of pressure from certain sections of our own party, Mr. Freeman had been retained as Treasurer, Mrs. Joslyn was still Superintendent of the Silk Department, and Mr. Henry Allen was representing the Company in Canada. He had taken the place of Mr. Eldridge as Sales Representative. These three had been leading members of the opposing party. More important still, I sensed at Oneida a new and hopeful confidence in youthful management.

The net result of all these factors was an uncontested election. By agreement, our five candidates and the four opposition directors were re-elected without competition.

A slight disagreement (better, perhaps, a misunderstanding) arose when my salary came up for consideration. If disagreement, it was certainly nonpolitical. It stemmed

116

from the lifelong habits of thrift and the equalitarian training of our elders. The fifteen hundred dollars I had been receiving seemed to them a large salary for any man twenty-four years old. How could it have seemed otherwise to Perfectionists who, for forty years, had reserved important positions—without pay—for the wisdom of age, and who, when salaries were started in 1881, voted the same pay for the manager of the homeboarding establishment as they gave to the superintendent of leading manufacturing departments?

This salary incident had its humorous side. I left the room, as was customary for a director while his salary was being discussed. Upon my return, someone whispered to me that a raise of fifty dollars a year had been voted, if I "maintained the same profits during the coming year." I was outraged and I told the directors so. I informed my assembled elders, I fear truculently, that if that was all they thought I was worth, they could keep their fifty dollars.

I know now, and should have known then, that no ungenerous thought governed their action. At this distance of time, I can acknowledge that I lacked perspective and gave way to uncalled-for heat. They promptly sent me out of the room again and voted a salary of eighteen hundred dollars. A raise of three hundred dollars was a large one in 1896.

I have always believed that it was a subconscious attempt to excuse that raise which led the directors to ask that I interest myself in the problems of the Trap Department, since, politically, this was the breaking of new ground. Already I had acquired management of three of the six manufacturing departments. We were still living in the Victorian era, a social and economic morass wherein men assumed that existing systems were finalities. It would have fitted with the times and the personalities involved if, in 1896, my elders had hesitated to suggest that I take a hand in the management of our most profitable department. They might easily have feared that they were paving the way for the elevation of extreme youth to a dictatorship; always suspect at Oneida. It occurs to me that the idea that I might edge myself into the top management may have originated in the innocent-sounding suggestion of Dr. Noyes that I interest myself in trap problems.

Perhaps it would not come amiss here to give briefly the history of this Trap Department which, forty years before, had saved the Oneida Community from bankruptcy, and was still our major source of income. This had now been added to my responsibilities.

It was in 1852 that the Oneida Perfectionists discovered —what many other community groups discovered too late— that agriculture and horticulture were not producing enough income for their support. An inventory showed that their assets had shrunk more than fifty thousand dollars in four years. Being practical people, mostly New Englanders, tradespeople, mechanics and farmers, they looked around for a more profitable field in which to employ their labor, and someone suggested the manufacture of a trap invented by one of their members, Sewall Newhouse. It was a new venture, but evidently those hardheaded Yankees, with the 1852 inventory staring them in the face, were willing to take a chance. The manufacture was undertaken, much of it hand labor in those early days, and Mr. Olds, one of the Community's "peddlers," was sent to Chicago with a trunkful of traps. Timidly he showed samples of the different sizes to the buyer of Chicago's leading hardware wholesaler, Blair & Company, afterwards Hibbard, Spencer, Bartlett & Company. When this buyer said to Mr. Olds, "I'll take all you've got," he unknowingly transformed an agricultural Community into an industrial Community.

Since the sale of canned fruits and vegetables had, until then, been its major source of income, the Community still maintained a lively interest in farming. A Farm Department was organized, and its management turned over to men who were more attracted by, and more adapted to, farm work than to factory work. During the ensuing years, more and more land was bought, until many hundred acres were under cultivation or used as pasture land for what was rated, during the 1880's, as the third finest Holstein herd in the United States.

It was, however, the manufacture of steel game traps that turned the financial tide threatening to swamp the Oneida Community in 1852. Soon, men, women and even children worked at trap-making. For many years all the work was done by Community members, but during the 1860's, when trap sales passed the hundred-thousand-dollar mark and the manufacture of silk thread had been added to the Community's industries, the hiring of "outside" help was begun. The trap business grew by leaps and bounds, in spite of Mr. Newhouse's grudging acceptance of helpers and his fierce opposition to any change in his patterns or improvement in his processes. I have been told that my father's tact saved the situation. When a machine was devised to take the place of some hand operation, or when a useless detail of Mr. Newhouse's design was abandoned, my father alone could persuade the old trapper to permit experiments with such novelties.

Sewall Newhouse, himself, deserves more than passing mention. He was one of those socially eccentric individuals who, in the early years of the last century, clung to a life of hunting and trading in furs; a life even then being gradually outmoded in central New York by the spread of farm clearings in a region which, only a few years before, had been the happy hunting ground for the Red Men.

The Oneida tribe, one of the Five Nations of the Iroquois Indians, had for three hundred years claimed as their territory the land in this section of the state. One of their large stockaded villages was at one time near Nichols Pond, where the famous defeat of Champlain by the Oneida Indians took place. Later, the tribe moved to the hills farther south, then to the present location of the village of Stockbridge and finally to Oneida Castle, through a region which later became the Oneida Community Farms. The Oneidas, like all Indian tribes, moved every twenty-five or thirty years, forced by the fact that the country around each camp became less desirable as game was killed off and the corn lands, never improved, became barren. The origin of the word Castle, which still persists in the name Oneida Castle, is interesting. The Indian stockades were called castles.

In the 1840's, in his blacksmith shop at Oneida Castle, Sewall Newhouse made steel traps and other articles which could be swapped for furs. His shop was still a favored haunt for such Indians as had been left behind when, in 1825, Eleazer Williams, Indian captive, Christian missionary and thought by some to be the lost French Dauphin, led the main group of Oneidas to their new reservation in Wisconsin.

In 1848 or '49, Sewall Newhouse joined the Oneida Community. Why he joined, even more why the Community let him join, is a mystery to me. Behind his gnarled face was a gnarled character. Perhaps his wife, whom I remember as a very religious woman, persuaded him and persuaded the Community.

When, as a boy, I knew him, he was in his sixties. His

A group of cyclists in the 'eighties. Pierrepont Noyes is fourth from the left. Elliot Hinds is atop the old-fashioned high bicycle.

The "Sand-Jig" Orchestra, 1888. Left to right: Pierrepont Noyes, Berton Dunn, Clifton Inslee, Stephen Leonard.

Pierrepont Noyes at Colgate.   Corinna Kinsley at nineteen.

Their wedding in June, 1894. The front row is the wedding party; the back row, the rest of their group of young people.

NOYES BROTHERS,

56 WARREN STREET, NEW YORK,

Oneida Community

SILVER-PLATED WARE

AMERICAN CHAINS, DOG COLLARS, ANIMAL TRAPS.

Presented by

Advertising card for Noyes Bros.

Page from an O.C.L. trap catalogue.

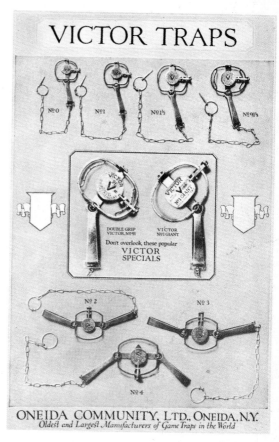

VICTOR TRAPS

Nº 0   Nº 1   Nº 1½   Nº 91½

DOUBLE GRIP
VICTOR, Nº 91

VICTOR
Nº 91 GIANT

Don't overlook these popular
VICTOR
SPECIALS

Nº 2   Nº 3

Nº 4

ONEIDA COMMUNITY, LTD., ONEIDA, N.Y.
Oldest and Largest Manufacturers of Game Traps in the World

The "Stone Cottage" at Niagara. This was the house to which John Humphrey Noyes retired after the breakup of the Oneida Community. Later Mr. and Mrs. Pierrepont Noyes lived here as a young married couple.

The Canadian factory of Community Plate, which was built on the site of the Stone Cottage.

Board of Directors, 1909. Seated, left to right: John Freeman, Martin Kinsley, William Hinds (President), Pierrepont Noyes, Mrs. Harriet Joslyn, Henry Allen. Standing: George Noyes, Stephen Leonard, Paul Herrick, Holton Noyes, Grosvenor Allen. (Taken on the Mansion House Lawn.)

Board of Directors, 1926. Seated, left to right: Holton Noyes, Miles Robertson, Martin Kinsley, Jr., Grosvenor Allen, Pierrepont Noyes, Gerard Wayland-Smith, Wilber Earl, Louis Wayland-Smith. Standing: John Noyes, Stephen Leonard, Chester Burnham, George Noyes, William Rich, Jack Milnes, Albert Kinsley, Jared Allen, Martin Keller. (Taken in the foundation of the new office building at the laying of the cornerstone.)

The old Trap Shop, eighteen nineties. The women worked in the Silk Department upstairs.

The factory at Sherrill today. The two projecting buildings in front are the old Trap Shop.

The Mansion House in winter.

Aerial view of the Mansion House. Buildings clockwise around the Quadrangle, starting with long building on left: The Tontine (dining room and kitchens), the Lounge,
the "New House" (built in 1877), the North Tower, the Big Hall, the Mansard, the
South Wing (formerly the Children's House), the South Tower, the Nursery Kitchen
and Ultima Thule.

Pierrepont Noyes and his son Peter in the Colosseum, 1925.

Aerial view of Saratoga Spa Reservation.

face was grim, his whiskers gray, and he moved with a shuf-
fling gait that I associated with the Indians who stole through
the forests in the pages of *Nick Whiffles* or *Frank in the
Woods*. He seemed still a woodsman; something of a hero
to a boy. For years he had been allowed to make trapping
expeditions to the North Woods each winter, and his book,
The Trapper's Guide (written by Mr. Hamilton) was read
and reread to help boys' trapping and excite their imagina-
tions for Indian scouting in the local woods.

He was not a dishonest man in the ordinary sense of the
word. I think that the ethics of his Indian-trading youth survived the Community's religious influence, and he still believed that things desirable must often be obtained by skill-
ful divagation. As an instance: Mr. Newhouse had a gun,
but no one in the Community was allowed to keep a dog.
Occasionally he was surprised in the neighboring woods or
"slashings" with both a gun and a dog.

"Oh, *that* dog!" He would brush aside the accusing question. "That's Sol's boy's dog. He *will* follow me."

His accuser may have had doubts, but it was left for my
brother Holton, in later years, to learn the truth. When questioned, Sol's boy laughed. "Yes, yes," he told Holton. "I always kept one or two hunting dogs for Newhouse."

Many good-natured stories about Sewall Newhouse circulated when I was a boy. They suggested that the Community recognized his peculiar psychology and made allowance for it. Following their custom of studying the talents
and even the preferences of members when allotting work
or encouraging a vocation, they permitted Newhouse to put-
ter with his trap-making long before it had occurred to anyone as a commercial project for the Community. When, in
their hour of need, it came to their rescue, it must have

seemed what my father used to call "a special providence," and so it continued after the old Community had ceased to exist, as the financial mainstay of the new Oneida Community, Limited. Unfortunately, in the hands of the elderly men then in charge of it, its sales were wobbling around one hundred thousand dollars annually, and in the early 90's, shrank considerably below that figure. This was the "trap problem" that Dr. Noyes so delicately suggested I should solve.

Something had happened late in 1895 which, early in 1896, gave my new and tenuous association with the Trap Department its first coloring of reality. This happening also led the Oneida Communty, Ltd. into the first move of a career of expansion which has continued, except during periods of depression, down to the present time, and which still shows no signs of becoming anemic. I will add that, if my youthful urge for expansion, at times brought worry to our directors, it also kept me, during those years, on a treadmill of hungry profit-seeking. It was all very well to present to the directors unanswerable arguments for each forward step, but the financial nemesis was always threatening, just a few steps behind me, and calling for increased net profits.

Looking back, it seems a bit of fortuitous good luck that a threat to our Trap Department collided with the excellent profit showing of 1895. For a great many years the Oneida Community, Ltd. had sold practically all the steel traps used in Canada. We owned no factory in that country except a little old one-story chain-making shop, created out of Carnachan's sawmill in Niagara Falls, Ontario, and had been obliged to import traps from the American factory. Those importations were subject to a heavy duty.

Now Mr. E——, the same Mr. E—— whom I had displaced as Canadian salesman, thought that he saw a chance to make some easy money and get revenge at the same time. Knowing the Canadian situation, he persuaded some local capitalists to invest with him and commenced the erection of a factory at Niagara Falls, Ontario, for the manufacture of traps. He gave out that he had secured the services of one of our former machinists to make the necessary tools. More important, I discovered that he had already quoted cut prices to some of our Canadian customers. It is safe to say that nothing but the evident need to protect the good old trap business would have led my elderly associates to authorize the building of a brand-new factory in Canada, but they did it with enthusiasm, and I lost no time in starting the work.

Mr. Daniel Kelly was given charge of factory construction, Ferrand Ellis with his fellow machinists made the tools and Jack MacQuade, long a foreman in the United States factory, planned the machinery layout. Jack also became the first superintendent of the Canadian trap factory. We moved so rapidly that the first Canadian traps were turned out of our new factory early in the fall before Mr. Eldridge had even completed his building.

He had figured on competing with American-made traps plus duty. The price we now quoted on Canadian-made traps was very discouraging to him, and to this discouragement was added the fact that he was unable to deliver a single trap during 1896, while we could supply all our customers from the new factory. Mr. Eldridge, or his partners, decided to turn their attention to other lines of manufacture. From my point of view, he had done the Oneida Community, Ltd. a favor by forcing us to build a factory in Canada.

While visits to Oneida brought renewal of my idealistic planning, back at Niagara commercialism resumed its sway.

If what I have called our idealism (a word somewhat too flattering for our ambitions) always hovered in the background, at Niagara, in 1896, it concerned itself largely with the problem of underprivileged workmen, rather than with development of the social group at Oneida. Also, I feel obliged to add that back at Niagara the old political cleavage was emphasized. There, I found myself an invader of enemy territory. In the factories, old allies of the former management and those financial leeches whom I had eliminated or was certain to eliminate, did their best to block my plans, and, over on the Canadian side, Corinna and I found ourselves socially unpopular.

It would be neither accurate nor fair to characterize, without qualification, the group of ex-Perfectionists at Niagara as political opponents. While, politically, they might hope that my success would never be so great as to establish me and my party permanently in power, this negative was somewhat offset by their desire for dividends. Their hostility to me was, I believe, more than half spiritual.

When Corinna and I tried to cultivate the friendship of their young people by keeping "open house" on Sunday afternoons, the parents did their best to keep their children from attending our parties. I can easily excuse those parents now. Quite aside from political hostility, they felt that I was what the Community called "worldly" and irreligious, hence spiritually dangerous.

However, the lure of our gatherings, always attended by young friends from the ex-Community families over the river, proved more than a match for parental opposition. As time went on, most of them joined us. At Niagara was begun the social—I had almost said the spiritual—integration of a younger generation whose fathers and mothers had lost much of that "spirit of agreement" which had animated them for more than thirty years as members of the Oneida Community.

Business-wise, the year 1896 opened with excellent prospects, but ended dismally. On the eighth of July, the Democratic Convention met in Chicago. For two long days, the usual oratorical persiflage was duly reported by Western Union and amplified by extra editions of the newspapers. During those same days a convention-calloused electorate followed listlessly the strategy of rival political groups. Then, suddenly, like a thunderclap from a clear sky, the country learned that a certain William Jennings Bryan on July tenth, with his "crown-of-thorns" and "cross-of-gold" perorations, had grabbed the Democratic presidential nomination. A little later, there trailed behind his nomination a platform in which most of the good old Democratic formulas, free trade, Jeffersonian individualism (in which it always seemed to me that an economic and social *laissez faire* was imperfectly concealed) and sound money, were submerged in the flood of radicalism.

Following that convention came the unforgettable Bryan campaign. The candidate kept himself always in the limelight, but it was an expansive Midwestern light which illuminated a host of grimy-faced soapbox orators, and in its penumbra revealed many so-called intellectuals, dogmatizing in clubs, colleges, forums and coffeehouses. (I bet one of those intellectuals fifteen dollars that Bryan would not be elected, and have never seen the man since—or his fifteen dollars). In September, it seemed as though the stern face of William Jennings Bryan stared at us from every window.

By October, the captains of industry (a new product), the capitalists and the citizenry in general feared that Bryan had captured the imagination of the working population as well as the farmers, and many of the capitalists, meta-phorically speaking, took to their cyclone cellars. Leading bankers announced that on the day after Bryan was elected they would not open their doors. For nearly five hectic months business was almost at a standstill. The candidate and his political pals were committed to the "free and unlimited coinage of silver at a ratio of 16 to 1," and campaign speakers told of a dozen other radical experiments to be tried. The country held its breath.

The business stagnation struck us, unfortunately, just after I had put into effect at Niagara a general raise of wages. My cousin George, quoting Fred Filby, originated the dic-tum that the best form of "welfare work" (extensively dis-cussed and advertised by industrialists in those days) was good wages. Having searched the minutes of the Directors' Meetings for record of any disturbed criticism of our wage raise, I find a suggestion that "the directors should have been consulted before such an important move was made." I also remember that the Bryan campaign, with its promise of poor business, left me, as they say in bridge, with a "weak de-fensive hand." My guess is that I apologized and bragged about our business prospects at Niagara.

The directors could hardly be blamed for alarm, since the greater part of our products were sold normally during the later months of each year. This made profits seem doubt-ful. Furthermore, when in January, 1897, inventories had been completed for the three Oneida departments, the di-rectors found that their worst fears had been realized. Those departments showed an aggregate credit of $18,665, while Mr. Freeman's general expense ledger turned this into a loss by a debit of $22,718. The future certainly looked dark.

Many of our older people were living on their dividends, and the substantial loss suggested by these partial figures foreboded no dividends. Gloomily, "our folks" awaited the Niagara inventories.

At Niagara we worked on those inventories nights and Sundays. There were hundreds of articles in different stages of completion to be weighed or counted and priced, and in spite of our most strenuous efforts a final figure was not reached for nearly two weeks. With the precious sheets in my bag—footed, classified, and indexed with Mrs. Barron's proverbial neatness—I arrived at Oneida via the Canajoharie Local and the O & W Evening Express. It was a dramatic moment, both for the home folks and myself. My inventory totals must be combined with the Niagara ledgers. The result was a shock—a pleasurable shock.

Fortunately, I had kept the Levison orange-spoon business, and during the year had been able to add several other promotional customers. As a result, the Silverware Department showed a profit $2,207 more than in the good year, 1895, and the combination of my three Niagara departments turned in a net profit of $36,568. Oneida emerged from its gloom. A 5 per cent dividend was possible.

Incidentally, although it did not seem incidental to me, at the Board meeting in January, 1897, the foundation was laid (but only a foundation) for revision of the Oneida Community, Ltd. organization. I had long been convinced that we needed a new managerial formula. Each department had been ruled by a superintendent who resented the co-operation of other superintendents and accepted with bad grace any interference by the Board of Directors. My conviction that we needed "centralized management" was shared by Dr. Noyes, and, led by him, the directors at that January,

1897, meeting took the first official step toward the creation of a single-headed management.

It came about in this way. Trap Department profits had been especially disappointing, as might have been expected under a superintendency which had not done too well even in good times. It will perhaps be remembered that at the beginning of the year the directors had suggested that I interest myself in trap problems. At Niagara I was, however, too far away to accomplish anything of importance and, anyhow, I had only been asked for "advice." Now, however, a desire was evidenced, both within the Board of Directors and among the stockholders, for an importation of Niagara management to rescue this old-time profit-earner, the Trap Department.

And yet, tradition barred the way. Eyebrows were raised. "Pierrepont already has three departments. Add a fourth?" Even my well-wishers shrank from such a break with custom. Further, my youthfulness must have been a stumbling block, for I was still only twenty-six years old, and for nearly fifty years superintendencies had been reserved for the wisdom of greater maturity.

Eight gray-bearded directors discussed the problems while I absented myself from the room, and their discussions ran around in circles until Dr. Noyes ingeniously, and I might add ingenuously, solved it for them. His solution resembled Alexander's cutting of the Gordian knot. I cannot believe that any director failed to detect the employment by the Doctor of some kind of cutting instrument, but they were evidently thankful for any solution which promised revival of the trap business.

What the doctor proposed was this: that the real management of the Trap Department be turned over to a "trap

committee." Quite brazenly, he named that committee—
himself, Mr. Freeman and me. It was brazen only because
everyone knew that he would take no active part in the actual
management and, even more, knew that neither Mr. Freeman's ambitions or qualifications warranted expectation that
he would mix in commercial or manufacturing problems.
Thereupon I became Superintendent of the Trap Department in everything but name.

And that was not all. The political appeasement, so ear-
nestly sought by Dr. Noyes and myself, had proceeded faster
and farther than I believe could have happened with any
other people. The Doctor's impartial and nonpartisan policy
in all matters and the success of youthful management at
Niagara had turned our former opponents' complacency into
a desire to co-operate. When election day arrived, we found
everyone willing to back the administration.

A slate was agreed upon, and a single block of stock was
voted for it without opposition. At this election in January,
1897, the stockholders of the Oneida Community, Ltd. voluntarily adopted a one-party system, and that system has
preserved political peace and strengthened the hands of the
Company's management from that day to this.

Our election system complied with every legal condition and every ethical standard. Each year the polls are open
for any stockholder who wishes to vote his or her stock *for*
the slate, *or in opposition*. The fact that, during more than
sixty years since then, no vote has even been cast in opposition
to the slate can be credited to two factors: First, each new
nomination for a director has been really impersonal and has
appealed to the great majority of the stockholders as logical
and in the interest of the business. Since then, young men
have been appointed only as their positions and responsibili-

ties made it patently desirable that they be added to a Board of Directors which really directed. Second, there is the accumulation of evidence, available to any stockholder, that political peace, which permitted the basing of advancements strictly on performance, has been a prime factor in the steady improvement of management efficiency.

CHAPTER X

DURING 1895, my dream of a new industrial organization built upon the old foundations had been forced to struggle with tradition and vested interests, just as a timid seedling struggles with older shrubs and the tall weeds round about. By 1896, it had grown into a sturdy plant, but still there was nothing about its growth to alarm its neighbors. It was in January, 1897, that my seedling forced its way above its surroundings and, in the sunshine of opportunity, spread outward and upward so strongly that our elders recognized it as a reality with revolutionary possibilities.

Personally, I had attained to a general managing position; effective, if ambiguous. Public opinion was not yet ready to accept the appointment of a General Manager (with capital letters), but directors and department heads sought my advice and assistance on all company problems. No important move was made without my approval.

George Noyes was recognized as my first assistant at Niagara. As a matter of fact, he was more: he was my confidant and good right hand, who often accompanied me to Oneida for directorial consultations. The January, 1897, meeting appointed Stephen Leonard assistant superintendent of the Trap Department. "Assistant" was as far as I could tactfully go at the moment, but Stephen then became superintendent in everything but name. Holton was officially recognized as understudy to Mr. Hinds in the Fruit Department, and Humphrey had been made assistant superintendent of

131

the Silk Department. With these lieutenants I consulted and conspired.

My home-staying time was divided between Niagara and Oneida. I say "home-staying," because I spent more than half of my time on the road, traveling east and west, in the interest not alone of my old departments, but now working very actively to rebuild our trap trade which had fallen from its high estate. The fact is that, from this time on, my most important work was selling; this, because with only Mr. Miller in New York, Mr. Myron Kinsley in Chicago, and Alfred Clark covering the rest of the United States for silverware there was much to be done if I were to continue the gains at Niagara and accomplish what was expected of me for the Trap Department.

During the year, necessarily, our sales force was enlarged. We added substantially to the staffs in the New York and Chicago Offices and employed Clifton Inslee on the road. But above all else I needed, for the tough trade battles I was waging, this efficient backing in the factories.

I owe it to Stephen to add that, during the years that followed, his management was all his own. During those years we increased trap sales by leaps and bounds, and we did it largely because of his management of the factory. I have often said—and without exaggeration—that whenever my campaign called for a cut of 2½ per cent in the price of traps, Stephen's initiative cut the cost 5 per cent, and he accomplished this in spite of our policy of steadily advancing wages. It was during those years that a prominent manufacturer in the neighboring city of Oneida told a meeting of the town's employers that our wages were ruining all the manufacturers there. He added, "However, it won't last long. They'll go broke."

It was during 1897 that I was given my first opportunity

to match myself against the commercial diplomacy which, during the nineteenth century, had built up a certain supremacy for Yankee industrialism. Somewhere in my conscious or subconscious, there lay an instinct which told me, first, that I had no genius for horse trading and, second, that frankness and honesty could succeed where subtlety and equivocation were still prescribed by tradition. I remember a formula I then adopted. It ran something like this: "Early in your struggle with an adversary, throw away your gun; if you do that, he will, in the end, throw away his, and then it will be the best man who wins." In simple words, the idea was to surprise your adversary with frankness. My first personal meeting with difficult competitors convinced me that I was right.

The so-called "tie-out chain" business had grown to surprising proportions. In four Southern states, which had "no-fence laws," cow owners, who pastured their cattle wherever they could find grass, were obliged to picket them. Twenty foot tie-out chains became the standard for picketing. Small hardware jobbers in those states bought one and even two carloads of tie-out chains each year.

We had struggled with our Yankee competitors for this business and had been reasonably successful. Finally they became alarmed. Mr. Edwards, owner of The Bridgeport Chain Company, invited me and also Bob Garland, owner of a Pittsburgh chain company which had shown signs of seriously invading the field, to meet with him in New York City. I had never met either Mr. Edwards or Mr. Garland. The conference took place at the old Manhattan Hotel. Mr. Edwards and Mr. Hill of Bridgeport conducted the meeting along lines prescribed by tradition for dealing with "Western-ers." Bob Garland and I were "Westerners."

Having come to discuss honestly plans for doing away

with threatened cut-throat competition, Bob and I laid our
cards on the table. They repeatedly asked for our figures and
we gave them. But when we asked for theirs, Mr. Edwards
looked at Mr. Hill and Mr. Hill looked at Mr. Edwards, and
they agreed that they had such figures but "unfortunately"
had left them at Bridgeport. So ran the whole interview.
However, those were the days when the Sherman Antitrust
Law was considered a dead letter, and before we left the
Manhattan Hotel we had all agreed on a fixed price for tie-
out chains. Mr. Edwards and Mr. Hill expressed themselves
as well pleased.

For myself, I was upset by the meeting and, as we
emerged on the street, I noticed that Bob Garland had something on his mind. He suggested, "Let's go into that saloon
on the corner and have a glass of beer." We went. I remember his saying as we sat there, "I don't like it." I assured him,
"Neither do I." Then we talked matters over.

Garland said, "They think we are suckers. They have no
idea of keeping their agreement. All they wanted was to get
us hog-tied." Again, I had the same thought as Garland, and
said so.

To make a long story short, we formed a little league of
our own. We divided the tie-out territory into two parts and
agreed that each would confine his efforts to his own territory.
It was further agreed that we would wait for the inevitable
price cut on the part of our New England friends, and whichever of us first obtained documentary proof of their price
cutting would telegraph the other, whereupon both would
start instantly on a campaign offering 10 per cent below the
Bridgeport cut price. We became so interested in the plan
that we worked out every detail, to insure the utmost rapidity
of movement.

Evidence was not long in coming; a customer's letter in which the Bridgeport company "confidentially" offered tie-out chains at 10 per cent below agreed prices. Our league of "Westerners" went to work. Garland personally covered his territory and, for the Oneida Community, Ltd., three of us took to the road. In less than a week we had a signed up a large proportion of that season's business for the Garland Chain Company and the Oneida Community, Ltd., at 10 per cent below Bridgeport's cut price.

This particular transaction led, as did most of our successes, to another burst of expansion, which I shall describe later. It also led to a change of managers in the Bridgeport company, and to the appointment of a young man in whom I soon acquired confidence. For the next ten years this young man, Walter Lasher, and I dominated the chain business with profit for both companies.

During the summer I learned that the Jas. S. Kirk Soap Company of Chicago was about to put out a five-cent cake of white floating soap to compete with Ivory, and that they intended to promote it with a premium. Their scheme involved giving away a silver spoon with each cake of soap and the shipping cases were large enough to accommodate one hundred spoons in addition to the soap. They invited bids from silverware manufacturers. Necessarily, the spoon would be a cheap article, but in the 1890's we specialized in cheap spoons.

Hopefully I entered our bid, but, visiting the firm on the day before decision was to be announced, my hopefulness received a severe shock. Mr. Kirk—it was Mr. James Kirk himself—showed me a spoon which another manufacturer guaranteed to be plated on a "white metal" base. The base metal of our cheap spoons was brass. This salesman had dramatically, in Mr. Kirk's presence, filed a deep notch in his sample which did reveal a surface white and silvery.

I knew the maker of this particular spoon and I knew that spoon was made of steel, but my statement to that effect did not seem to impress Mr. Kirk until I added, "If you wet that filed spot you showed me, it will be red with rust overnight." He laid his hand upon my arm as a friendly elder will do to encourage youth. I remember the twinkle in his eye as he said, "You tell me that this spot on the spoon will rust overnight. All right, we'll try it." Calling for a glass of water, he put a drop on the filed spot and placed it in a pigeonhole of his desk. "Now," he said, "you can come back in the morning and we'll see if you are right."

There was nothing left for me but to say, "Good." I knew that the metal was steel and would rust, but I did not know how long it would take it to rust. I think that I left Mr. Kirk's office with a sinking sensation in the region of my solar plexus. I had staked my success or failure on my statement that steel, if wet, would rust within twelve hours. Meekly I asked Mr. Kirk, "What time shall I come here in the morning?" "At any time after seven," the old gentleman said, with a suggestion of pride in his tone. "I'm always here at seven o'clock."

I have described those early memories as colorful. At this distance of time the color is usually pleasing, but I do remember that on that morning I entered the Kirk factory with anything but a light heart. Mr. Kirk greeted me cordially and with the same amused twinkle in his eye that I had recognized the day before. He settled himself in his chair.

"We'll now examine the sample," said Mr. James S. Kirk.

My heart was in my mouth. Very deliberately he took the spoon from an envelope and held it to the light. "God be praised!" (I did not say that, but I felt it.) Covering my competitor's white metal was a fine red coating of rust.

There remains one other interesting memory in connection with the deal. Although Mr. Kirk told me I could have the business and seemed really pleased that I got it, he raised one question. "I shall need a hundred gross of spoons every day, and I *must* have that many every day or my soap shipments will be held up. Can you guarantee to ship a hundred gross *every day?*"

I said, "I can." Not that we had ever manufactured a hundred gross in a day, but I made up my mind that we would do it, anyway. I remember that the old gentleman, at the last moment, alarmed me by saying thoughtfully, "Perhaps I ought to arrange a second source of supply."

I begged him, "Give me a chance to show you."

Back home at the factory I said to Fred Filby, "It's up to you," and Filby never let the factory quit work at night until he had shipped a hundred gross. In the end we actually got ahead of the soap, and were asked to cease shipping for a few days while they caught up.

Which reminds me that business enthusiasm threatens omission of what was perhaps the most important happening in 1897; the birth of our daughter, Constance. I withdraw the "perhaps." Her joining our family meant more to Corinna and me than any business success. From that day to this, Constance has been a marvelous companion for both of us, and always a colorful inspiration. Our family seemed complete.

As the year 1897 was nearing its end there occurred an incident which, while on its face personal, proved of great importance for the development of our new Oneida Community, Ltd. There comes back to me a vivid picture of three young men sitting on the snowy bank of a half-frozen stream, eating sandwiches and drinking hot coffee. George, Stephen and I, tramping over the hills from Kenwood to nearby Clinton, had halted beside the brook to eat our lunch.

When we had finished eating, no one arose to go. George or Stephen—one of them, I have forgotten which—asked, "What is it?" He looked hard at me. "From one of your remarks, I gathered that you proposed this expedition with a definite purpose in view."

"You're right," I said. "I've decided on a rather radical move. Do you realize how little of this Company's stock is owned by our generation of men? Do you also realize what a marvelous growth and what prosperity is coming to the Oneida Community, Ltd.? We, who will have contributed most to that success and who are most concerned as to the kind of an institution we create, not only have little Company stock but we stand to inherit little. Our generation should, in the end, own enough stock to direct the Company's policies as we want them to go. If we don't, others will dictate those policies, and our dream of a co-operative industrial organization will vanish like other dreams."

The others agreed. "But how?"

"Salaries," I said. "We must have larger salaries."

Again George and Stephen agreed, but I saw that they did not suspect the radical nature of my plan. I dropped generalities.

"At the January meeting I am going to ask for a salary of twenty-five hundred dollars and raises for the rest of you in proportion."

That was something else! The boys were startled. I was still drawing the eighteen-hundred-dollar salary voted me two years ago, and a seven-hundred-dollar jump in one year was unheard of. Furthermore, eighteen hundred dollars had been the top salary paid by the Oneida Community, Ltd. up to that time.

Stephen, I think it was, exclaimed, "Twenty-five hundred dollars!"

I rubbed it in. "Yes, twenty-five hundred dollars, and don't think I'm going to stop there. That's only a starter. A range of twenty-five-hundred-dollar salaries will never enable our generation to buy enough stock to influence the future of this Company."

The logic of our situation prevailed. It is, of course, easier to convince even a naturally conservative young man that his salary should be raised than—let us say—that it be lowered.

The year 1897 was one of rapid progress in the relationship between the eight older directors and the rising generation whom I, alone, still represented on the Board. The older Board Members all became very cordial toward my dream of the future. On my side, I must have compromised with their traditional conservatism in matters not affecting the business, for I find in the directors' minutes two curious resolutions.

The first reads: "Card-playing in the Company's rooms, only by permission; none on Sundays."

The second: "Smoking within 100 feet of the Mansion House is prohibited."

Don't laugh, my young readers! Those men had genuine and persistent religious convictions which, as with their New England ancestors, had become hopelessly entangled with ethical and social taboos. Smoking was forbidden in Community days, and, while Community members indulged in simple card games, betting had emerged with our generation.

During this year another relic of the political—perhaps

I should say spiritual—cleavages of the breakup was abandoned. The "F & Co." [Freeman & Co.] dining establishment, which the Noyes Loyalists organized in 1881 to separate themselves from the Dissidents, was turned over to the Company which, from that day to this, has maintained it for the convenience of residents of the Mansion House and the Company's guests.

The end of this year found the Oneida Community, Ltd. at the beginning of a steep climb toward a new social integration and financial prosperity. In addition to the special accounts I have described, we had made good progress with the regular silverware trade. Filby had introduced modern methods in the Niagara factories, and Stephen had done the same at Oneida. Also, business in general was improving. As a result, in January, 1898, the directors looked at a very satisfactory balance sheet; a net profit of $59,906.

It was a very cheerful group of ex-Perfectionist stockholders that foregathered at Oneida on January 11, 1898, for the annual company meeting. They were not only cheerful but, directors and stockholders alike, radiated a new cordiality toward the transfer of management to our generation of young men. The best evidence of this was a unanimous agreement upon Stephen as a director to replace Mr. Hinds, who had announced his temporary retirement from the Board. Mr. Hinds was evidently planning a sabbatical year. He had substantial real-estate holdings in California and many friends living there whom he desired to visit. Also, I think that his shrewdness told him the nature of the evolution taking place in O.C.L. affairs and its inevitable end, since later in the year he asked to be relieved of responsibility for the Fruit Department.

As a matter of record, the increase of huge commercial

canning institutions, with up-to-date machinery, had during recent years made the possibility of profits for our small, essentially "hand-made" industry increasingly difficult. For the first time in its long history, the Fruit Department showed a red figure at the end of 1898.

Mr. Hinds's action brought the centralization of management nearer. Dr. Noyes proposed a Fruit Committee, along the same lines and with the same membership as the Trap Committee; i.e., Mr. Freeman, himself and me. When Mr. Hinds cordially endorsed this arrangement, I knew that he had, perhaps regretfully, buried tradition. His political instinct saw my general managership not too far ahead.

So the stage was set for our attack on small salaries. After explaining to the directors the point of view of my generation, I asked for the twenty-five hundred dollars. This, as I anticipated, was a shock. Twenty-five hundred dollars! Where were we headed!! Silence met my suggestion.

Thereupon I took the bull by the horns. I said, "I may as well be frank; this is only a beginning. When results warrant it, I shall ask for further raises." I seem to remember seven blank faces when I walked across the room to leave the meeting, as was customary. I carefully refrained from looking at Stephen.

I was told afterward that the realistic Mrs. Joslyn, our only woman Board member, recovered first and proceeded to rationalize my proposition. She said, "The fact is that Pierre occupies a position that has never existed in this company before. He has been made manager of a majority of our departments and, for myself, I am willing to work with him in the management of the Silk Department. During the last two years he has helped me, notably in the negotiations with Gudebrod and in the closing of a favorable contract for the manufacture of Marshall Field's special brand of silk. If we recognize that Pierre is practically General Manager of the Company now and give him that title, this salary will not seem unreasonable."

The quotation is not exact, but is in substance what Dr. Noyes reported to me after the meeting. Whatever may have been the misgivings of individual directors, I was appointed to the new position of General Manager, and the salary was voted. Not only this but, when the salaries of other young men came up for discussion, I detected a new liberality.

In still other ways the directors showed at least complacency toward my ideas. In the Board minutes, I find that, later in the year, Mrs. Joslyn asked permission to raise the wages of her workers, especially girls working at the looms. Another minute records approval of my plan for workers' vacations with pay. Then, in June, a committee was appointed to "see that our tenant houses [average rent $6.50 to $9.00 per month] be kept in prime sanitary condition, without much reference to cost."

That phrase "without much reference to cost" struck a new note. Economy was part of the religion of the older generation, and, a few years before, with the best of intentions, that resolution would probably have ended, "keeping costs down as much as possible." I also find in the minutes that the directors voted to pay employees who had enlisted for the Spanish War the same wages they had received when working, payments being made to wives or family.

During January, 1898, we held our first Agents' Meeting and banquet; the two elder Kinsleys, at either end of the table, carved turkey, and their two boys, Albert and Mart Kinsley, waited on us. Later, the directors voted payment for this banquet. We were branching out. During the spring, I attended my first hardware convention in Buffalo, with directorial approval and their vote that the Company stand the expense. If, during 1898, all departments prospered under my new General Managership, a liberal credit must be given to increasing prosperity in the country. The business tide was rising.

On the other side, I was guilty of a piece of cowardice whose results arose to plague us later. We had a chance to buy the Blake & Lamb Trap Company for twelve thousand dollars. Unfortunately, the B. & L. Trap Company had two other ancient lines of manufacture—cowbells and organ springs—and the older directors objected to our acquiring these. I think I was trying to be too clever, to offset my insistence on expansive planning by a little conservatism, and this seemed an opportunity to please the older directors in a rather unimportant matter. I deducted an amount representing cowbells and organ springs from my offer to the Company. The deal fell through.

This later became a threat to those very essential trap profits when a man named Hawkins bought the old Blake & Lamb assets we had refused and began a campaign to spread their sales in the Western market. The B. & L. "jump" pattern traps had always enjoyed a substantial sale in New England but were little known in the West.

We found that Hawkins had a very tight little manufacturing proposition. He had built a sizable factory on a little water-power development near South Britain, Connecticut. The upper floor of this building was devoted to living quarters for his family and the family of his son-in-law who was the active foreman of the plant.

I tried without success to buy Hawkins out. He was what we often refer to as a "character." His huge, loose-jointed, farmerlike figure, with clothes to match, and his slow New England speech would fool you, but you soon discovered that he was shrewd and that he knew exactly where his advantage lay.

At the end of a long day of negotiating, we made a contract with him whereby we undertook to handle the sale of his traps on a small commission basis with an agreement to keep all his New England customers with total sales never less than those of the present year. On the other hand, we were not bound to sell any of his traps in the Western market.

This arrangement worked to our mutual satisfaction for nearly ten years; so greatly to Hawkins's satisfaction that when, in 1911, we decided to get closer to the Sherman Anti-trust Act by resigning from all the price-fixing trade associations to which we belonged, which included the abandonment of our arrangement with him, he felt very bad. He urged us to continue as his selling agency, making any modification of the old contract in our own favor that we thought necessary. We refused, but always maintained a friendly attitude toward his sales in New England.

The records show that three important and fortunate happenings in 1898 helped along a prosperity for which we were receiving much credit. The first was Mr. William Wrigley's premium business. Those were the days when the foundations of the Wrigley chewing-gum fortune were being laid, and the very forthright Bill Wrigley (I knew him well throughout the rest of his life) made important use of premiums.

Perhaps I ought to tell of the odd incident which led to my acquaintance with Wrigley. One day the following telegram was laid on my desk: "Where is the hundred gross of butters and sugars you promised?"

An order for a hundred gross of butter knives and sugar shells! The telegram was addressed to the Oneida Community, Ltd., but I knew, of course, that it was a mistake. We had never received such an order. However, early the next morning I arrived in Chicago. I entered Wrigley's office, then located on Michigan Street (not Michigan Avenue). The boy, who had taken my card, came back. "Mr. Wrigley will see you."

Bill Wrigley told me afterward that, on principle, he saw everyone who called on him; that he did not intend to miss anything good. However, he made decisions quickly, and the average caller got from one to two minutes of his time. Looking at my card, Bill said, in his best rapid-fire manner, "Oneida Community! I never dealt with your firm, but I've been having trouble with my other supplier and I nearly wrote you yesterday."

I produced the telegram, saying, "Oh, that explains it, Mr. Wrigley. This wire evidently came to me by mistake. I've called today, first, to find out where it should have gone. But, second, because I'd like a part of this butter-knife and sugar-shell business myself."

Bill looked at me with a sparkle in his eye that I later came to know. "You're a fast worker," he said.

I parried the thrust. "How else can anyone get anywhere?" Then I charged straight at the mark. "Your other order hasn't been delivered. I can make a hundred gross of butters and sugars for you, and I can keep my promise about deliveries."

Before I left Chicago he had given me an order and I had made a friend. From that day until Wrigley died, I had all his silverware-premium business. On one occasion I shipped him a solid carload of teaspoons, which went as premiums to his dealers.

The second important happening was an offer from Bob Garland to sell me his chain outfit. He and John, his brother, had a growing business in the manufacture of insulated tubing for electric wiring, and their chain business was small by comparison. It had become merely a nuisance. The Garland automatic wire chain, "Eureka," was not as symmetrical as our "Niagara" chain, but we knew it could be made more cheaply. Also, Garland had machines for much larger sizes of chain that we could make. I presented his proposition to our directors. The project was expansive— my second really expansive project—but the directors encouraged further negotiation, and, early the following year, we bought the Garland Chain business and moved the machinery and inventory to Niagara.

It was after the sale had been consummated and documents signed that I spent an evening with the Garlands at Bob's house in Pittsburgh, and it was during that evening that they offered me fifteen thousand dollars to come with them. (I was making twenty-five hundred dollars at the time!)

I was flattered but not tempted. I thanked them, adding, "I left the old institution once, but I shall never leave it again."

Bob was evidently interested. He said, "I knew that you left. You never told me why you went back."

After a few moments consideration I said, "A feeling and a thought together took me back. This feeling was that I still loved the Mansion House where I was born and brought up. I still loved many of those elderly friends whose struggle for unselfishness in the old Community had left its deep imprint on their character. I pictured living with them and for them as a more satisfactory life than any possible wealth."

Neither Bob nor his brother broke the silence that followed. After a little I continued:

"My 'thought' was that the great change in business conditions now going forward could presently put an end to the Oneida Community, Ltd. The kind of men . . ." Then I hesitated. It came to me that I was overdoing it.

Bob spoke quickly, "Go on, Pierre. We're interested."

"Well, the kind of men who made the Oneida Community were the kind of men who built up the United States. Those were the days when an able and honest man could build up a prosperous manufacturing business around one of the small water powers that abounded in New England and New York State. Such men brought their talents to the Community.

"Now—I needn't tell you—mass production is changing all this. In the end these elderly men hadn't a chance to survive. The institution needed younger men and, having effected a friendly working relation between the two generations, I intend to do my part to make it a success *together*."

The third happening, whose importance achieved recognition only later, was the addition of Grosvenor Allen to my staff. After leaving Yale, Grosvenor, following a theory of his own which called for experience outside the home company, had taken a position with the Pope Company in Hartford. Now, on the thirteenth of December, 1898, he applied for work with the O.C.L. I was greatly pleased and our directors hailed his return with cordiality.

As a matter of fact, Grosvenor's joining us at that particular moment was another of those timely happenings that have contributed largely to the Company's success. In his character a critical faculty which insisted upon studying every angle of any proposed plan of action was combined with a tact which rendered all his criticism impersonal and therefore not offensive. He completed the character, so to speak, of our little group of young men to whom the future of the O.C.L. had been committed and added to the confidence of both directors and stockholders.

I remember hearing of a remark made at the time by a stockholder, a woman, who said, "I don't mind their turning control of the Company over to Pierrepont, as long as he has George and Stephen and Grosvenor hanging on to his coattails."

CHAPTER XI

IN THOSE DAYS, each year ended for me only when the January closing of the General Ledger at Oneida revealed profits and progress. The General Ledger! I can still recall my feeling of mingled hope and dislike when I thought of it. Would it be, this year, friendly or hostile?

On January 16, 1899, that accursed ledger showed almost exactly the same profit as the year before, $59,588. This was approximately 10 per cent on the capital stock, but one of the penalties of a position erected on success is the expectation, not to say demand, for ever-increasing success. Hence, in January, 1899, explanations were called for—and given. I think that by 1899 I had necessarily cultivated the art of "explaining."

The directors asked, tactfully, of course, why so? Sales were one hundred thousand dollars larger than in 1897. I explained that, due to the employment of additional salesmen, selling expenses were larger but, enveloping the meeting in a warm, sunshiny atmosphere of optimism, I urged, "This will bring rich returns in the end."

Our Treasurer, Mr. Freeman, came to my aid. He pointed out that, with the Board's approval, he had made substantial reductions in our real-estate inventory, and had charged off certain large amounts (one, the Wanzer-Lamp debt, sixteen thousand dollars, contracted during the previous regime) which had been carried as assets in the Bad-

and-Doubtful Ledger, for years. Discussion and analysis occupied one entire session. Our explanations must have been convincing, since I find in the minutes: "Comparison of 1897 and 1898 gives a fair showing of profits."

This reconciliation between expectations and results, and the renewal of directorial hopes was essential, since the purchase of the Garland chain business was on the fire. That confidence was restored is evidenced by a resolution in the February meeting, authorizing me to make Garland a cash offer and calling for a stockholders' meeting in March to approve the purchase. We paid Garland thirty-two thousand dollars cash, plus a royalty of 3½ per cent on the sales for ten years. This royalty was later compromised by a further cash payment.

The older directors, by unanimous vote, confirmed my position as General Manager. There was no change in my salary, which suggests that I, myself, was feeling a little modest over the profit showing for the year, or suspected that it was a poor time to push my salary plans. However, they did add: "And the sum of $250 additional, in half-yearly payments, to meet his expenses in maintaining a home both at Niagara and Oneida."

Stephen was named full superintendent of the Trap Department, and Holton of the Fruit Department. Further expansion of the selling organization was approved. Mr. Myron Kinsley was appointed "resident agent" in Chicago, with an office allowance of twenty dollars per month. An increase of salary for Alfred Clark was voted, but his application for office space in St. Louis ran into an economy sandbank: "Business not sufficient to warrant." George was encouraged to establish for the Oneida departments the cost system he had installed at Niagara.

On March tenth, a stockholders' meeting approved the Garland Chain Company purchase. Then, four days later, a friendly Board of Directors naïvely registered the mingled feelings of hope and fear with which they were following (and backing) my upward flight. The record of the March fourteenth meeting closes with a pronouncement which, while at the start cool and businesslike, ends on an earnest, almost wistful, note. Here is the minute:

"Some conversation followed concerning our swelling investments. Finally the idea was expressed, substantially, that, as our great businesses are now in good shape, the result of much study, liberal expenditure, and push for several years, and, as the country is entering an era of prosperity, we may say that we are now prepared to reverse our policy and hereafter devote our net earnings, above running expenses and a reasonable dividend, almost entirely to getting receipts in full from our creditors, until the last dollar of our indebtedness is discharged."

I am touched, partly because I was very fond of the Mr. Underwood who wrote the paragraph; partly because it takes me back to the emotional atmosphere of those early years, when lifelong conservatism was struggling with a newly born confidence in me; and partly because none of those men lived to see that "receipt in full," which, as a matter of history, awaited the successes of a generation younger than my own.

The year 1899 saw the only strike of any importance in the history of the Oneida Community or the Oneida Community, Ltd. It came about in this way. Early in July of that year, the Metal Polishers and Buffers Union decided to move in on the two silverware factories at Niagara. Mr. Jamieson, formerly our own drop room foreman and at this time manager of the Wm. A. Rogers Company, a competitor, announced that he would "burn his factory down" before he would submit to unionization. For my part, I made no public statements.

I shut down the plant and called our work people together in the buffing room. I told them why I was unwilling to have ours become a union shop. Standing on a buffing bench and looking down on a roomful of eager faces, I said, "I believe that the labor unions have done an immense amount of good in this country. If this Company planned to do no more for its people than the other manufacturers, I'd welcome a union into our plants. But fortunately, I have plans for the future of the Oneida Community, Ltd. and the prosperity of its working people which go far beyond anything the unions can do for them, and these plans cannot be carried out with a union shop. Therefore, I shall not admit a union, and I ask you all to stand with me."

It was only a few years ago that a gray-haired man said to me, "I was a boy when you told us that day up in the buffing room that you would not have a union because you had better plans. You certainly have made good what you said."

Our people stood firm for a while, but picketing, arguments and threats started desertions. Then Mr. Jamieson broke down completely. He accepted the union and discharged his superintendents and other men marked out for discharge by the union. This, of course, led many of our workmen to believe that I would ultimately cave, and that, if they stuck by us, they would lose their jobs. For ten long weeks we suffered a combination strike and lockout. Every week on Monday morning, four of our managing group who had been working in different areas brought in a group of workers from other cities, to take the place of such employees as had been frightened away, and every Saturday night we found that we had lost half of these.

That was a trying time for a young man in his twenties. My two-year-old, Constance, was very sick at Oneida, and I could not leave Niagara on account of the strike. My only solace was daily reports by telegraph. To make matters worse, the Oneida directors became alarmed or doubtful regarding my policy. As the result of a "special meeting to consider labor troubles," Dr. Noyes (alas! my hitherto unwavering backer) wired: "Directors here think you may have to give way to the union."

I hope that my answering telegram was dictated as much by belief in the rightness of our cause as by irritation. I wired: "If that is the Board's decision, you can send someone out here to unionize the shop and take my job. I am through."

I read in the minutes only this, that "the Board discussed the labor situation at the Falls in its various bearings, but no action was taken." I suspect that the original draft of this minute read a little differently, since I find the following in the record of the next regular meeting: "The minutes of the special meeting, July 22nd, were read, *amended*, and approved." I say "suspect"; as a matter of fact, I know that the motion was originally, to say the least, directive. Dr. Noyes told me so.

I cannot refrain from relating one incident which showed that, in spite of the terrorism and disorders generated by the strike, men never lose all of their sportsmanship. One of the new workers whom Grosvenor had brought from Rochester was an ex-prize fighter. Among the strikers, also, was a fellow with a local reputation as a pugilist, and the two groups, union and non-union, arranged a "mill," between these two, on which sizable wagers were made. The fight was to take place in the opera house. Unfortunately (or perhaps fortunately) the police interfered. They assured me that, with feeling running so high, there would surely be a riot, whoever won the match. The police were undoubtedly right, but I can remember a secret regret. I felt sure our man would win.

The spirit of the strikers was a little different from many we read about. The picket lines were noisy, but neither I nor any of our managers were molested when going through them. There were threats, but my philosophy—perhaps my optimism—told me that men intending to hit didn't threaten.

The Rogers boys, having been unionized now, were so rough with our workmen when they passed the Rogers factory at quitting time that we let our men out fifteen minutes before five o'clock. One day, three of our men were late in leaving and as they passed the Rogers exit the crowd rushing out the door attacked them. The chief of police told me the result. One of our three men was the pugilist Grosvenor brought from Rochester and, as the attackers reached him, he hit each man just once. The policeman told me that within two minutes four men were lying prostrate in the street.

The hero of that strike was Fred Filby. Fred was everywhere. He could be found in the factory or somewhere on the grounds from dawn to midnight. He walked boldly through the picket lines, speaking to lifelong friends among the picketers, but never allowing himself to be drawn into an argument. As I remember the finish, a committee of strikers sought an interview with Filby and me. We knew that the end was approaching when their leader asked, "Will strikers be taken back?"

My answer had been agreed upon. It was Filby's plan. I said, "Yes, all of them, ultimately. But some will have to wait. The troublemakers may have to wait a year."

That was the end of the only serious disagreement between Oneida, Ltd. management and men through the more than half a century that has ensued. In the end, the union gave up, and practically all our workers came back to us. I hope they have never regretted my stubbornness.

My first meeting with Doctor Noyes at Oneida after the strike had been settled was typical of him and of his relation with me. I remember well that interview.

When I entered his room, he was sitting by a window looking out upon the green expanse of the children's playground. He started to rise. I prevented him and drew a chair to his side. He was silent for a moment, then turned to me eyes which were suffering. All he said was, "We're old fogies, Pierre."

I grasped his hand and pressed it, saying, "I don't blame you at all." That was all that was said about the strike. Nothing could really disturb the relation of confidence and affection that existed between the Doctor and me.

In August, Mr. Lord died and the cordiality with which the directors unanimously elected my cousin, George Noyes, to fill the vacancy on the Board told me that our youthful adventure was finally accepted.

During those first years, although I had boldly violated the conservative traditions which kept superintendents close to their factories, the Mississippi River had been my farthest West. Now, I threw traditions to the winds. I personally investigated every territory.

We had no representative in San Francisco, and I had long suspected that the Coast states offered a rich field for the expansion of our silverware business. Visiting San Francisco, I arranged with William P. Morgan to represent us in all the states west of the Rocky Mountains. This was a rather daring enterprise, and when I returned home, our directors, some of them, did more than raise their eyebrows.

Mr. Allen asked, "William P. Morgan? Isn't he the agent of our largest competitor, the Meriden-Britannia Company?"

I replied, "Yes, but if you'll trust my instinct, he's the kind of man who will hold an honest balance between two principals."

"Also," spoke up another director, "isn't he the brother-in-law of Horace Wilcox, head of the Meriden-Britannia Company and a dominating figure in the silverware business?"

I admitted the relationship and, also, that Horace Wilcox had been called the czar of the silverware business, but I repeated my confident belief that we would profit by the arrangement with William P. Morgan. As a matter of history, Mr. Morgan for fourteen years "carried water on both shoulders," as they say, without spilling a drop.

Even when, a year later, the Meriden-Britannia Company, with a half-dozen other Rogers Companies, disappeared into one of the early trusts, under the name International Silver Company, Mr. Morgan maintained a satisfactory balance between the two accounts. In the end, however, the lines became too competitive. A newly organized firm, Morgan & Allen Company, took over the William P. Morgan business, and the sales staff was divided. Horace Allen and several other salesmen became exclusive agents for Oneida Community, Ltd. products, and Roland Allen became sales head of the International Silver Company account. Briefly, during those years we broke into the Pacific Coast market and profited very largely through the friendship and conscientious handling of our account by William P. Morgan.

It was on this, my first trip to the Pacific Coast, that my inexperience led to what then seemed a tragedy. I was traveling from Seattle to Vancouver, British Columbia. A man came through the train seeking a partner for cards and, having nothing better to do, I accompanied him to his stateroom. It was the old "Army game." There I found two other men, apparently strangers to each other. One could not play whist, and another could not play poker, which resulted in our settling down to a game of euchre. Five cards!

The tired-looking man, who had played poker the night before, grumbled over his good poker hands until another asked, "Do you mean it? I'd go a dollar with you on a show-down."

Small bets passed back and forth among the others until I could not resist a "full house" dealt me. I won several small bets. Then, winding up with four aces to my four kings, they cleaned me out. Presently one of the players expressed a fear that the conductor had noticed our betting, whereupon we all returned to our seats in the parlor car.

A few moments later, the train stopped at Sedro-Woolley and it happened that the southbound train passed ours at this station. The other three men boarded that train. As I stood there watching them disappear in the distance, a man at my side remarked, "A bunch of beauts!"

Up to that time, no suspicion of crooked dealings had crossed my mind, but with his words I instantly saw it all. The gentleman at my side remarked casually, "They tried to get me into their game." When I finally acknowledged that they had taken me for every cent I had, he offered to finance me until I could get some money in Vancouver.

Perhaps the reader can imagine my feelings as I stood there at the Sedro-Woolley station. My first long trip, heading for unknown regions in Canada, dead broke, and contemplating what, with my current salary (and a two-year-old baby at home), looked like a very real loss of money—perhaps sixty or seventy dollars. However, I have, since that time, congratulated myself on the experience. No crook has ever got a cent of my money since that Western trip.

Reading over the directors' minutes reminds me of our simplicity in the closing years of the nineteenth century. I confess to a wave of nostalgia when I read that, "Filling lamps by lamp-light in any of our buildings is prohibited" and, again, "It is the duty of the directors, as well as the officers of the Company, to stop boys from throwing stones at the buildings or from anything that will damage the property of the Company."

This attention to homely details was a hangover from the old Community life. The problem of living together in peace and comfort—I think I should say the art of living together—was still a matter of prime importance to the directors of a business corporation. Our generation of young men were also near enough to our childhood in the Community so that we joined our elders in giving much thought to living conditions. I know that George and Stephen and Grosvenor and I, who had come to be reckoned a sort of executive committee of the Board, were determined that prosperity should insure comfort for the old Community members still alive.

In those minutes I also find ample evidence that we were equally determined to share that comfort with all who worked for the Company. A "Sick Benefit Association" was at that time formed by the employees and managed by them. The Company contributed on a fifty-fifty basis. Also, I read of a dance for the employees, which we all attended and which was financed by the Company. Prizes for suggestions for improvement in manufacturing technics were offered. And, in 1900, recesses from work, forenoon and afternoon, without loss of pay, were voted. A committee was appointed "to study ways and means for ameliorating conditions and encouraging the progress of our employees." Lastly a committee was voted to arrange for "building houses in the neighborhood for employees who live at the Castle and Oneida and have to arise very early to get to the factory at seven o'clock."

Beginning in 1896, golf became a favorite sport among the younger generation and some of the older ones. Dr. Noyes, at the age of fifty-six, became an enthusiastic golfer. It began when our doctor suggested golf as an exercise for my wife. Our first links consisted of three holes; the first hole was a short one on the old children's playground. The second went over the hedge and across the Cragin meadow nearly to the Creek. The third came back over the hedge to the playground again.

When youth took hold of it, three more holes were added in the "Island Meadow." All the work on these new links was done by the "boys." I can remember much fun in "shovelling and levelling *bees*" (a name for joint work inherited from old Community days and by our forebears from early New England customs).

We played all winter with red balls, across country and often in six or eight inches of snow. An objective was decided upon, usually a barn, often a mile away, and the winners were whoever, after going around this barn, returned to a home hole first. I used the plural—winners—because we played in pairs. One partner went at least two hundred yards ahead and watched the ball bury itself in the snow. He dug it out, then it was his turn to drive.

On one occasion this winter game almost resulted in a tragedy. Our home journey—my partner's and mine—took us across the frozen creek above the dam. There was no special indication that the central strip was mostly slush not yet frozen hard. As I, attempting to cross, stepped on this narrow strip, I went through—bang!—through to my arm pits where my arms and shoulders were held by the stronger ice. Unfortunately, due to the mass of slush I could not raise myself at all. I could only hang there by my arms.

I yelled to my brother Holton, my partner, who also had broken through the ice below, where the water was shallow. He yelled to the other players who had gone beyond us. I shall never forget Albert Kinsley coming over the bank with his eyes fairly popping out of his head. He thought I was about to drown. Quickly, he, with the other boys, brought a small tree to the stream and pushed it out until I got hold of its branches. Then they pulled me out and onto the bank. After that, our winter golf lines were laid where there were no streams.

Oddly enough, the golf enthusiasm led directly to a new swimming enthusiasm. It was the Doctor's suggestion that the stream above the dam maintained a level that, when diverted into the Cragin meadow, would create a lake deep enough in parts for diving as well as swimming. Again all hands took hold and created a very attractive little lake now known as Sunset Lake which has furnished summer bathing for hundreds of neighborhood children for half a century.

The incidents that I have recounted may seem trivial in the history of a rising business corporation, but they were not trivial in the life of the times, and they are far from trivial in my memory. If Oneida Ltd., in 1958, differs at all from other corporations, it is because the Community's conviction that "life is more than meat" carried over to another generation, and, for themselves at least, has modified the twentieth century's worship of wealth.

In spite of the strike, the year 1899 turned out the largest profits in our history up to that time, and more than doubled the $60,000 of the two previous years; to be exact, profits were $130,347. Everyone was happy; the stockholders, with their 7 per cent dividend, employees after the strike, the workers with their new benefits, the younger generation with their prospects, and my baby, Constance, was again well.

CHAPTER XII

In a recent book written by a well-known author, I found a hint—or perhaps something more than a hint—that good autobiographies can be written only by introverts. I am not an introvert, yet here I find myself trying to combine with my autobiography a story of the youthful, semi-socialistic ambitions and commercial strivings of myself together with a group of our young men. We were descendants of Oneida Perfectionists and were attempting to carry into a modern setting as much of the principles taught by our forebears as seemed to us practicable.

I have persuaded myself that an account of our struggle to enlarge our business—if associated with the workings out of youthful dreams of a better life through that struggle, when commonplaces seemed to us romantic—would leave the reader with a truer impression of the present Company, Oneida Ltd., than any merely descriptive words could convey. For I believe that we really have, in our organization at Oneida and Sherrill, a quality differing from that existing in any other industrial concern.

We ourselves feel it, and outside people who come in contact with us often volunteer, "You have something different at Oneida." Yet I have been unable, and others who have tried have been unable, to define that difference. It is not enough to say that it lies in the special psychology or the inherited idealism of our people. It is more real, and our

162

relations with each other are more realistic, than either psychology or idealism.

So now, lest the exciting memories of those days of commercial struggle black out the really more important object of my writing, I shall delay that part of the story in order to bring up to date at least a partial inventory of our social progress. In spite of our absorbing interest in commercial adventure, we did make progress along social lines during those years.

Recalling the principle, announced by my cousin George and emphasized by Fred Filby in 1898, that good wages were the best form of welfare work, I am interested to find in the directors' minutes that in 1898 I apologized to the Board for having announced at Niagara (without consulting my elders) a nine-hour day—then unheard of—with ten hours' pay. This *fait accompli* must have justified itself, since the nine-hour day, with 11 per cent raise in wage rates, was soon extended to the Oneida factories.

Another statement in the 1903 minutes surprises me. Our secretary made a rather elaborate report of a discussion wherein our elders revealed their fears of overexpansion and stressed the desirability of higher prices for the new silverware. Dear old Mr. Underwood, the secretary, added to the minutes: "A statement was made that our wages have advanced thirty or forty per cent."

It may seem like youthful optimism that in 1901, just when we were planning an ambitious and expensive campaign to create through advertising a national demand for our new line of Community Silver, we should add another ambitious campaign to improve the living and working conditions of our people.

Our first step was to build eight simple but comfortable

houses to take the place of the aged "tenant-houses" left by
the Community. These were rented to employees at low rates
and within a few years had been sold to them for twelve
hundred dollars each. Later, nine more houses were built and
sold on partial-payment terms. Most of these houses, with
some improvements and additions, are still, in 1958, considered desirable residences.

This was promptly followed by the opening of new
streets on which building lots were sold to employees at only
slightly more than farmland prices and a cash bonus of one
hundred dollars given. There and then was born the present
City of Sherrill which, today, has a population of around
three thousand individuals.

It was not until June 1905 that a complete plan for the
proposed "city" was laid out on the Community Farm by a
surveyor named Jenkins, and streets were opened as needed.
Since the Company had plenty of land, the lots were given
a depth of 165 feet, and a width of 88 feet, leaving room for
sizable kitchen gardens. The Company either loaned money
when necessary for building or helped employees to get time
loans in Oneida which were gradually paid off by payroll
deductions.

Today practically all of the one hundred acres of the
Company's old "Hitchcock Farm" area is filled with attractive homes, and the four streets opened across Sherrill Road
are also full. New streets are opened only when the last one
is completely filled. The building bonus has crept up through
the years until it is now one thousand dollars per house. Six
hundred dollars is given for the land, which includes side-
walks and services such as sewers, electricity, city water,
etc. Four hundred dollars is given in cash. No bonus is paid to
executives for building.

This building plan has worked out advantageously both for the workers and the Company. Our little city, the smallest in the United States, is located conveniently near the factories, Club House, the playing fields, and the shopping center, where stores of several kinds, in a building erected by the Company thirty years ago, really anticipated the "shopping centers" now becoming so numerous and popular. The Real Estate Department told me a few years ago that, in Sherrill at that time, 90 per cent of the houses were owned by the people who lived in them and more than 60 per cent were fully paid for.

John Ruskin whom, as a young man, I greatly admired, said in describing his ideal community for workers, "We will try to take some small piece of English ground, beautiful, peaceful and fruitful. We will have no untended or un-thought-of-creatures on it; none wretched but the sick, none idle but the dead. We will have plenty of flowers and vege-tables in our gardens, plenty of corn and grain in our fields— and a few bricks."

When I walk through our little city my mind goes back to this quotation. There can be seen from the many windows of our factories as well as from the streets of pleasant homes, "flowers and grain in our fields—and a few bricks." As Ruskin insists, the surroundings of a factory need not necessarily be ugly.

In those early days another aspect of our relation to the Company worried me a little, but in general was submerged by what I may call the "previous question," *i.e.*, survival— survival of the company under the managership entrusted to me "on approval," so to speak. In 1900, with every year add-ing to the Company's size and reputation, another aspect engaged the serious attention not only of the original managing group but of a dozen or more younger men working their way into important positions. More and more, with success, the question was being asked, "Who will own this company? Who will own its stock?"

There was only one answer to this question: that, while a certain amount of stock could be inherited by the "group," a majority would automatically go outside to absentee owners.

Here was a situation created by our tradition of comparatively small salaries plus the rapid and inevitable increase in the value of the stock as a result of our own labors. The only solution that presented itself was dangerous but since it was the only one, we adopted it. We borrowed money on the collateral we had and bought more stock. We borrowed the limit on this new stock and bought still more.

Two stock dividends during the first decade of the century which, together, doubled the common stock, helped us, but this only meant more collateral on which to borrow, and more debts. We were fortunate enough to find friendly citizens of Oneida and prosperous farmers along the "West Road" who were glad to get 6 per cent interest. Few of those loans were ever "called." Our youthful association made it a business to cultivate lenders and followed up our own borrowers to ensure prompt payment of interest. Our salvation was a steady increase of company profits so rapid that the demon of vanishing "margins" never quite caught up with us. By 1910 our financing had become entirely respectable.

By 1912, Stephen estimated that nearly 90 per cent of the Company's common stock was held by members of the organization (including employees) or friends.

The Mansion House with its grounds lies in a bend of Oneida Creek, in Madison County. One quarter mile to the south is a bridge over the creek. Beyond, in Oneida County, lies the Knife Plant and many acres of our farm land. A full half mile to the north there is another bridge leading to the company's main silverware plant in Sherrill (again in Oneida County) and more acres of farm land.

In 1910, inside this loop of the meandering stream, twelve privately owned residences clustered around the old Mansion House and its lawns. Today, there are thirty-seven such houses, together with a number of company-owned multiple apartments, able to house eighteen families in all. The Mansion House is still, in 1958, somewhat crowded, partly because many of the single rooms have been combined into suites, and partly because some of the present older generation, including myself, have moved back into it, turning our private houses over to descendants.

This group of buildings is known as "Kenwood," and it has proved to be the means of uniting old members of the organization and what I have called joiners. Today at least two thirds of us are joiners.

All this, of course, was far in the future at the time of which I am writing. A little incident of the early building is full of the friendliness and simplicity of those early days. Stephen, having built his house in "The Vineyard" (so-called because in Community days the area was largely occupied by Mr. Henry Thacker's grapevines), learned later that George was building in that new site on the other side of "The Orchard." He was very fond of George. In the end he paid to have his own house moved cross lots, and over the highway, three hundred yards to a site near his friend. The feeling of comradeship in a joint enterprise, which is so marked a feature of our organization today, was born during those early years.

Better schools became a prime interest with all of us. When we found our plans blocked by the fact that we shared a school district with two other localities, we put up a fight for separation. In 1901 the vote went against us. Our little red schoolhouse (it was not red, but otherwise belonged to that genus) was all that trustees of those other school districts thought necessary for their children or ours, and they had no wish to lose our taxes.

We gritted our teeth and decided on a real campaign, for we took the matter very seriously. Before the opportunity for another vote came around in the fall of 1906, we had personally canvassed every taxpayer in the three districts, and we brought to the meeting at Oneida Castle what we hoped was a winning majority.

How well I remember that meeting held in the old Oneida Castle Congregational Church! Feeling ran high on both sides. Aggressive leaders of the opposition were a retired farmer and an Oneida Castle lawyer. As the church filled with voters, a feeling assailed me which has often occurred to me when victory has been in sight. I pitied the losers. Perhaps a less creditable emotion was mixed with this pity, namely a fear that we ourselves might lose. Memory does not include this, but the frailty of human nature suggests it. In any case, I decided to try for a compromise.

The suggestion of compromise appealed to the opposition. Three men from each side adjourned to the lower regions of the church and I made them this offer: the Company would buy the little schoolhouse, paying the other districts fifteen hundred dollars for it. In addition, the Oneida

Community, Ltd. would give the other districts one thousand dollars in cash, if they would agree to separation. When the compromise was announced to the assembled voters, it was greeted with cheers, and the vote to separate the districts was unanimous.

It was my cousin George who, at that time, took an effective part in the development of new schools, and he acted as Chairman of the School Board for many years. A modern building was built for the grade school and, later, in combination with the Sherrill School District, we erected a fine high school and another grade-school building. The cost of these new schoolhouses and the teachers' salaries were at that time shared half-and-half between the taxpayers and the Company. Thus, early in the twentieth century all our Kenwood and Sherrill children enjoyed school opportunities as good as any city afforded.

Grosvenor Allen suceeded George as Chairman of the local School Board, and for the many years of his incumbency the schools continued to flourish.

The year 1900 opened hopefully. Business had been increasingly good since 1896, and the spirit of enterprise, stimulated by the merging of rival American companies into huge units of production, gave a fillip to the ambitions and expectations of most businessmen. The era of mass production had begun.

Oneida Community, Ltd. stockholders were happy. Our own Company's net profit for 1899 was very satisfactory, and prospects for the new year also seemed favorable. Yet I found myself dissatisfied. As a matter of fact, faint twinges of anxiety had, even in our years of triumphant progress, intruded upon my self-satisfaction. If, at times, when there was a temporary slackening in business, doubts had assailed me, the gap had been filled by my temperamental optimism— or nearly filled. But occasionally, from somewhere down in my consciousness, suppressed questionings would force themselves to the surface.

I confided my worries to George and Stephen and found that the same questions were disturbing their minds. I remember that Stephen emphasized the many young men who had confidently entered our Company full of expectation for the future; and George reminded me that, at the time of the strike, I had told our employees that I had a plan for the future which would bring them something better than any union could offer.

As for myself, before the end of that January, in 1900, I had become fully awake to the fact that I was staking the future, not alone my own future but the future of all these young men and our employees in general, on the returns from dexterous salesmanship, and I saw, with disturbing clarity, the fragile nature of the foundation on which we were building a new and much larger Oneida Community, Ltd. On the threshold of the new century, my satisfaction over previous successes was dissolving in doubt.

I called together my little management committee, which now included Grosvenor Allen. All agreed that we were faced with a major problem. I summed it up. "We are building a house on the sands."

Stephen made a suggestion right to the point, but at the time we all missed it. He said, "We ought to make something else as popular as our traps."

George shook his head, "The old Community was happiest in hard times."

Grosvenor had just come with us and modestly declined

to comment except to remind me of a statement he had heard me make at one of our Oneida get-togethers when he happened to be at home on one of his periodical visits from Hartford. "You told the home folks that saving the institution with whatever was left of the old Community's friendly family spirit for our own and future generations had no small part in your determination in 1895 to return to the old Company."

I thanked Grosvenor for reminding me of that statement. It was true that in 1895 my idea of the future Oneida Community, Ltd. anticipated no growth beyond that which the successful development of our old business would support—having especially in mind the trap business.

George was greatly stirred. "If we made an integral part of our ambition the preservation of the old home and the 'spirit of agreement' (to quote Mr. Miller) it will bring added strength and—for me—validity to our struggle for success."

These quotations are not word perfect, but the occasion was so dramatic that I have remembered the details of the discussion.

After that, the four of us had many sessions, some of them lasting far into the night. Then one day I called them together and announced, "I have a solution—advertising! We need, we must have, a line with large sales so well liked by the public that we can count on a certain modicum of sales in bad times as well as good. Only advertising will accomplish this."

My three associates agreed with this solution, but differed as to which of our lines of manufacture should be selected for the experiment. Our oldest, canned fruits and vegetables, was rapidly running into destructive competition with the huge new corporations whose mass-production methods allowed them to sell at much lower prices than we could afford. Forgetting the veal in their canned chicken and the pumpkin in their strawberry jam, our survey told us that to compete with these leviathans we must have plants in many widely separated localities; in Maine for corn, in Wisconsin for peas, in Maryland for tomatoes, in Western New York and California for many kinds of fruit. This meant diffusion, and our ambitions called for concentration at Oneida.

The manufacture of silk thread was still, in 1900, our largest business, although the least profitable. Studying the possibility of establishing with the consumer a demand for "Community Silk," we arrived at a negative answer. The cost of raw silk was nearly half the price obtained for the finished product, which promised little margin for advertising and merchandising.

The manufacture of steel traps and chains was our most profitable business. At the time, we were rapidly increasing our sales of both these lines, but felt bound to recognize that their possible volume was limited, while our ambitions were unlimited.

The net result of this survey was a conclusion that silverware offered the most promising field for the growth and security we needed. We knew very well that in the silverware market there were old trade-marked brands, firmly established with the consuming public; so firmly established that when, in 1902, we brought out advertisements of the new "Community" line of silverware, neutral and even friendly observers in the trade referred to our enterprise as brave but suicidal, and our leading competitors laughed uproariously.

It is easier to arrive at a conclusion as to what needs to be done, than to devise the means for doing it. Fortunately, the four men who, in the year 1900, devoted themselves to solving this problem of "means," were in temperament so different that our little managing group had what might be called an intellectual balance.

George Noyes was chiefly interested in the human—I might almost say the spiritual—aspect of our discussions. Stephen was a doer; he believed in our aims and devoted himself to making the factories produce results absolutely necessary for success. Grosvenor Allen, our latest addition, was by nature a critic. During the ensuing years I used to say that it was more difficult to get my schemes past Grosvenor than any of the older directors.

My project had always been a double-barreled one: first the creation of a semi-socialistic manufacturing institution and, second, a business plan sufficiently profitable to keep it alive. The double quality of our managing group was fitted to handle both problems. But before beginning the story of our struggle to build a commercial bridgehead which would make more secure our growing industrial area, I am inclined to review briefly the development of our semi-socialistic ambition.

Webster calls socialism a "system which contemplates . . . more just and equitable distribution of property and labor," but adds, "the term is often employed to indicate any lawless revolutionary social scheme." We were, of course, interested only in the first half of Webster's definition. We were not revolutionists, lawless or otherwise. Memory adds, also, that we had no ambition for the role of "reformers"; that we aimed only to work out that "more equitable distribution" in our own little industrial island or, as another writer said, "to provide a new social existence for the mass of the workers."

My dream had started with that sudden antipathy for getting rich *alone* which, as noted in a previous chapter, seized upon me when, at the age of twenty-three, my own natural optimism suggested a lonely personal success. Following that, my fortuitous injection into the political struggle at Oneida in 1894 and 1895 turned into a practical channel ideals that might otherwise have evaporated, as youthful ideals are apt to do.

Our aims were still narrow in 1895. This sharing only with friends the better living to be secured by joint success, I can see now, was merely a dilution of selfishness. It was the close association with workingmen which came to me as manager that led to a radical change in my outlook and the outlook and plans of our group. This may have been a hark-back to childhood that made it easy for us to recognize that all labor was equally honorable and that all laborers have a right to share in the comfortable living provided by successful accomplishments. In the old Community days, men and women were shifted from job to job until their aptitudes were found. Early experience may have had no conscious part in shaping our plans, but it surely eliminated the intellectual negative which causes most people to regard as radical and revolutionary any approach to a fair sharing of the proceeds of success with all who work for it.

My memory refuses to bring back to me any connected series of steps leading up to the later policy of sharing profits with our employees before declaring dividends to our stockholders. I am sure, however, that we early decided to keep salaries well below the range provided for successful ex-

ecutives elsewhere, in order to make certain that there would
be something to share.

I remember many discussions with George at the Stone
Cottage in those early years. Often we presented our con-
clusions to Doctor Noyes. He warned us not to go too fast,
but he also supplied, from his own experience, encourage-
ment for the direction we were taking.

I remember his saying, "People fool themselves; they
think that sharing with others will deprive them of part of
their own means for happiness. They don't know, as we
learned in the Community, that working for something which
will benefit others as well as one's self can multiply the pleasure of work and the enjoyment of success by the number of
friends benefited." That was the burden of his comments.
"It is hard for people to believe that 'it is better to give than
to receive.'"

Then there were further talks with the ever-faithful
Fred Filby. He fully sympathized with our plans but as always was extremely practical and would simply reiterate his
old slogan, "The best kind of welfare work is good wages."

This confirmed an opinion which, all through the years,
has served me in good stead: Generous wages are the first
and most important part of sharing. In adopting other forms
of benefits, do so as a matter of fair play and because they
are deserved, not as so-called "welfare work" for which those
benefited will thank you.

I think I was wise enough to accept this principle far
beyond its immediate application, and the experience of
life has confirmed my opinion that it applies universally.
Doing for others, being unselfish in the hope that you will
be repaid in the coin of gratitude, is certain to bring disap-

pointments. Giving freely, from the heart and without thought of return, can benefit the giver, but giving with the expectation of return cannot benefit the giver and may be a personal offense to the receiver. It was not long, however, before we dropped all talk of "giving." We quickly became convinced that all we were "giving" was really deferred wages due our people as their share of any surplus profit from our joint efforts.

From all these experiences and discussions there emerged a principle which has been basic in the industrial philosophy of this Company's management for more than fifty years. It can be stated: "Strive not to buy gratitude; strive for confidence. When your employees really believe that you take a true interest in their welfare and that you *mean what you say,* you will have acquired an asset of price-less value." There is a corollary to this principle which has also been fundamental with us: "Act always and only because you believe that Company success should add to the comfort and happiness of every member of the working group."

This brings me back to the year 1900. The attainment of security and the ability to pay good wages was now con-fronting us as the most necessary accomplishment. We were on the brink of a plunge into the uncharted waters of national advertising, in order to create an Oneida Community, Ltd. that would promise permanence.

CHAPTER XIII

We were now fairly committed to a campaign aimed at putting a solid foundation under our rapidly growing industrial organization. For weapons, we designed and began to manufacture a line of silver-plated ware of a quality superior to anything ever before offered the American public, and in patterns more attractive than had hitherto been thought necessary for plated ware. The weapon on which we counted most, however, was advertising.

Both theory and experience had told us that our sales of "Community Silver" would be, for several years (it turned out to be eight years), too small to pay for the amount of advertising absolutely necessary to establish acceptance by the consuming public. Our steel trap and chain departments were counted on to carry this financial load. Hence, the reader will recognize that any considerable shrinkage in hardware profits would have put an end to our advertising, and will understand, if not altogether excuse, the seeming ruthlessness with which, during this period, we attacked would-be invaders of our trap or chain field.

The first threat to our trap sales seemed to some of our people not too serious, but I could take no chances. A man named Harding, in Gallipolis, Ohio, had built up a following among trappers in the United States and Canada for his monthly magazine *Hunter, Trader, Trapper*. Hundreds of readers wrote him letters about their "catches," with pictures of skins nailed to barn doors. These pictures were published in the magazine, and what attracted my attention was the frequent reference to the brands of traps these writers preferred.

One might suppose that we would welcome a magazine which was evidently increasing the interest in trapping. We did, but there was in the offing an able and very aggressive Illinois manufacturer of mousetraps, named Schultz, whose ambition to get into the game-trap field worried me. If he were to form an alliance with the magazine owner, such a combination could be dangerous.

I first tried to buy a half-interest in the magazine, but Mr. Harding would not even discuss a sale. So I started another magazine, the *North American Trapper*. From a literary standpoint, our magazine was a much better product than the *Hunter, Trader, Trapper*, but the ungrateful trappers preferred the Ohio sheet, which printed their pictures and letters and talked their language—never literary and often not grammatical.

It was fear of the *North American Trapper*, however, that presently persuaded Harding to sell us a half-interest in the *Hunter, Trader, Trapper* or rather, a half-interest in the combined magazines. We paid him around eight thousand dollars as the difference in the value of the combination and after adding our list of subscribers (about one fifth as many as his) the *North American Trapper* was abandoned. I still get some satisfaction out of the fact that during the years that followed we had much to do with making the magazine profitable beyond Mr. Harding's wildest dreams.

This magazine consolidation came none too soon. Within a few months we heard that our Illinois friend, Schultz, having merged three mousetrap companies into one, which he controlled, had hired an ex-machinist of ours to make the dies necessary for the manufacture of game traps. Aside from Mr. Schultz, the stockholders in his new concern were largely Dunkards and Mennonites, whose mousetrap enterprise in Lititz, Pennsylvania, had been merged with his. A large amount of new stock had been issued, and, with the proceeds, a fine new factory was in process of building. We also discovered that Schultz had already offered the leading hardware jobbers of the country a price on game traps 10 per cent under our prices. It was time we struck.

On a certain wintry morning Stephen Leonard, Bob Kinsley and I landed in Lititz. We engaged the services of a Mennonite real-estate firm and, in snow nearly a foot deep, walked down the railway to Schultz's half-finished factory. For his use, the railroad had extended a siding. Also abutting on the siding, beyond and behind his property, was a large vacant area. This was ideal for our purpose. By noon we held an option on this land adjoining his factory.

It was in the dining room of the Lititz Springs Hotel that casually, to all appearances, we met our would-be competitor, whose acquaintance I had made a year or so before. Naturally he appeared both surprised and suspicious to find me in Lititz. He demanded, and his tone was almost menacing, "What are you doing here?"

I told him that we had always planned to make mousetraps, and had now decided to build a plant where the technique of mousetrap making was so well known. I added, as though it were an afterthought, "We've already bought a site for the new factory down beyond your plant."

Schultz sputtered for a moment but presently pulled himself together and asked, "Could we have a talk?"

"Certainly," I replied. "We'll be at the Stevens House in Lancaster this evening. Come and see us."

He came. When he arrived at the hotel, he seemed much perturbed, and I added to his perturbation by telling him that during the afternoon we had made a contract with a Lancaster builder for the speedy erection of our new factory. He urged a "friendly" discussion. I told him that we would discuss but could not negotiate except at home, where our directors would be available. I invited him to visit Oneida for the discussion.

Mr. Schultz was a Missourian, able, tough and hard. He had the extensive "burnsides" of a camp-meeting preacher, but between those luxuriant whiskers was a poker face with steely blue eyes which looked you through and through. On this occasion they registered suspicion. He brushed aside my invitation, fearing, I decided, that this was an attempt to get him away from his trap campaign while I stole a march on him. However, in the end he agreed, with evident misgivings, to visit Oneida.

Mr. Schultz and his wife were our guests in the Mansion House at Oneida for a week. He had the bargaining technique of a Missouri horse-trader and the negotiations were long drawn out. I had to satisfy a tough negotiator on the one hand and a somewhat timid Board of Directors on the other. I vibrated between the two, with modifying or compromise proposals. In the end, agreement was reached.

After taking care of Schultz's investment, we agreed to give the Lititz stockholders a premium of 2½ per cent on their stock, which, since they had paid only an installment of 10 per cent of the share price, gave them a profit of 25 per cent on their investment.

Together, Albert Kinsley and I, with Mr. Schultz, journeyed to Lititz. While on the train, Schultz asked, "If they will not accept the 2½ per cent, what are you going to do?" I assured him that 2½ per cent was our limit. Then he surprised us. "We have gone so far," he said, "I should like to see the deal go through. If it's not too much, I'd be willing to pay any additional percentage they insist upon."

Our negotiation next day with the directors of the Lititz Trap Company was the oddest one in which I have ever been engaged. The Lititz directors were also directors of a Lititz Chocolate Company, and our meeting with them was held in an office of the chocolate factory. Albert and I were repeatedly called into the directors' room, where Mr. Schultz edified his associates by arguing emphatically for more money. Following each appearance before the directors, Albert and I would retire to the chocolate-factory workroom to discuss their offer. After a reasonable interval, we would return and listen to another argument by Mr. Schultz. Again we assured him that 2½ per cent was all our directors would pay.

This negotiation went on from about four o'clock in the afternoon until eight o'clock that evening. Always, I watched Mr. Schultz for a signal. In the end, he called us in and said, "We still don't think 2½ per cent is enough. Now, Noyes, you want to get this settled, don't you? If your directors positively refuse to go beyond 2½ per cent, you boys can afford to pass the hat around among yourselves and pay the additional 1½ per cent, which is all we ask."

When I looked Schultz in the eye, I saw the signal. He was willing to pay 1½ per cent himself.

Albert and I, with due solemnity and shakings of the head, retired again to the factory. For at least twenty minutes we occupied ourselves by eating chocolates. Then we went back to the meeting and announced that we had decided to accept the offer. I said, "If our directors will not agree, we will find some way to raise the money without them." I remember that Albert and I got back to Lancaster around ten o'clock that night and celebrated by ordering the largest sirloin steaks the hotel could afford.

As I noted before Mr. Schultz had very impressive, what I would call ministerial, sideburns. After he had become manager, a very competent manager of our Lititz business, he frequently visited Kenwood to consult with us. We came to value him and his services very highly and we aimed to make him feel an important member of the management of the Company. One incident will illustrate this new friendship. After nearly fifty years, reference to it among the older men still brings laughter to them.

It was Ab Kinsley's idea. Mr. Schultz would visit Kenwood about two months later for Directors' Meeting, and Ab suggested that for a joke, all our men should raise sideburns like his. When Schultz landed at the front porch of the Mansion House, the first person he met was Bill Earl. Bill's luxuriant sideburns astonished him. Then came Ab from the house with equally remarkable ones. Presently one after another of his Kenwood friends appeared with the same elegant adornment. We had all done our best. When the joke dawned on Schultz, it brought loud and long laughter. He once said to me, "You know, P.B., that was my ticket to a seat in the inner courts of the Oneida Community, Ltd."

I cannot leave this rather curious chapter in our history without saying that our Missouri friend, with all his toughness, turned out to be a very honorable man, a good friend and an able manager. He was superintendent of our Lititz factory for the next three years, and did a wonderful job. Furthermore, he showed his character when fire consumed the old Mast mousetrap factory, then in use as a workmen's dormitory.

As our Lititz business grew, we had been obliged to go outside Lititz for workmen. A Greek padre in Brooklyn sent us men as we needed them, and these were housed in the old Mast mousetrap factory. Mr. Schultz had received verbal permission from all the insurance agents for this use of the building, and all but one had given him written permission to house the Greeks in the factory. After the fire, the company that had given only verbal permission refused to pay. Three times Schultz sent me his personal check for something over three thousand dollars to reimburse us for the loss, saying, "It was my fault." I sent the checks back. His failure to get written permission had been due to overwork.

I was always touched by Mr. Schultz's description of the character and habits of those ninety or one hundred Greeks who had undoubtedly been out of work when gathered in by the Brooklyn padre. They were as clean as workers in a factory could be. They were industrious and orderly and what impressed me was the fact, as Schultz told us, that every evening before retiring they had a season of prayer.

Our chain business had, in the meantime, grown until its profits were very substantial additions to the trap profits. I had several clashes with dangerous chain competitors, and these I handled as I did threatened invasions of our steel-trap market. The continued success of our hardware departments was absolutely vital to our other, larger plans for the future, and only the protection of our trap and chain sales could allow us to persist in advertising, from 1903 to 1910, on a scale sufficient to establish our silverware as a nationally known product. This was our single-minded ambition, the goal we were bound to reach, toward which we fought our way doggedly for eight years.

We were satisfied; we had made a good beginning. "Next year," I told the directors, "with the addition of Grosvenor's new floral design, our gains will surely be large."

The years 1900 and 1901 were, for our youthful junta, years of suppressed enthusiasm. We were planning a coup. The shadow of our coming adventure excited not alone the four of us most responsible for the Company's operations, but thrilled a younger generation, then just starting their business careers.

Perhaps "suppressed" is not exactly the right word. Enthusiasm really waxed, but we restrained our natural impatience while we made a careful study of ways and means. Those of us who traveled brought home information regarding trade conditions, which we mulled over in endless discussions. We added quantities of advice from our advertising friends, also pinches of our own earlier observations, and we hoped that the mixture would finally jell into a successful plan for gate-crashing silverware's exclusive aristocracy. We even explored negatives. Why were our forebears' earlier attempts to sell high-grade silverware with a Community trade-mark unsuccessful?

Looking back, I am surprised that we did not adopt one or another of the ingenious selling campaigns that emerged from those studies and discussions, and I am just a little proud of the skepticism that told us our plans were *too* ingenious.

At times we were baffled by the magnitude of our problem. And then, near the end of the year, there came to us what my father would have called an "inspiration." Someone —I have forgotten who—suggested that we could not beat powerful competitors who were selling trade-marks long established with the buying public merely by employing some variation of their game, however ingenious that variation might be; that we must play a game all our own and hope to make our competitors play it, too. Thereupon, we threw the bulk of our "surveys" out the window. We asked ourselves, what is "our own game"?

The business fathers of the old Oneida Community, Perfectionists as they were, had successfully developed four industries by refusing to make any but the *best* of each article produced. Only their youngest enterprise, begun in those later days when worldly encroachments were shaking the foundations of the Community, was the exception. They made cheap silverware. What more logical, now, than for us to go back to the earlier traditions of our ancestors and make our competitors play the game of better quality silverware? That, we decided, would be our new game. From then on, our discussions were confined to discovering ways of making better silver-plated ware than had ever been made before.

Oddly enough, however, the first forward-looking detail that caught our imagination had nothing to do with the wearing qualities of the product. Somone—it might have been the wife of one of us—suggested that once the interest of women, with their natural love of the beautiful, was directed toward their dining tables, they would value silverware more for its beauty than for its wearing qualities. Certainly, no other accessory—linen, glassware, china—would lend so much richness to a dining table as really artistic silverware.

It was generally agreed that American plated-ware manufacturers had, in the matter of design, failed to move with the new age. Old, time-tested patterns were still thought good enough for plated spoons and forks, with the result that, whenever something new was called for by their sales departments, diesinkers simply altered the details of ornament or outline of some design which had already proved popular and, presto! a new pattern.

I am not sure but that the absence of beauty and especially of interest in the plated-ware patterns of the nineteenth century could be laid to the same human frailty that dictates "keeping up with the Joneses." Plated-ware esteemed itself a sort of Cinder Wench, but unlike Cinderella, it had tried to imitate its more fortunate elder sister, Sterling. American Sterling, in its turn, had imitated the products of English conservatism, which today still finds century-old spoon designs popular.

Whatever the cause, in the year 1900, manufacturers were offering housewives in this country plated-ware designs hopelessly outmoded if compared with American women's taste in other lines. These designs belonged with hoop skirts and poke bonnets. It was as though an architect today insisted on presenting plans based on the florid motifs of the capitol at Albany or the old post office in City Hall Park, New York. Here, surely, was our opportunity. Late in 1900 we started work on a design which now seems crude but was then artistically in advance of the times.

For more than forty years it has been a standing joke at Oneida that I designed this first "Community" pattern, the Avalon. I must own up that I did not design it—I constructed it. We then had no designers; only diesinkers. I showed Mr. Bruns or Mr. Schultz a spoon whose top I liked, another whose side ornaments seemed to fit with that top, and still another whose contour might lend itself artistically to a combination of the first two. I asked him to work out a spoon pattern along those lines. The result was our Avalon pattern.

Our new *quality* we built around a theory our very own. Again, it seems odd that it was left to us, comparative newcomers, to discover the reason why so little "triple plate" was sold. The wise men of Connecticut knew the answer. They said, "People able to pay the price of 'triple plate' silverware will buy Sterling."

But a girl, a clerk in a jewelry store, knew better. Her simple statement to one of our men suggested something that became the keystone of our plan and, later, the most effective argument for our salesmen and copywriters. She said, "The trouble is that the other manufacturers make the *same* patterns in single plate that they do in triple plate. Ladies would not pay a big price for patterns their hired girls might buy at a fraction of the price."

"Splendid!" Our group became enthusiastic. "We'll make Oneida Community patterns in one quality only, and that quality even *better* than triple." This added the finishing touch to our blueprint of Community silverware. We settled on a plating of silver heavier than the six-ounce plate called "triple."

I remember the reaction of some of our older directors when I told them of this better-than-triple plate. Mr. Allen or Mr. Hinds asked rather dubiously, "Can you sell any quantity of this new line at the high prices necessary for a profit?"

We were prepared for this. I told them that the price need not be high, and, to clinch the argument, I produced Amos Reeve, our head plater, who explained to the Board of Directors that by far the largest part of the spoon's cost had been expended when it had been shaped, polished and made ready for plating: that, once in the plating bath, the cost of keeping it there until seven ounces had been deposited would be little more than the bare cost of four or five additional ounces of silver. He assured them that our new Community "Triple-Plus" plating of silver (as we called it then) would not add a proportionate amount to the cost of the ordinary "extra plate" of commerce.

"Why," asked Mr. Allen, "do all the silverware catalogues list 'triple plate' at a price more than double the 'extra plate'?"

I told him that, in my opinion, the Connecticut manufacturers, who had monopolized the silver-plate market for years, were not interested in "triple," and their Yankee instincts suggested getting "all the traffic would bear" for the small quantity of "triple" sold. They traded on the certainty that Mrs. Consumer would believe that triple plate cost three times as much to manufacture as single plate. Beyond that, the price had become a tradition, and the six or seven fiercely competing companies in those days saw no gain in starting a new competition they might not be able to finish profitably.

But that was not all. Searching for our competitors' weak points, we found one that led us to forge a weapon which, during the first three or four years, helped us with dealers more than either beauty of design or quality of product. For several years I had noted a growing rebellion on the part of merchants against the callous disregard for their profit—or for their lack of profit—shown by the owners of established silverware trade-marks. These manufacturers traded on the fact that every first-class jeweler must, of necessity, sell their silverware because consumers called for it.

I had not only noted, but I had already profited by this

point. The larger retail firms who, as they told me, were obliged by competition to sell a $3.50 set of Rogers knives and forks for only 25 cents more than they paid for it, had listened eagerly to the idea of buying from us a pattern with their own firm name on the back. In 1900, these "special brand" lines represented a very profitable part of our business.

So, we adopted "resale prices" to protect the dealers' profit. This was not original with us. Manufacturers in certain other lines were insisting that both jobber and retailer maintain fixed "resale prices" which gave them a reasonable profit. We simply were the first to add resale prices as a dealer attraction to a line of silverware.

One memory still makes me smile. In 1902, the president of the largest silver concern in Connecticut told a friend of ours that we would "get our belly full of telling customers what to charge for their goods." I smile because, four years later, both this firm and others adopted "resale prices."

If 1900 was the year in which Community Plate was born, 1901 and 1902 were devoted to providing facilities for the manufacturing and selling of it. The first step was accomplished in January. Our directors voted an appropriation of thirty thousand dollars to build a new silk mill at Oneida, thus enabling us to move our chain business from Niagara to space in our Sherrill plant vacated by the Silk Department, and releasing the entire chain building at Niagara for additional silverware equipment. The move seemed logical to everyone. Our steel-chain business had become very profitable in proportion to investment, and could be combined advantageously with steel-trap making. Silk sales also had grown to a point where the need for more room was apparent to all.

In spite of the logic of this extensive move, I can only

account for the thirty-thousand-dollar appropriation by assuming that the older directors failed to anticipate the expense involved in our proposed assault on Connecticut's monopoly of the silver-plated ware business. I may have employed a little—what shall I call it?—diplomacy. Certainly I tried.

As a last stroke of preparation, we revised and enlarged our sales organization. Grosvenor was sent to Chicago as manager of that office and was given an assistant, Leon Mac-Kown. Bob Kinsley was added to the New York City staff. Clifton Inslee had a roving commission between New York and Chicago. "Pop" Beers covered the South, and the Morgan, Allen Company, the Pacific Coast.

Grosvenor's transfer to Chicago not only revealed a salesman with something new in the way of sales technique, but it prepared the way for his future career as our designing genius. When he talked with a customer or anyone else on serious business, he impressed his listener with the conviction that he had a well-thought-out idea or plan. The result was that customers listened to him, even though they had intended to say "no" in the end.

In 1901, Grosvenor convinced Mr. Brampton, Advertising Manager of the American Cereal Company, and Mr. Crowell, its President, that they could afford to forget their policy of "no premiums on Quaker Oats" and at least consider his proposition. Then he interested them in our new Community quality silverware. They asked him to show them a special piece in this special plate.

Grosvenor was at his wits' end. He had sold the Quaker Oats people the idea of *real* art. He studied, as he always did, and in the end, sought out an artist, Miss Julia Bracken, who afterwards became famous. Together they developed the "Cereta" design and a cereal spoon, which resulted in eighty thousand dollars' worth of sales to the American Cereal Company.

But that was not all. Grosvenor's artistic enterprise led him to an intensive study of general designing, as well as the specific designing of silverware, a study which, in the ensuing years, brought to our Company benefits incalculably greater than that original eighty-thousand-dollar sale. Incidentally he—still with the aid of Miss Bracken—designed the first big pattern-success for our new Community line. But that is a later story.

During the fall of 1901, we exhibited fourteen pieces of the Avalon pattern at the Buffalo Exposition, and early the following spring were prepared to experiment with the market. The directors gave us an appropriation of five thousand dollars to advertise the new line.

To be sure, we could buy very little advertising space with five thousand dollars, and we spent our money largely on pages in dignified monthlies of small circulation and correspondingly low rates, *The Century*, *Harper's* and such. These pages served largely as textbooks for our agents. They were filled with reading matter telling of the quality merits and value for the money to be found in Community silverware and, whenever a prospective customer permitted, the salesman read it all impressively to him.

We made progress slowly in 1902; very slowly. In fact, most of our first jobbing customers were hardware firms, to whom "Pop" Clark had sold traps and chains for years. Grosvenor and Clifton were the only two salesmen besides myself who sold any appreciable amount of Community silverware during 1902.

It was during those early days that our competitors spoke slightingly of us as "good blacksmiths—iron trap makers." However, we were not at all discouraged. We did not expect large sales. We were feeling our way and knew perfectly well that until we showed signs of extensive advertising to the consumer, few jewelers would take the chance of stocking goods they might not be able to sell. Our efforts were aimed, much as reconnaissance expeditions in war are aimed, at getting profitable information leading to additions to, or revisions of, their plans.

The first thing this reconnaissance told us was that we needed more than one pattern. We found that our competitors had brought out, or were about to bring out, "floral" designs. We decided that we must have a floral pattern. That was where Grosvenor's experience with the Cereta Cereal Spoon saved us. With the aid of Miss Bracken, the Flower de Luce pattern was conceived and designed and, thanks to a factory group ready to turn somersaults in the interest of our project, it was ready for delivery late in 1904, when we were fairly embarked on our serious-minded campaign. But that again is ahead of my story.

One other factor seemed important for that critical moment when we intended to spring the complete plan on our Board of Directors. Company profits of 1902 must be large enough to give these directors a comfortable feeling about the future. For this purpose, trap and chain sales were our best bets. I filled all my companions with a determination to boost hardware profits.

Recalling those years I find myself a little surprised to note the patience with which we took time to look before we leaped. My own reputation is not that of a patient man. As I have confessed before, I am the victim of hunches, and, once convinced of the desirability of a move, I am impatient for action. . . . We had plodded through nearly three years of study and experiment before we took the final plunge.

CHAPTER XIV

JANUARY 18, 1903! It sounds like a diary date, but in 1903 I kept no diary. Had I kept one, however, the entry would probably have read something like this: "Today Stephen, George and I disclosed to the older directors the (to them) alarming financial dimensions of our proposed campaign to establish Community Silverware as a nationally known product."

We had kept the Board generally informed of our progress in developing the Avalon sales, and I had told them repeatedly that increased advertising would be a necessary feature of our plans; but I had soft-pedaled the *amount* of that increase. On the whole, it seemed reasonable and tactically sound that, during our long period of preparation, the interest of those elderly men, whose business training and instincts had always kept them away from anything like gambling, be centered on the prospect that this branch of the Company's business was about to be converted from production of the poorest grade of silverware to production of the very best. We agreed that nothing would be gained by a premature discussion with the Board on the cost of our proposed enterprise.

More than fifty years have passed since that memorable Directors' Meeting, but I can still re-create for myself the excited hopefulness with which we three younger men faced the six senior members of the Board on that January morning. For the record, those seniors were Dr. Theodore Noyes,

William C. Hinds, Martin Kinsley, Henry Allen, John Freeman and George Kellogg; the younger men were George W.
Noyes, Stephen Leonard and myself. My mind even pictures
the room. We were meeting in the Directors' Room, on the
southeast corner of the first floor of the Mansion House. From
the windows could be seen the great south playground of my
childhood. Eastward loomed the enormous shaggy butternut
tree of Indian tradition.

After election of the officers for the ensuing year and
the usual reports, I was given the floor. I assume that I became oratorical. I certainly bore down heavily on our current
reputation as manufacturers of the worst silverware in the
country and appealed to the feelings of ex-Perfectionists
who had always prided themselves on making "good goods."
I reminded them that our traps were so superior to any others
that trappers in the Adirondacks and the Canadian forests
would accept only Oneida traps; that with practical trappers,
price meant nothing, when compared with confidence that
their traps, after being toted on human backs many miles
through deep snow, could be counted on to do their work.
I reminded the meeting that our care in canning Community
fruits and vegetables enabled us to sell all we could put up,
at prices well above that of our competitors. And, finally, I
reminded them of the high reputation of Oneida Community
sewing silk.

Having thus established a favorable background, I enlarged upon the amount of advertising needed for the undertaking. I bore down on this point too, and gave a glowing
account of what large advertising had done for other firms.
Frankly, I admitted that there was an element of gambling
in this enterprise. Then I broke the news—thirty thousand
dollars to be spent in advertising during the year 1903!

There was silence in the board room. My statement must

have struck like a bombshell among expectations conditioned by the five-thousand-dollar advertising appropriation the previous year. To shift the metaphor, it certainly had the effect of a dash of cold water thrown upon our elders' enthusiasm for better silverware. Finally, Mr. Hinds asked, "Where will we get the thirty thousand?"

Years later, when Community Silver was established with the consuming public as, I make bold to say, the best silver-plated ware in the country, a keen-eared boy, my nephew, Howard Noyes, sitting beside me in a New England dining car, whispered, "Those men across the aisle are talking about us. I heard one of them say, 'They took it out of their traps and put it into their silverware.'" That man was a good guesser, or else he had inside information. What he said was true. Our Trap Department was the little gold mine from which we took most of the wherewithal to finance a seven-year silverware campaign. For it was seven years from that day in 1903 to the day when Community Silver emerged from the "red" and took its place as the principal earner for the Oneida Community, Ltd. and the greatly desired guarantee of security for its members.

Observation of existing conditions in 1902 had convinced me that a big expansion of trapping was just ahead, induced by the fashionable demand for furs. Sure enough, during 1902, trap sales increased 50 per cent, and profits considerably more, thanks to Stephen's management at the factory.

During the preceding six years, our trap campaigns had been tough. I had refused even to talk with our competitors. Now I took advantage of this situation to get the necessary ammunition for the silverware campaign. Drawing a paper from my inside pocket, I said to our directors, "I have the thirty thousand here. This is a signed agreement with our trap competitors. We have all raised prices 15 per cent, for the year 1903. I estimate our sales at two hundred thousand. There you have it—thirty thousand dollars." I got the appropriation, albeit only one third was to be spent during the spring and summer months.

After the meeting Mr. Hinds came to my room. He was very much my friend and through all the years of my management had backed my plans, even, I sometimes suspected, when he felt misgivings. Now he had one more question to ask regarding the silverware campaign. "How long will we have to advertise?"

I really hated to dash the hope evident behind his question, a hope that this expenditure was temporary, but I decided that extreme frankness was indicated at the moment. I remember placing a friendly hand on his shoulder as I said, "Just as long as we are in business."

He repeated my words with a rising inflection decidedly suggestive of disappointment, "As long as we are in business?"

"Yes," I said, still determined to have the bald truth out. "And more and more each year." Then, seeing his discomfiture, I added, "But presently it will be only a percentage on sales, and not a burdensome percentage."

Mr. Hinds had lived all his business life with "sales" and "percentages," and, after a moment's thought, he brightened up. "That will be all right; if it can be confined to a reasonable percentage on sales."

I might have reminded him that I had said "presently," but thought best to leave well enough alone. The other directors were usually satisfied if Mr. Hinds was satisfied.

In 1903 we were, as advertisers, "lambs to the slaughter." The small advertising appropriation of the year before had been placed by Mr. Miller with one of the country's largest agencies, and the same agency was continued through 1903.

Its head was a dignified gentleman. I remember his lecture on the theory of advertising and especially the well-worn platitudes and unconvincing paradoxes with which he tried to impress our committee.

This Agency's copywriters proceeded to fill magazine pages for us with statements and arguments certainly not sufficiently pointed to impress magazine subscribers or get themselves read beyond their banal subtitles.

As I look back on that first year of our campaign and note the real progress made in spite of totally uninspired advertising, I give much credit to our salesmen. I am reminded of reports telling how American soldiers, at times, have fought and held their own without the backing of tanks or airplanes. Good advertising might have done for us what those weapons do for fighters. But our first agency's copy created neither tanks nor airplanes.

In May, Dr. Noyes's illness resulted in the appointment of George Noyes, as President *pro tem.* One month later, the Doctor passed away. Mr. Hinds was my choice as his successor. At the time of that critical election in 1895, he had voluntarily stepped aside in favor of the Doctor, but I knew that he still cherished an ambition to become President of the Company.

On my part, I was bound to make sure that he would be the same kind of President that Dr. Noyes had been. My real acquaintance with this lovable half brother had begun, as I have said, in 1892, when Holton and I moved to New York City to seek our fortunes. During the next three years, that acquaintance ripened into deep affection, but our positions reversed themselves, so that during the last few years of his life, my role was that of elder brother, although Theodore was thirty years older than I. He was by nature a philosopher, a brilliant mind with an insatiable intellectual curiosity, but a thinker rather than a doer, and always a non-aggressive man, to whom the rough-and-tumble of the business world was uncongenial. He had accepted the presidency because I asked him to and had always made my ambitions his own and my problems, his problems, but he had never interfered in the practical management of the Company's business. I kept him informed regarding all my moves. I often went to him for advice and spent many profitable evenings in his room, where he slid easily from dull business to the metaphysical area so dear to him and Mr. Frankland, in the old New York days.

Now I had a frank talk with Mr. Hinds. I told him that he was the logical candidate for the presidency and was *my* candidate, but that, if elected, it was necessary that he recognize that the relation of our President to our business management had changed radically since the 1880's and early 1890's; that, as general manager, I could not work with a president who interfered in details, as Mr. Hamilton and Mr. Campbell did in the early days. Mr. Hinds was equally frank. He said that he did recognize the change, fully approved of my management and desired only to back me. On June twenty-third he was elected president.

At the same time, Grosvenor's election to the Board of Directors completed the junta of four young directors who, during the next ten years, were accorded the unofficial standing of an Executive Committee. Mr. Francis Wayland-Smith, who, as a departmental superintendent, had served the new Company well during its earlier years, and had left in 1893 to establish a private business in New York City, now returned to Oneida. He was appointed Secretary to the Board and, with his strong personality, he added strength to the conservative element.

During this year, Grosvenor designed the new Flower de Luce pattern and turned it over to the factory, where work was begun for its issue in 1904. That ended Grosvenor's career as a salesman; he was too valuable elsewhere. My superintendency of the Niagara Silverware factory, while living at Oneida and traveling a great deal, had persisted up to this time. Now it became evident that, although I still must travel from my central headquarters at Oneida, my duties as General Manager would absorb all the rest of my time and energy. Grosvenor was recalled from Chicago and sent to Niagara as superintendent.

I traveled a great deal in those days, and many details of my travels come back to me; uncomfortable sleepers alternating with dirty day cars and cheap hotel bedrooms. By actual count, kept during two years, I spent over eighty nights each year on sleepers. However, I was at the age when touching elbows with every kind of traveling man, even in the foul smoking compartments, attracted me. There I listened to, and sometimes took part in heated arguments, and these contributed to my education, general and business-wise. I enjoyed arguments.

Some of those hot smoking-car sessions I remember in detail. One night a fiery Protestant partisan harangued us, insisting that the Catholics were getting into all prominent positions and would soon run our government. The very next evening I struck an equally fiery and alarmed anti-Semitic, who assured us that the Jews were about to take over the United States. In the end I pleased the audience, if not the Jew-baiter, by telling about my experience the night before. "It couldn't be both ways. The other fellow," I said, "was just as sure he was right as you are."

On another occasion I found myself in a smoking compartment filled with eminent Southern educators, returning from a convention in Atlanta. They told such interesting stories that I longed to make notes, but I was wedged in tight and did not dare. In spite of a deliberate attempt to fix these stories in my mind only one of them stuck.

A man named Sawney told the tale, and it ran something like this. It seems that there was a college trustee's meeting in his town at which a typical, hardheaded farmer delivered a tirade against what he called "fanciful education." The old fellow wound up his speech, as Sawney said such men always do, with, "When my boy gets through college, I want him to be able to milk a cow." Before he was fairly seated, Sawney was on his feet. "When *my* boy gets through college, I want him to be able to do something that a calf can't beat him at!"

My recollection of drummers' confabulations in stores, and of my own sessions in the offices of wholesale customers, is one of endless and repetitive arguments. I believe, however, that I did learn something from them—if only the force of suggestion. For example, in order to re-enforce my statement that other silverware manufacturers had neglected the artistic in their productions, I would hold a competitor's spoon in one hand, our Avalon in the other. "Look at this," I would say dramatically, waving my rival's spoon before the customer's eyes. "You can see for yourself—just a lot of lumps and sausages thrown together by a diemaker! Now— look at *this!* The work of an artist!" I was careful not to reveal the name of this artist—myself—and, as I think of the dear old Avalon pattern today, I am bound to admit that it was a real tribute to the power of suggestion when cold-hearted buyers often agreed they saw the difference I claimed.

Clifton Inslee's persistence often resulted in a reluctant

dealer's listening to the page of really excellent arguments for Community Silver buried in the *Atlantic* or the *North American Review*. I say buried, because the readers of those serious-minded magazines were few. As late as 1917, Dr. Harry Garfield told me he regretted that such publications accepted *any* advertising. There were a few jobbers, as well as retailers, among Clifton's successes.

Grosvenor succeeded in getting more sympathetic hearings by a totally different route. I have listened interestedly, not to say doubtfully, while he agreed with at least 50 per cent of the objections advanced by a dealer and then deftly extracted from the remaining 50 per cent enough favorable arguments to sell our silverware. It was all done quietly and with courteous appreciation for the other man's wisdom. Often, in the end, the merchant found himself asking for information from a man whose knowledge he had come to respect. Grosvenor sold his full share during those lean years.

With apologies, I must include myself in the "successful three." My methods differed from either of the other two but were aimed at the same result; namely an *interview prolonged* until hope was gone or success attained. Sometimes I got my second wind and outstayed even reasonable hope. My technique involved selling our institution and myself to the man across the desk, before bringing the silverware attack to its climax.

Our actual sales of Community silverware during 1903—34,589 dozen—will seem small today, but, in spite of the fact that this did not begin to pay the expense of the advertising and sales campaign, it encouraged us.

CHAPTER XV

I REMEMBER 1904 as the year when our hopeful voyage in search of a safe harbor for our rejuvenated successor to the Oneida Community, became very definitely a struggle with the winds and waves of fierce opposition and discouragement. Our competitors were jocose rather than alarmed by our enterprise. They wept crocodile tears of sympathy for our rashness, and, at the same time, launched stinging attacks upon our product. They still told the trade we were blacksmiths; that we could make good traps, but good silverware —no. Even our trade friends fed us discouraging advice. They said, "We admire your courage, but we fear you cannot sell high-grade silverware without the name Rogers on it."

We, ourselves, were not discouraged. Our only answer to discouragers was, "We're going to, though!" and we worked harder than ever. I think that we were never filled with more determination and hopefulness than in 1904.

We were learning rapidly. We continually revised our plans in the light of experience. We traveled the country tirelessly and, when necessary, even spent more money than was actually voted us by the directors. We boldly exchanged the huge advertising agency, employed by Mr. Miller, for a small organization run by one man who interested himself in our real problem. Paul E. Derrick, our new advertising agent, spent much time with us at Oneida. He had been employed by the Quaker Oats Company and there had learned that a company's advertising plans must be dovetailed with its sales plans. In that period, this was a youthful idea not taken seriously by the tradition-infested larger agencies, but now a fundamental principle with all advertisers.

Incidentally, it was Derrick who suggested our trade name, "Community Silver." We were then stamping our ware, "Oneida Community Triple Plus Plate," which was not only too long for convenient stamping on the back of a spoon, but, as a trade-mark, lacked "punch." We had spent a long evening, Grosvenor, Derrick and I, searching for a short, dynamic trade name, when Derrick suggested tentatively, "Why not simply 'Community Silver'?" We grabbed it. Within two weeks Community Silver was registered in Washington as our trade-mark, and those two became the magic words which, for ten hectic years, inspired hard work and labeled our adventure.

Some of our younger salesmen will ask why we later changed to "Community Plate." Perhaps it was unnecessary. We were influenced at the time by the Canadian law which obliged us to omit the word silver on blanks sent to our factory in that country, and which suggested the probability that the same law might be passed in the United States. Of course, no such law has ever been passed.

I find my sense of humor slightly tickled by the strokes and counterstrokes of the struggle in those early years. We advertised a silver plating heavier than the old-fashioned triple plate and heavier than any plate our competition offered. Some bright sales executive of the enemy's produced a word intended to neutralize this argument of heavier plate. Their salesmen said, "Yes, a little more silver, but it is what we, in Connecticut, call a 'mush plate.'" That was a stroke of genius. Consumers could logically assume that there was little wear in a "mush plate."

Our answer was a "wear-test" machine. This consisted of a large wheel, perhaps six feet in diameter, which whirled horizontally above a platform covered with many substances, wood, iron, cloth, etc. From the eight arms of the wheel depended strings to which spoons were attached. With each turn of the wheel, the spoons were loosely dragged over these abrasive surfaces, to duplicate the wear they would receive when sliding over tableclothes, drainboards and sinks, and a recording instrument showed how long they had been dragged before a spot was worn through the silverplate on the back of the bowl. We published the result in miles. Community Silver spoons ran so many miles—I forget the exact figure—before the silver coating was worn through. Our competitor's spoon ran much fewer miles, and we introduced impartial testimony to prove this.

Noting that a successful sterling pattern had popularized floral design, as I have said, Grosvenor, with the aid of Miss Bracken, created the Flower de Luce pattern. We brought this out during the fall of 1904, and it proved an instantaneous success. The Flower de Luce gave Derrick something really artistic to work with in his advertising. During the year we rapidly enlarged our sales force. We also enlarged our factory, and with Grosvenor there as superintendent, it was, year by year, adapted to our ambitions for the future.

It was during 1904 that Berton Dunn, the Children's house companion of my boyhood, gave up his practice as an eye, ear and nose specialist in Syracuse and joined us. At first, he was employed in a minor capacity, but suddenly and unexpectedly he emerged as an advertising genius. Nowadays, when every agency in the country claims its staff of geniuses, this epithet may sound commonplace, but Doc was the father of them all. During the ensuing fifteen years his unique imagination took him far from the "canned" advertising of that period into new fields of original creation.

Doc's first outstanding success was his series of "lace-background" ads. He nosed around museums, art galleries and stores where artistic merchandise was sold, and his faculty for making acquaintances served him in good stead. He was able to borrow from the curator of the Metropolitan Museum priceless laces and, using full pages in the magazines, exhibited our latest designs with these museum pieces as background.

Incidentally, he is credited by the advertising profession with being the first advertiser to use full magazine pages regularly. Later, in 1911 or '12, his Coles Phillips pictures made history as the first pin-up girls. This series was so popular that it gave him a number-one standing among advertising men, and, later still, his sponsored dining-table ads intrigued those same men. They asked, "How did he get such society leaders as Mrs. Vanderbilt and Mrs. Belmont to permit the showing of their dining rooms and their names in his advertisements?" At that time it seemed miraculous, but the secret—photographer Baron de Meyer's ingenious handling of contacts with his friends in international society— must have leaked out. I suppose that the modern rash of Junior Leaguers sponsoring cold cream and "men of distinction" commending whiskey must be laid at Doc's door.

Doc originated the theory that the only audience we could afford to spend money on was youth, especially girls in their teens, who were the brides of the future and hence prospective customers. This theory was made the basis of his

copy and was given effective substance by Coles Phillips'
attractive pictures of young people enjoying themselves and
each other. Old-line advertising men, brought up on the
rule that every inch of a page must be crammed full, criticized his waste of space, but Doc was sure of his thesis. It
was the lace background and the full pages that first brought
our heads above water, so to speak. In 1910, Community
Silver, which had been in the red for eight years, emerged
as a profit line.

Recalling memories of those six years, 1903 to 1909, I am
bound to give a large amount of credit to our salespeople and
to Gerard Wayland-Smith, who early became our dynamic
Sales Manager. Gerard was a huge man, six feet four inches
tall, two hundred thirty pounds weight, with an unquench-
able enthusiasm and a physical drive that spread to all his
sales force of young men. More than all, he had a personality
that no one could resist. Customers became his ardent friends,
and his fellow salesmen set no limit to the hard work they
would do for him.

In those days we were all spartans. In our Agents' Meetings, I told young men—and they took it seriously—"Don't
tell me why you didn't get the order. I'm not interested." I
added, "If you came to a ten-foot ditch which must be leaped,
and jumped nine feet, you would be no better off than another
man who jumped six feet. You would be at the bottom of
the ditch with him. Only the man who jumps ten feet and gets
across is a valuable member of this gang."

I shall not go into detail about those six years of climb-
ing. One theory that I insisted upon will interest advertisers.
I told our directors, "Once we start advertising, it must be
continuous." A large manufacturer of unadvertised silver-
plated ware started advertising in 1902 and advertised page

for page with us until 1907. Then that year's financial panic alarmed his directors, and they decreed no advertising. In 1910 this firm tried to pick up where they had left off, but they had lost so much ground that they found it difficult to resume. Luckily, I was able to persuade our directors to continue our advertising straight through the depression of 1907.

Since I am writing this story largely to describe for a later generation of Oneida Ltd. members not only the evolution of an ideal but the development of the team that "carried the ball" during those early fighting years, this seems to be the place to call the roll. Some of these men, now white-haired, are still to be found in the Oneida Ltd. factories or offices.

It was during the early years of the new century that we definitely initiated a policy which has had much to do with the success of Oneida Ltd. I write "definitely initiated" because, while there was no rule denying this policy in earlier years, the record shows that until that time we searched almost exclusively among our own rising group of young people for additions to the managing staff.

A list of those early additions to our group will illustrate my point. In 1900, H. V. Noyes was promoted to Superintendent of the Canning Department. Paul Herrick became head of the Silk Manufacturing. Bob, Albert and Mart Kinsley were given semi-managing or sales positions while still in their teens. Chester Burnham and Ray Noyes started their executive careers during this period.

Later, in 1901 or 1902, we agreed not only that we must invite capable "outsiders" to join us, but that, if we would have an integrated organization, we must consider "joiners" just as much "our folks" as those descended from Community parents. As a matter of fact, that was the real story of membership in the old Oneida Community. When I was a child, I thought of my elders as a united band of founders, but I discovered afterwards that a majority of them were later additions to the original eighty or ninety men and women who, in 1848, had settled on the Oneida reservation.

A list of the "joiners" who came during those first ten years of O.C.L. would include Eugene Kitendaugh and Leon MacKown in 1902, William Life in 1903, Wilber Earl in 1905, Carroll Austin, Orville Cumings and Jack Milnes in 1906. Martin Keller, as Lititz Superintendent in 1906, made such an outstanding record that in 1913 he was drafted to become Assistant Superintendent of the Sherrill factory and later became the managing head of all the Company's factories. A little later, William Rich, Leon Hill, Joseph Bliss and Reay Milnes joined the group.

Quite inevitably, the expansion of our business since that time has involved a very large number of joiners, including in 1913, Dunc Robertson, now President of the Company. At least two thirds of our present executive group have come from the "outside," and the Company has been truly fortunate in the character, ability and loyalty of its joiners.

There is another list of joiners whose work and enthusiasm played a part as important as that of our sales organization in the fight for Community Silver. It would be unfair to omit their names from this record. I refer to the hardworking superintendents and foremen who had none of the stimulating incentive of our romantic selling adventures. In what must sometimes seem to them the obscurity of factory lives, they never spared themselves. In addition, they carried to every man and woman under them their enthusiasm for the management's ambitions and the Company's success. At their head was Stephen Leonard, Superintendent of the Trap

Factory. His mechanical genius, his ability to pick the right men and his infectious enthusiasm had much to do with creating the profits which paid for Community Silver advertising.

The list of his leading assistants (that was more than fifty years ago) would include Rollin Hurlbut, Jack McQuade, Jerry O'Neal, Ferrand Ellis, Clarence Ward and Jim Graves, all men in charge of the workrooms; also Louis Morrison, who connected those rooms with the office. I am bound to add to this list Fred Filby, the man who superintended the silverware factory at Niagara Falls during these strenuous years; also Amos Reeve, head plater and Filby's assistant. There were other men who deserve mention, but I lack the space to complete this loyal and much-valued roster.

Before writing this chapter, I interviewed several of these men; rather I shared with them memories, both serious and whimsical, of the early years. Those talks were not only informative but, for me, they added new color to memories of that first decade of the twentieth century.

They told me that, while they were fighting to help build a firm foundation for the Company, they strove to enthuse the entire membership, foremen and workmen, with a feeling that more, even, than the achievement of business success, they were helping to create a new kind of industrial organization, one in which all were partners.

They reminded me of forerunners of our modern twice-yearly Lounge meetings; of gatherings in the big Mansion House Hall when salesmen, factory people and the large "Community Family" listened to talks emphasizing the common interests of all. Their reminiscences also brought back memories of picnics on the Mansion House Lawn, enjoyed by all, and they recalled the allotment to employees of plots of Company land for vegetable gardens during bad years. I was, naturally, pleased that they placed value on my own frequent tours through the factories, to keep up my acquaintance with the men. Those were the days before increasing numbers made a close, personal acquaintance with every employee impossible, but I believe that to this day all our people know I am their friend, as I know they are mine.

In November, 1906, came the most important joiner of all—to me: a daughter, my little Barbara. Just as the arrival of that first daughter, Constance, had doubled my urge for success, so now Barbara redoubled it. I *had* to make good!

Nineteen hundred and ten! The year I personally celebrate; the year when our new Oneida Community, Ltd. came of age, so to speak; the year when the emergence of Community Silver as a warranty of the Company's financial soundness ended fifteen years of what our older generation must have regarded as an experiment.

Looking backward: Until the year 1861 the old Oneida Community, founded in 1848, might have been considered an experiment, the badge of experimentation being its life in a wooden house—the original Mansion House built in 1849. In the autumn of 1861 when the Community family moved into the brick "Mansion House" built with their own hands, then and only then did they know it was no longer an experiment. Just so in 1910, the character and quality of our new institution was no longer in doubt. Recognition of all who worked for the Oneida Community, Ltd. as partners was firmly established, and it added strength to the Company's human frame work. We all admitted that we had a long way to go to reach our ideals, but our direction was set.

It is the birth of a new Oneida Community, Ltd. with

new ideals that I have tried to describe in the preceding pages. The rest of this story will be a story of growth not only in size but the growth of those ideals. Which leads me to issue a warning to the reader. Although our young company had inherited from its parent, the old Oneida Community, the ideals of brotherhood, of social equality, of sharing the fruits of its labor, it turned its back squarely upon what my father had called "Bible communism." My own generation, in our youth, had witnessed its inevitable breakdown. We could testify that even under the most fortunate conditions, under an inspired leader, peopled by absolutely dedicated members and under a strict religious discipline, such a system could not succeed. Today, when the word "communism" has for the whole world a different and sinister meaning, it is the extraordinary fact that our group and our company, descended as they are from another kind of communism, are, by the same token, vaccinated against it. We are immune, so to speak, because we know from incontrovertible evidence that no kind of communism can ultimately prosper or endure.

The next four years, 1906 to 1910, were years of steady grind. They were not romantic like those earlier years when we plunged and learned to swim, but the urge forward never slackened. They were marked by enlarging sales, more advertising and a rapid increase of our sales force.

The fact is that the Oneida Community, Ltd. by 1906 had emerged as a young man's company and its management—men still in their thirties—had matured in the rough struggle. The romance of adventure and the rather delightful feeling that we were adventurers was gone. We had learned of the necessary balances and the inevitable drudgery involved in maintaining a place in the sun, to say nothing of growing, in this new day of corporate leviathans manned by that hard-boiled generation of business men who in the 1890's had invented mass production.

We had, in a way, graduated from being amateurs into being professionals. Not that we had abandoned what we called the "amateur spirit in business." It was only that the informed judgment of many minds was substituted for the hunches and sudden decisions of the earlier years. We had acquired immense respect for twentieth-century competition and competitors.

During this period there was one break in our steady progress. A business panic struck the country in the fall of 1907—a real panic. Sales fell off that year, but the panic's full force was not felt until 1908. The extent of this business depression can be gauged by the drop in our total company profits from a high of $271,000 in 1906 to $89,000 in 1908.

However, the basic soundness of our growth was shown by our quick recovery—$280,000 profits in 1909 and $381,000 in 1910. This momentary dip might not deserve a place in this story were it not for two incidents. The first was a positive gain from the panic conditions. During the panic, several companies cut their advertising. We did not, and instead, picked up business which they lost. It may not seem in the best of taste to call another's misfortune your own good fortune, but that is exactly what it was.

The other incident had a personal character. Certain men, somewhat disappointed in their positions or progress, decided in 1909 that the bad statement of 1908 profits offered an opportunity to unseat me as General Manager. Their campaign petered out before the annual election and peace was restored, as was evidenced by the fact that when our revered President, William A. Hinds, died in the spring of

1910, the directors unanimously insisted on electing me as President.

It was Holton V. Noyes who insisted that provision should be made for a park with baseball field and tennis courts adjacent to the site of our proposed clubhouse in the young city of Sherrill. His plan was ambitious, but its approval by the directors shows how important this development of recreational facilities was considered. H.V. employed a professional builder of baseball diamonds, and this man's work was so good that on several occasions professional teams, doing early training nearby, obtained permission to use Noyes Park for their practice games.

The Company's directors showed how important they considered the development of recreational facilities by approving an expenditure that turned out to be larger than anticipated, and later by authorizing the building of a grandstand and a bandstand where for many years the Community Band gave a public concert every Monday night. H. V. Noyes's foresight made possible the baseball teams, football teams, tennis clubs and a score of other athletic and recreational enterprises that have expanded and entertained the growing membership of the Oneida Community, Ltd.

CHAPTER XVI

WRITING OF THESE later years, I shall aim to keep autobiography within reasonable limits. I say reasonable because, since I continued to be the responsible head of Oneida Limited for another sixteen years, during which the Company's adventures were my adventures, a certain amount of my own life story will inevitably creep in.

For example, our export business which later carried our goods all around the world, got its first real impetus from some of my early trips to Europe. These journeys were not strictly business, however. I remember a particularly interesting incident that occurred in 1910 when a half-vacation, half-business trip landed my wife and me in Europe. While we were in London, H. G. Wells honored us with a dinner at which, among the many notable guests, were George Bernard Shaw and his wife. I happened to be seated next Mrs. Shaw, with her husband just beyond. During our conversation I could sense that Mrs. Shaw was stumbling somewhat over a question she apparently wished to ask. Her husband leaned across with a suggestion.

"Perhaps I can state the question for her. We should both like to know whether you were born under the old Oneida Community system? Were you what your father called a 'stirpicultural' child?"

My answer would have been the same in any case, but I instantly recalled Shaw's footnote to *Man and Superman* in which he described the eugenic experiment of the Oneida

Community as the only attempt by mankind to breed what he called the Superman. In this note Shaw had added: "The question as to what sort of man they should strive to breed being settled by the obvious desirability of breeding another Noyes." He had before him now another member of the Noyes clan, and he may have been curious to know how I regarded my parentage.

I was, as I have always been, proud of my descent not only as a child of my parents but as the product of what I believe was a great experiment, and I had no hesitation in saying so. "Yes, I was one of the Stirpicultural children. I am 'another Noyes.'"

My candid reply seemed to break the ice, and the silence which had followed Shaw's question was dispelled by a deluge of questions from the other guests. All these I answered freely, abetted by Mr. Wells who had visited us at Kenwood some years before and been interested and impressed by what he saw. For Mrs. Noyes and me, at least, this was a delightful and memorable evening.

The news of Mr. Hinds's death reached me in Paris. It saddened me, as was to be expected, but it did more. It raised those general questions as to human relations and in particular to the part that Mr. Hinds and the old members had played in shaping life for the generations that followed them. It led me to dwell affectionately on a picture of Community "folks" as I knew them.

With the passing of Mr. Hinds, I knew that I was expected to suggest his successor, and since the position of General Manager had for nearly fifteen years given me all the authority I needed to carry on the responsibilities of leadership, it seemed an opportunity to honor another of the older men who had helped to make a success of the original Oneida

Community. Dr. Noyes and after him, Mr. Hinds, had, as Presidents, co-operated with me wonderfully.

Of that older generation there was still left Mr. Henry Allen, Grosvenor's father, who had been rated one of the Community's leading businessmen. I cabled Grosvenor that I should like to see his father elected President. The answer came within a few hours: "All here believe you should now become President and you have been elected." So, at the age of thirty-nine, I became both General Manager and President.

My earlier visit to Europe in 1901 had been exploratory and accomplished little, but I crossed the Atlantic in 1910 on a definite errand. This journey was made to rescue the very considerable game-trap business we had enjoyed in Russia. For many years a Russo-German manufacturer's agent had handled this trade for us, visiting Oneida once a year to arrange a new contract. These negotiations always involved exasperating dickers over prices.

During this agent's visit to us in 1909, he and I failed to come to an agreement on prices, and he left in high dudgeon. Later we learned that, with a rolling mill in Riga, he had persuaded a small firm in Pavlova to adventure in trap-making. This firm made a very rough grade of house hardware, and the traps they turned out were equally rough. They would have worried us little had not the Riga German, using some kind of political influence, persuaded his government to impose a 58 per cent duty on imported game traps. Up to that time, all traps had entered Russia free of duty, as "vermin exterminators."

My journey to Moscow was uneventful, except for a regrettable error. Corinna, my wife, loves travel and had looked forward eagerly to accompanying me to Russia. On the boat going over, someone warned her that the Russia of 1910 would prove a very uncomfortable place for a woman, and so, reluctantly, she gave up the idea of going there. Actually, I found that she would have been very comfortable in Moscow; able to go sight-seeing to her heart's content—even to visit the Kremlin. I stopped at the Hotel Metropole and found it much like any other good hotel in New York or London, except for the fact that even in midsummer my bedroom windows were not only locked tight but also puttied, to guard us from the night air.

Arrived in Moscow, I consulted a Russian banker with whom we had done some business. I told him of my problem and my plan; that I intended to tell the Pavlova men that they did not know how to make a good trap, that we did, and that we would send them the necessary machinery, with a man who knew not only how to make but also how to sell good traps and that we would give them half the profits.

The banker asked the names of these manufacturers. I answered, "Orgozev and Poushov." (I have forgotten the spelling of their names.)

"No!" he said emphatically. "Not Russians! If they were Germans, or Jews, your scheme might work, but not Russians! They would cheat you before you got out of their yard!"

I must say that I was surprised at a Russian warning me against his own countrymen, but I heeded the warning, gave up my plan and went on to St. Petersburg, where I had learned of an American named Lenke, a Pennsylvania Dutchman, who had large metal-working factories there. I discussed with him placing our machinery in one of his plants and sending a man to oversee the trap-making. He was not unfavorable but wanted many details. In the end, I left with nothing more definite than a promise by Lenke to communicate with us later.

The end of the story came two years afterwards. Despite his promise, we heard nothing from Mr. Lenke, and increasing activity at home allowed the matter to drop for two years. Later, in 1913, Mart Kinsley and I visited Russia with a definite proposition. We showed Lenke an inventory of the machinery we would send. We told him we had a man, Bob Hurlbut, who knew trap-making from end to end, that all we would need was factory space and power.

Lenke seemed even more favorable than on my earlier visit, but insisted upon more time to arrange space in his plant where such machinery could be placed. At home again, negotiation dragged, and when in 1914, the great war broke out, we dropped our Russian enterprise forever. As a dramatic finis—in 1917 Lenke turned up at Oneida. He told me that his factories were all seized by the Russian government and that he had barely got out of Russia with his life.

My own negotiations ran into the crookedness that characterized Russian officialdom during the last Empire. Lenke's success in building up an enormous manufacturing business was due, I am sure, to the fact that his directors were members of the nobility or the "court set." One of these directors was present while I enlarged on the profit to be made by a good manufacturer of traps.

The next morning, when I called to hear Lenke's decision, this director, Prince X, was again present. Lenke pointed his finger at him, saying rather disgustedly, "After you left yesterday the Prince suggested that if trap-making is so profitable, we ought to take it over ourselves. Why share with you? He'd cheat you out of your eyeteeth if he could." The Prince simply smiled—a friendly smile. He was not in the least embarrassed.

My most colorful memories of that first visit to Russia result from my friendship with a very capable American engineer, Robert McCarter, who was then manager of the Westinghouse factories in Moscow. He was a very forthright young man and his experience in managing an element of Russian industrialism was not only interesting but informative historically.

For instance, he had a strike in his factory. He was quickly informed by the authorities that if he would name the leaders of the strike, they would "disappear" secretly. He declined, telling his informant that he would handle the strike the "American way." Under his management a small library had been accumulated in the factory. When a delegation of the strikers asked if they could still draw books, he said, "Certainly," and there were continually strikers in the factory drawing books. This undoubtedly helped in a reasonable settlement of the strike.

Another of McCarter's experiences with the old Czarist regime seems worth telling. One of the Czar's discarded favorites knew too much. She gave out details of the bribery accompanying the building of the St. Petersburg tramways which had been constructed by Westinghouse under McCarter's management. Presently the accusation spread so widely among the "court set" that they became alarmed, and an investigation was ordered.

McCarter, as head of the Westinghouse operations, occupied the witness box for two weeks, with all the Corporation's books. Every transaction with the government was there in detail: "Five hundred rubles to Count Z." "One thousand rubles for Prince D," and so on, *ad libitum,* until half of the most prominent Russians were tarred with proof of guilt. There was a near-panic in the Moscow court set.

Then the heroic savior appeared. The intermediary—

nowadays we would call him a "stooge"—took the witness stand. He swore that all the ledger items were correct, but calmly claimed that he, himself, had kept all the money; that he had used those illustrious names to cover his own thefts. He saved his country by taking the blame for the "higher-ups" who had actually received the bribes. Bob told me that this man had become the most honored man in Russia. People asking any favor from the government found it profitable to get his name on their applications.

Another story I was told concerned an American who, many years before, had built some of the first railroads for Russia. In return he received a permanent contract for a royalty on every wheel turning in that country. This became *very* profitable and Moscow, growing jealous, sent parties to negotiate a settlement ending this contract. The American laughed at them. In the course of the argument he said, "You can bribe any man in Russia, even the Czar."

This remark was reported to the young Czar, whose reaction was, "That's a very clever man. I'd like to meet him. I know that every man in Russia, besides myself, can be bribed. I don't know what *I* would do, because no one has ever tried to bribe me."

Although this visit was disappointing, I had not given up the idea of export trade, and with this project in mind, went to England with Mart Kinsley in 1913. He had been appointed the Company's export manager with instructions to investigate the possibility of developing a profitable market for our silverware in Great Britain and the larger British Colonies. Clifton Inslee was appointed resident British salesman.

Mart and I arrived in England a week earlier than Clifton, partly to "investigate," but more, hoping to encourage him by actual sales made. However, when Saturday came and we, with our best efforts, had not made a single sale, we were both disappointed and embarrassed. We were embarrassed because we knew that the failure of two managers to make a sale with a week's efforts would serve any salesman as an excuse for making no sales. We were desperate.

We proceeded to Glasgow. While eating breakfast, I suggested that the best way to pull ourselves out of our slump and start the day with a winning spirit was to tackle the toughest proposition first, which meant the largest jeweler. This company had three gorgeous floors of display. We found, however, that their purchasing office was in an adjoining building which looked like a warehouse. We mounted to the third floor of this building and were met by an office boy, who disappeared with my card into a dingy hallway.

Presently he returned and handed back my card with the curt statement, "'He doesn't want any silver.'"

Having softened the boy up a little I said, "Go back and say that we are executives of a large American Company. Ask him to spare a few minutes just to see these unusual products."

With evident reluctance, the buyer presently appeared. I introduced Mart and myself with what I hoped was a mixture of British formality and American enthusiasm, and told him that we had samples of the very latest thing in silver design. I urged that for his own information he should at least have a look at it.

After a little more talk he came up to the gate that separated us, saying resignedly, "I'll look at it."

I spread out my roll of spoons and forks. By a stroke of luck there was no place for this open roll except to balance it on the inch-wide edge of the gate. I held it by one end, but with Mart purposely backing away, the buyer was obliged to hold the other end. After that, he could not let go his end of the roll without spilling all the silver out onto the floor, so, perforce, he listened to Mart and then to me, becoming momentarily more interested. Finally he said, "You have some excellent merchandise here, but I hate to trouble the head of the firm."

The situation was improving. I urged "Won't you ask him to take just a moment to see this new American silver?"

Mart tactfully relieved him of his end of the roll and he disappeared. It was an exciting but a trying moment for Mart and me. Would he come back?

He did come, and with him came a nice old gentleman, the owner of the business, who proved to be deaf and dumb! Our new friend, the buyer, communicated with him by lip reading. I ventured comments spoken slowly with the hope that he could read at least a few of my words.

In the end both men left. Our hearts were in our throats! Then the buyer came back. He spoke in a very friendly voice, "I am instructed to order a small quantity of these two patterns."

Later, while the buyer and Mart made out the order, the old gentleman took me through a door into the retail store and showed me proudly the merchandise that he had just brought back from Japan.

This company was for many years one of our best customers in Great Britain. They may still be. At present our Export Department has spread so wide that our agents cover Europe—except for Russia and her satellites—Mexico and the West Indies, South America, Australia, Japan and American bases in the Pacific. We have a factory in Sheffield, England, and two in Canada. All of this, grown, of course, far be-

yond our possible accomplishment in those early days—but
not beyond our dreams. Although this has largely come about
since the days of my active participation, it is gratifying to
remember that I helped in its beginning.

The years from 1910 to 1917 saw a steady growth in the
Company's sales and in the strength of its organization. Its
commercial progress may be measured by the addition of
$1,325,425 to the Company's "surplus" during these seven
years, in spite of rapidly increasing expenditures for social
services, large contributions for schools, churches, etc. and
liberal dividends.

In 1913, it became very evident that, for efficiency's sake,
we should move the manufacture of silverware from Niagara
Falls to Sherrill. Plans were made for erecting a suitable
building behind the trap factory. It was also decided to bring
all the trained employees to Sherrill to look the ground over;
all who chose to make the change were offered their old positions. A special train was chartered for these employees.
Upon their arrival in Sherrill, they were handsomely entertained and were given a tour of the Oneida buildings and
the site for the new factory. A gratifying number of employees decided to make the move to Sherrill. Within the year
forty houses were built for the men and their families, and in
the meantime the new factory was completed. By 1914, the
move was complete. This loyal and enthusiastic group of
employees added immeasurably to the O.C.L., and I hope
that none of them has ever regretted making the move.

The growing strength of the organization stemmed from
the election to the Board of several men belonging to a generation younger than my own, and the emergence of these
and others into important executive positions.

Already in 1909 membership of the Board had been increased to eleven in order to add P. B. Herrick, Superintendent of the Silk Department and Holton V. Noyes, Superintendent of the Canning Department. In 1911 Albert Kinsley, Mart Kinsley and Louis Wayland-Smith became directors and a few years later Burton Dunn and Gerard Wayland-Smith were added. This completed the transfer of responsibility for management of Oneida Community, Ltd. to a Board of the younger generation.

It is worth while noting that, with responsibility and policy-making entirely in the hands of our youthful junta, all elder directors from 1895 to 1915, excepting one, served as long as they lived. Mr. Henry Allen resigned in 1911 to make possible the election of a young man.

To complete the personnel history of this period: in 1911 George Noyes became Treasurer; Albert Kinsley was made Manager of the Silverware and Hardware factories in 1912 and the next year Manager of all factories; Mart Kinsley became Manager of Sales for the Silverware Department; Louis Wayland-Smith Auditor and Purchasing Agent and Gerard Wayland-Smith Manager of the Sales Force. A little later Mart Kinsley was made Export Manager.

In 1912 we sold the chain business to Walter Lasher. It had been a very profitable department, but by this time Lasher, a manufacturer of tire chains, was making all his parts excepting the "side chain" (four or five million feet of chain), which he had left with us because of a longtime friendship, and I knew that he must soon take this business from us.

The technique of this sale was very unusual. We met in a room of the old Belmont Hotel and out of a clear sky I announced that I was going to sell him our chain business. I said, "You know the conservatism of our inventories. You are going to pay me the amount of the chain inventory, machin-

ery and stock, plus a stated amount in cash. You can run the
business in our chain factory until you have built one for
yourself, staffing it with the men you will employ later." Walter said, "All right." We employed no lawyer to draw up the
contract of sale, but during the year, while he occupied our
factory, there were no arguments or misunderstandings, and
the transfer was made on the terms I proposed.

It became evident that silverware for the Canadian trade
should be made in Canada. Not yet being ready to build at
the time, in 1916 we bought the Stone Cottage property, with
its six acres of land. We found we could adapt the old stone
house, long connecting shed and huge barn to our temporary
use.

But the expanding business soon outgrew these make-
shift quarters, and with sentimental regrets we tore down the
old cottage buildings in 1925 and made way for the handsome
stone factory which stands on the site today.

In 1916 we sold our silk business to the Hemingway
Company. Competition with the big silk manufacturers had
been steadily decreasing our profit and, in any case, we were
at that time concentrating on the silverware development.
We needed the money to expand that department. Also, we
were, in spite of ourselves, neglecting smaller departments.
The later history of the then-very-profitable one-hundred-
yard spool-silk sales made me thankful that we sold at that
time.

In the summer of 1914, when panic threatened at the
outbreak of the European war, we cut the higher salaries in
two, reduced wages, and put the factories on short time. In
1916, however, we refunded to employees their losses through
the cuts and the short time.

One of our most successful accomplishments was proposed by the "Plant Committee"—Albert Kinsley, Lou Way-land-Smith, Mart Kinsley and Gerard Wayland-Smith—and was worked out by Albert and Lou. This was the "High Cost of Living" plan. It called for a second envelope, marked "H.C.L.," given out at the same time as the regular envelope. It was an additional wage based on .25 per cent of the base wage for every five-point rise in the weekly cost-of-living circular issued by the Bradstreet Company.

At one time during the war the additional pay in this H.C.L. envelope amounted to nearly 50 per cent of the regular envelope. This obviated all questions regarding rates of pay. Our employees were more than satisfied with the arrangement and waited expectantly for the Bradstreet weekly telegram which was posted in all of our factories. I even heard that there was betting on the increase in each bulletin.

Several Washington departments became interested and asked for details of the plan. I remember that Dr. Harry Garfield, Federal Fuel Administrator, discussed it with me, hoping to find in it relief from the strikes and wage struggles in the mining industry.

Three important events belong to this period. The first calls for only brief mention at this point in my story. It was the joining of Miles E. Robertson who, after graduating from Syracuse University and its Law School, and being admitted to the Bar, went to work in our factory at a wage of thirteen dollars per week.

It has never been satisfactorily explained to me why Robertson made this sudden about-face. He was a friend of Albert Kinsley, and Albert was an enthusiast for our social plans, also an enthusiastic believer in the future of the Company. Something in that future must have struck Robertson as more worth while than a career with the Standard Oil Company which had made him an attractive offer. His joining I have called an event because fourteen years later he was unanimously appointed General Manager and in 1950 became President of the Company.

The second "event" was more important to me personally than the other two. It was the birth of a son—Pierrepont Trowbridge. I will not enlarge on the happiness brought to the family by this addition, nor repeat the foolish things— mostly garbled—that tradition insists that I said when carrying the news to relatives and friends, but content myself with the statement that Peter has never disappointed me, and note for future reference that he has been just as devoted to the development of Oneida Ltd.—my kind of an Oneida Ltd.—as I have been myself.

The third event was the appointment on January 16, 1917 of Albert Kinsley to the position of General Manager. Early in life I developed a theory—some called it an eccentricity—that leadership, the responsibility for management of a Company, should be passed on to a younger generation before a man was fifty. I had noted that a man who skipped a generation often found it difficult to pass to his grandson the kind of leadership he desired. Somewhat whimsically, I called my theory, "The shingles on the roof." In my youth I worked as a carpenter, and I knew that if one course of shingles was omitted the roof would leak.

Whether or not I was 100 per cent right, I put my theory into practice by resigning the General Managership in January, 1917, at the age of 46, and with the approval of the Directors turned that responsibility over to Albert. I retained the presidency, but left Oneida with my family and rented a house in Santa Barbara, California, intending to remain there for the greater part of the year to give Albert a chance to get fairly in the saddle.

He was in his early thirties and had earned his promotion by vigorous handling of the Company's manufacturing operations and farsighted planning for the future. He had also shared in the solution of sales problems. He was especially satisfactory to me because of his ambition to make real my youthful dream of an honest-to-God "sharing Company" with no "rich" and no "poor."

So we seemed wonderfully organized for a new era of youthful enterprise at the moment when what we were approaching was an era of world wars.

CHAPTER XVII

In April, 1917, as all will remember, the United States entered the European War. Immediately on hearing this news, I made a hurried dash to Oneida, leaving my wife to close up the house in California and follow me home with the children.

At Oneida, I did not disturb Albert's position as General Manager. In the short three months of my absence he had organized his staff effectively and the factory was rapidly taking on war work. I was especially pleased with a plan to assist the families of employees who were leaving to join the Army, a plan which had been worked out with the aid of a Committee consisting of Louis Wayland-Smith, Mart Kinsley and Gerard Wayland-Smith.

Under this plan, volunteers and, with certain limitations, drafted men who were married or the sole support of a relative, were to receive sufficient wages to make their total income, including army pay, equal to their average before leaving.

Satisfied that all was going well with the Company, I hurried to Washington to find some work I could do to aid the war effort. My own first choice was to become a flyer. This may sound like a foolish ambition for a man at forty-six, but my old friend Elliott Hinds, the hero of that long-ago broncho race, was, at forty-one, flying an observation plane in France. However, the head of the Air Corps discouraged me. He said that the best I could hope for at my age was a teaching job on an American flying field. I decided that I could be more useful elsewhere, so I gave this up and looked for another war job.

My first service in Washington was with Vance Mc-Cormick's Foreign Trade Bureau, but after a few weeks I left the F.T.B. to join Dr. Harry Garfield's Fuel Administration. This shift was the result of one of those unbelievable coincidences that have, throughout my life, led to unexpected and interesting experiences.

Harry Nims, our Company lawyer and a warm personal friend, was paying a one-day visit to Washington to consult me on Company business when he accidentally met another old friend, Dr. Harry Garfield. Nims had been a favorite pupil of Garfield's during his undergraduate days at Williams College. When the United States entered the war, Garfield was president of the college but had been drafted by President Wilson to help in Washington. When Garfield saw Nims that day, he seized upon him. He had, he told Nims, been unexpectedly appointed Fuel Administrator but, having another week's work on the Wheat Committee where he had been serving, he had not been able to give time to this new job, with the result that an enormous amount of correspondence had collected, unanswered. He insisted, "You must come over and help me out."

Nims could not refuse, but he soon found himself hopelessly swamped by the avalanche of letters and telegrams pouring in from fuel users all over the United States. He had a bright idea. He told Dr. Garfield that he had a friend in Washington who was trained for exactly this kind of work and who, he knew, was dissatisfied with his present arrangement. Garfield said, "Get him." I was the man he got.

When I arrived at the new Fuel Administration and saw

the stacks of wire baskets filled with urgent but unanswered appeals for coal, I sent for my brother-in-law, Carroll Austin, and together, working sixteen hours a day for three weeks, we cleaned up this correspondence by form letters explaining the delay and promising early information. Dr. Garfield was a stickler for orderliness in the handling of business correspondence—and, for that matter, in all other relations of life. It was not until five years later that I dared tell him of the many letters and telegrams we dropped summarily into the wastebasket because they had lain so long unanswered that finally no answer was possible. At that late date, he laughed when I illustrated our dilemma with a case in point.

I said, "For instance, we would find an urgent telegram from the governor of a state, requesting an immediate reply —but already two weeks old. How would you have written him?"

After such a delay, of course, no reply was better than a lame explanation. Dr. Garfield must have understood that problem, even at the time, since I was never reprimanded for my arbitrary dealings with an impossible situation.

Actually, the work, for me, was both fascinating and exciting, and during those first confused and confusing months, a number of other unexpected—and sometimes unauthorized—jobs came my way. It is possible that a more cautious, or perhaps I should say a more orthodox, man might have hesitated to undertake such responsibilities, but it did not occur to me to refuse, and I must say that luck or the accident of perfect timing or whatever it was favored me throughout the whole affair.

During the next eighteen months, until the end of the war, in the confusion of the bureau-ridden and—I am sorry to say—sometimes politics-ridden City of Washington, I had

many interesting experiences and made a satisfactory progress
in responsibility. Through all the later months of the war I
was Dr. Garfield's first assistant and his personal representative on other war boards. The most interesting and important
of these was Bernard Baruch's all-embracing War Industries
Board, where, as the fuel member of his Priority Committee,
I made the acquaintance of that really great man and gained
a friendship which has lasted from that day to this.

During those months I found myself welcome to sit in
Baruch's office and listen to the succession of interesting and
often tough interviews which occupied his long working days.
I particularly remember his struggle with the heads of two
of the largest steel companies. I remember it because of the
cryptic remark of Baruch's right bower, Alec Legge, President of the International Harvester Company, which ended
the struggle.

Baruch had put up to these steel executives a program
for steel deliveries which they insisted was impossible. After
endless argument, Baruch turned back to his desk with a
final shot. "I expect you fellows to come across with that
steel."

The steel men simply shook their heads. There was silence. Presently Legge asked casually, "You say you can't do
it?" Again they shook their heads. Legge threw at them, "In
that case, gentlemen, my advice to you is to buy a couple of
German grammars and study up on the language of the future." The steel men finally agreed "to try," and I learned later
that they carried out most of the program.

I had one rather amusing experience when serving as
fuel member of the Priority Committee.

Baruch rarely attended the sessions of this committee,
but once, when I entered the board room, I found him pres-

ent, also Charlie Schwab, who had much to do with the building of ships for the transport of material and personnel to the war areas. Schwab had attended the meeting to propose the building of a large plant in which to construct oil tankers much larger than had ever been built before.

What interested me was that he proposed to build this plant in the so-called Philadelphia area of the Delaware River. So many war industries were already located here that the Fuel Administration had found it very difficult during the previous winter to keep them all supplied with fuel. As I had the actual job of seeing that they had the coal, I knew that if such a plant as Schwab proposed were built, either it or other of the plants located there would shut down during the coming winter for lack of fuel.

Schwab—everyone called him "Charlie," during the war —did not deny my statistics or argue at all. He simply reiterated the advantage of his huge tankers and brushed aside my figures proving "not enough coal" with a good-natured statement, "You'll find enough if you have to."

The discussion lasted nearly half an hour until Baruch, who had been sitting a little back of Schwab with a smile on his face which suggested that he was enjoying the struggle between him and me, suddenly spoke. "You seem, Noyes, to be in a minority of one. Perhaps you'll have to give way to the majority."

Quite unexpectedly Legge's voice broke in. "Not one! A minority of two! I think Noyes knows what he is talking about."

The net result, however, was a victory for Schwab. I accepted defeat but spoke directly to him. "We will get you all the coal we can but hope you'll remember that you once sold coal short."

Charlie Schwab was happy. He thanked me but, turning to Baruch, he asked, "What's that, Berny—what's 'selling short'?"

The entire committee laughed with those two Wall Street veterans.

The ending of the war in November prevented any proof that I was right.

If my employment as a member of the Fuel Administration staff was the result of remarkable timing, my later elevation as Director of the Bureau of Conservation and, later still, to first assistant to Dr. Garfield was—I can think of no word more descriptive—bizarre.

During the first weeks of Garfield's service as National Fuel Administrator, a sudden rash of mine strikes occupied most of his time, so much so that the men—important businessmen—whom he had appointed directors of the various Bureaus found it impossible to discuss their difficult problems with him. It was a youngish lawyer, a member of one of the prominent law firms on lower Broadway, who came to me with a proposition which only that word "bizarre" will fit.

He said, "Dr. Garfield has placed me in charge of the appointment of State Fuel Administrators. For example, there's a fierce political fight going on right now between two candidates for the Minnesota job. It must be settled quickly, but I cannot get an interview with the Commissioner. He is closeted all the time with miners and mine operators. If someone like you would take the responsibility for answering questions like this, which *must* be settled, it would save a lot of trouble and in many cases keep the distribution of coal going."

To the question of why I was chosen—or even more, of

why I accepted the responsibility—I have never since been able to find a reasonable answer, but I did accept. Perhaps the fact that my friend Harry Nims always attended the discussions in Dr. Garfield's office had something to do with it.

Dr. Garfield must have known what was going on, since, a week or so later, he called me into his private office and said, with an odd smile, "Mr. Noyes, this administration has no Bureau of Conservation. I should like to have you organize one. I have rented for you the building next door." (The Fuel Administration was then located in private buildings on 16th Street.)

I told him, with, I think, a mate to his smile, that I was enjoying my present work. Then he spoke seriously. "I know, but your rather anomalous position is making trouble in certain quarters."

This I could well believe, in view of my lack of any strictly official status in a situation supposed to be handled with due regard to protocol. We both thoroughly understood the difficulty, of course, but to me, at least, it was a tribute to the large calibre of Dr. Garfield's mind that, in the face of our necessity, he recognized the need for unconventional methods, gave me neither reproach nor reprimand for my temerity but instead offered me a promotion. From that time until the end of the war I became, officially, the Director of Conservation for the Fuel Administration.

After six months of hotel living, I sent for my family to join me in Washington and we rented a very comfortable house in the outskirts of the city. My wife has a genius for hospitality. She made our home the favorite gathering place, especially for Oneida men, a number of whom I had drafted into my Bureau, and helped with the entertainment of many of my departmental co-workers.

She has always been very much alive to public events, and I think she enjoyed Washington in spite of its noise and confusion. For her, however, there were, I remember, two drawbacks to our location. The first was the persistence on our walls of one hundred sixty-seven oil paintings—sixteen in the bathroom—all copies and all unbeautiful—painted by our landlady. Our lease bound us to leave them all where they were. The second drawback was the zoo just across from us in Rock Creek Park. At some time during each night, an animal or a bird would pipe up and then a chorus of all the beasts and birds would make life hideous, sometimes for an hour. However, I believe that the whole family enjoyed our stay in Washington.

Perhaps I could also call a drawback my inability, as a government employee, to help our Company get much-needed war work. However, Mart Kinsley, who for ten years had been our Export Manager, was put at the head of the department for procuring war work. He accomplished much and continued in this position until the war ended and our factories returned to civilian production. Later, Mart returned to his export position, traveling widely in all parts of the world. All his life he was an able and devoted member of our group. His death, in 1947, and that of his cousin, Albert Kinsley, six months earlier, were losses deeply felt by all of us. In losing them, we lost not only loving friends but men of the calibre we have always called "O.C.Q."—Oneida Community Quality.

My connection with the Paris Peace Conference in 1919 and 1920 and my appointment as the American Member of the Rhineland Commission came as an explosive propulsion from the normal orbit of my life. To be sure, World War I had disturbed that orbit, but war brings a hiatus to most men's careers and when it is over, they resume their former manner of living and thinking with little change and fast-fading memories of those hectic months.

So it was with me when, in December, 1918, I said good-bye to Washington and the Fuel Administration where I had spent a year and a half. In my case, however, an even more violent disruption of the aforesaid orbit was then in the making. A chain of events, already started, was about to plunge me into a career entirely foreign to my education and experience and so filled with strange activities and nightmare possibilities as to change my thinking and claim my interest for the rest of my life.

The first link in that chain was forged by my first trip to Italy in 1916, before the United States entered the war. The second link was the friendship and confidence of B. M. Baruch and other members of President Wilson's so-called "kitchen cabinet," which I had acquired in Washington. And the third link must be credited to luck—to landing in Paris at the very moment when, after six weeks' struggle, M. Clemenceau had given way to the British and American insistence on a Rhineland Commission "with teeth in it" and a matter of hours before the President was to send a telegram to a certain prominent American asking that he come to Europe to serve as American Member of that Commission.

At the war's end, having cleared up the affairs of my Bureau, I returned to Oneida in December 1918, where I found the shift from war work to normal civilian production proceeding satisfactorily. I suggested no change in Albert's position as General Manager, but devoted myself to getting ready for a second visit to Italy.

To go back a little, it had happened, during the summer of 1916 and before my Washington experience, that I made a somewhat arduous journey to Milan. On the face of it, I was hunting for future silverware business, but I suspect that I had not entirely lost my love of adventure and had an itch to see the war in Europe firsthand. We knew that most of the blanks for Italy's silver-plated ware were made in Germany and plated in Milan. Now, Germany was at war with Italy, and I thought I might capture this business. As a matter of record, I did make a tentative contract with one of the leading platers in Milan which was supposed to come into effect after the war.

That trip to Europe—England, France and Italy—in wartime was a very interesting experience. I happened to be in Paris on Bastille Day, 1916, when the population turned out to watch a great parade. Units from every front, including a company of American volunteers, marched along the boulevards. Beneath all the cheering, there was in the crowds an undercurrent of gloom, for the terrible battles of the Somme were then in progress. I was later told by an American colonel, who served as liaison with the British Army, that the Somme battles were fought as a diversionary measure to prevent German attacks on the Champagne front; that the British Commander had been warned by the French that defeatism was so general among the French troops that the line would give way under heavy assault.

Now, in 1919, with the war over, I decided to return to Italy with the intention of finishing the business I had begun three years before, and that is how I happened to arrive in Paris during April, 1919, with a trunk full of silverware samples and not the remotest idea of taking any part in the great international drama being enacted in Paris. The Peace Conference was then being organized with headquarters at the Crillon Hotel. Knowing that everyone was extremely busy, I delayed calling on the many Washington-made friends gathered there until, passing the hotel at noon two days before I expected to leave for Italy, I decided to risk a short visit with Baruch.

As it happened, I found Alec Legge in Baruch's office. Characteristically, as I entered, Legge got up with hand extended. "Well, I'll be damned! It's good to see you again."

Baruch also had risen. He turned to Legge, "The very man we want for the Rhineland."

Legge took up the cue. "Sure, Noyes. We've got a job for you."

Naturally, I did not take this seriously. "No."

Legge with his customary emphasis said, "Yes!" Then he told me of the situation.

"We've smoked out Clemenceau and got a Rhineland Commission with teeth in it. The President has practically decided on a man for the American member. In fact we have a cablegram all ready to send him tonight." He turned to Baruch. "Noyes will be twice as good."

This sounded serious. I explained, "I can't do it. I'm going to Italy on my Company's business."

"Like hell you're going to Italy." This was Legge as I knew him in Washington. "You're going right up to the Rhineland."

I lunched with them in Baruch's office and before that luncheon was over I had weakened. They sold me the idea that it was an important job, would be an interesting adventure and keep me away from my business not over three or four months. I promised to think it over.

When I called next day I found that the hard-hitting Baruch had not waited for my final word. He had obtained the approval of the other four American members of the

Supreme Economic Council who acted as advisers to the President, and the latter had already shifted the appointment to me.

I read in my diary that Baruch "found Vance McCormick enthusiastic, Robinson and Davis cordial, but Hoover rather cool—said he did not know me very well."

Under instructions from Legge I interviewed each of these four men, discussing the handling of their departmental affairs in the Rhineland. When I discussed food distribution with Mr. Hoover I found him, as my diary puts it, "loosened up." He was very friendly. He even took time to tell me "the story of his life" and read me paragraphs from his printed speeches in the S.E.C.

Vance McCormick offered some advice for which I was thankful later. He said, "There is a very able young man in Luxembourg serving as a member of the present futile Rhineland Committee. His name is Wallace Day, and you will do well to get him for your assistant if possible."

McCormick went on to tell me of Day's history. "He became head of one bureau in the War Trade Board in Washington and was so efficient that when other bureaus went wrong I added them to his responsibilities. When the war ended, he was in charge of three bureaus." He went further, "I'll tell you frankly that if Day were not so young—yes, if he did not *look* so young—he would be the new Rhineland Commissioner. Appointing him might be resented by the other three Commissioners since they are all 'big men.' But you'll find Wallace Day invaluable. Get him on your side of the table if you can."

As a result I asked McCormick to wire Day to come to Paris, and on Saturday I signed him up. That proved one of the greatest pieces of good fortune of my entire Rhineland experience.

Day helped me get together quickly a skeleton staff of helpers and all the paraphernalia for office work and traveling. I remained an extra day in Paris largely to get some instructions and advice from the busy Baruch. His instructions were typical of the man I had known in Washington, turning important matters over to assistants and apparently washing his hands of them. He said—I remember the exact words—"Hell, Noyes, if I knew what to do I would go there myself. Use your bean." That was all, except—just before I left—"Don't get us into any trouble."

CHAPTER XVIII

MY APPOINTMENT as Rhineland Commissioner was the beginning of a new era in my life.

Hitherto, although I had made several business trips to Europe my object was along familiar lines and my return home, within a definite time, certain.

Now before me were activities I knew nothing about and in a completely strange setting. Only remembrance of the enthusiam for public service that pervaded Washington during the war and Baruch's and Legge's confidence in me could have persuaded me to accept the position. Also, if further persuasion was needed, the reports from home assured me that our business was running smoothly.

I joined the Commission with some misgivings. Sir Harold Stuart, the British member, was a man of the highest integrity and of great ability, whose thirty years in India had carried him to an important position. Both he and the British Government agreed with the American hands-off-as-much-as-possible theory for the Occupation. Sir Harold and I worked harmoniously together through all my service with the Rhineland Commission.

M. Tirard, the French member and chairman of the new Rhineland Commission, had been a high government official in Morocco. He was a fine-looking man of medium height who, through all the year and half I remained the American member of the Commission, wished, I am sure, so far as French policy, dictated from Paris, permitted, to meet my

242

ideas. Unfortunately, the French and American ideas of the conduct of the Rhineland Occupation were very far apart. Hence we had many struggles.

The first Belgian Commissioner took little interest in occupational problems except to speak up continually for a rule prohibiting German importation into Belgium of articles which his own factory at Spa was manufacturing. Soon he was superseded by Baron Rolin-Jaequemyns, Professor of History in the University of Brussels, who was a very fine type of man but who, for some reason, took little part in our procedures except to vote always with Tirard.

Two of them, professional diplomats of long experience, one a noted scholar—and diplomatically I was a novice!

In Luxembourg City, our temporary headquarters, Sir Harold and I tried to arrange with M. Tirard for the organization of the Commission, but his reception of the idea was cool, and when, the next day, we pressed him, he said that he would go to Paris and find out just what "they wanted to do." On the morrow he telephoned us from Paris that he would not be back the next day and added that a plan was being discussed which would make the Rhineland Commission unnecessary. After a brief discussion, Sir Harold and I notified him by telephone that, whether he was there or not, we would the next day organize the Commission which was to be located at Coblenz.

It happened that within a month after joining the Rhineland Commission I felt forced to take a stand not only in opposition to the French and Belgian Commissioners, but one which my friend, Sir Harold, at first hesitated to back. I say "forced," because I have always taken responsibility seriously—perhaps too seriously.

The commanding generals of the five Allied Nations

were appointed as a committee to draft a "convention" which should define the relation between the occupying forces and the German inhabitants of the Rhine Provinces. The report of the Military Council, under the influence of Marechal Foch, turned out to be a brutal document. It decreed that "martial law with all its consequences" should remain in force in the Rhineland for fifteen years. It placed control of the German police and "the conduct of the occupation" in the hands of the French Military Commander.

Together, Sir Harold Stuart and I entered a strong protest against the military plan and were told to suggest modifying amendments. For two days Sir Harold and I worked over revisions of the document. At the end of that time I threw up my hands. I told Sir Harold, "It's bad, so bad that no amendments can make it good." Incidentally, I discussed this military convention with M. Tirard, the French President of the Rhineland Commission, and he admitted that it was bad. My diary quotes him as saying, "Just like the military mind."

Sir Harold worked out a modification of the Supreme War Council's convention and asked me what I thought of it. I said, "Still bad! The basic principle of 'martial law' with all its consequences, maintained in these territories by the Allied military authorities, means continuing war for no one knows how many years. I think I shall write a letter to President Wilson and tell him it is bad."

Sir Harold laughed, but said, "Go ahead, Noyes, and write him." I do not think he meant this seriously. It was too far from what the British system of governmental relations permitted.

However, I consulted Bernard Baruch and while he also laughed, he said, "Go ahead and write him."

I hesitated all day, but Felix Frankfurter, with whom I

lunched, insisted that I write. He said (I am quoting from my diary) "The President is tired out. He has been bullied and beaten, and he knows it. For the first time in his life he wants support. He has grown humble."

I quote from a book I wrote in 1920, entitled, *While Europe Waits for Peace:*

> This letter seems to have reached the President at a psychological moment, for he took it to the Supreme Council and obtained unanimous consent to the appointment of a committee instructed to draft a plan along the lines I had suggested. This committee, after a week of continuous session, presented to the Peace Conference the "Rhineland Agreement" which was finally signed by Germany and the Allies at the same time as the Treaty of Versailles. The French "White Book," containing the discussions of this special committee, states in Paragraph I:
>
>> "That a Commission composed of 'A representative of the United States of America who will be designated by President Wilson; Lord Robert Cecil, for Great Britain; Monsieur Loucheur, for France; Marchese Imperiali, for Italy'
>
> will be appointed to draft a plan of agreement concerning the Occupation of the Rhineland Provinces, in accordance with the scheme suggested [skeleton plan] in a letter dated May 27, 1919, from Mr. Noyes, American Delegate to the Interallied Rhineland Commission, to President Wilson.'"

The book also contains a copy of the letter, which I quote, since it states my position at that time—a position which I have since seen no reason to alter.

American Commission to Negotiate Peace
Paris, May 27, 1919

To the Honorable Woodrow Wilson,
President of the United States of America,
11, Place des Etats-Unis, Paris

Dear Sir,

After a month spent in the Rhineland as American Commissioner, I feel there is danger that a disastrous mistake will be made. The "Convention" for the government of these territories, as drafted by the military representatives of the Supreme War Council on May eleventh, is more brutal, I believe, than even its authors desire upon second thought. It provides for unendurable oppression of six million people during a period of years.

This "Convention" is not likely to be adopted without great modification. What alarms me, however, is that none of the revisions of this document which I have seen recognize that its basic principle is bad—that the quartering of an enemy army in a country as its master in time of peace and the billeting of troops on the civil population will insure hatred and ultimate disaster.

I have discussed this matter at length with the American Commanders of the Army of Occupation, men who have seen military occupation at close range for six months. These officers emphatically indorse the above statements. They say that an occupying army, even one with the best intentions, is guilty of outrages and that mutual irritation, in spite of every effort to the contrary, grows apace. Force and more force must inevitably be the history of such occupation long continued.

Forgetting the apparent ambitions of the French and possibly overlooking political limitations, I have sketched below a plan which seems to me the maximum for military domination in the Rhineland after the signing of peace. Our Army Commanders and others who

have studied the subject on the ground agree with this
program:

SKELETON PLAN

I. As few troops as possible concentrated in Barracks
or reserve areas with no "billeting," excepting possibly for officers.

II. Complete self-government for the territory, with the
exceptions below.

III. A Civil Commission with powers:

    a. To make regulations or change old ones when-
ever German Law or actions—

    (1) Threaten the carrying out of Treaty terms,
or

    (2) Threaten the comfort or security of troops.

    b. To authorize the army to take the control
under martial law, either in danger spots or
throughout the territory whenever conditions
seem to the Commission to make this necessary.

Very truly yours,

(signed)   Pierrepont B. Noyes,

American Delegate,

Interallied Rhineland Commission.

It is history now that M. Clemenceau on May
twenty-ninth seized upon this more liberal plan of "occupation" presented by President Wilson in order to
make more sure of the final adherence of the American
and British Premiers to the main principle of "occupation." Sitting in the meetings at the Quai d'Orsai as a
spectator, I witnessed the most intense and persistent
hostility to this "civilian" plan on the part of Marechal
Foch and his aids.

I believe that in the Rhineland a hostile military occupation is seen at its best; and at its best, I can say from personal observation, it is brutal; it is provocative; it is continuing war.

A temporary occupation was, as I have said, inevitable, and its continuance until the disarmament of Germany has proceeded to a point satisfactory to the allies is probably desirable, but its maintenance as a debt-collecting agency through fifteen years is unthinkable—it will be a running sore. America is today participating in this "occupation" with more troops than any nation excepting France, and yet we have elected to place entirely outside of our own influence the character of the "occupation" and the length of its continuance.

During the fourteen months in which I worked as a member of the Rhineland Commission, I became daily more shocked that any responsible man should be willing to curse the world with such a hatred- and war-breeding institution as this. I could multiply the details until every American would be equally shocked, but I will leave it to the imagination of my readers to decide for themselves what would be the ultimate result of a fifteen-year occupation of the New England states by victorious German or foreign troops.

I received a letter from President Wilson (quoted below) and, under his influence, my letter of May twenty-seventh was made the basis for the Convention with Germany. I have described this affair at length because my letter happened to change the occupation from a military to a civilian one. The President's letter was as follows:

Paris, 29 May, 1919

My dear Mr. Noyes:

Thank you sincerely for your letter of yesterday.

I find myself in agreement with you in what you say of arrangements that ought to be made with regard to military occupation of Rhine Provinces and I am sincerely obliged to you for your helpful letter.

Cordially and sincerely yours,

(Signed) Woodrow Wilson

Mr. P. B. Noyes
American Mission
Hotel Crillon

One of my most valued possessions, this letter now hangs framed above my desk, in memory of a great and tragically misunderstood leader.

To return to my story, I was told afterward, by a man very close to the President (one of his fellow Peace Delegates) that he greatly disliked the Military Convention, but "was at his wits end" and that my letter decided him. A committee of five, representing each of the Allies, was constituted, with instructions to "draw up a convention with Germany—exactly along the lines of Mr. Noyes' letter."

Lord Robert Cecil was made Chairman of this Committee. Marechal Foch represented France and John W. Davis, then Ambassador to Great Britain, was summoned to Paris to represent the United States. He insisted that I attend the Committee meetings and invited me to his apartment in the evening to learn whether I was "satisfied with the way the discussions were going."

Sitting there at the Quai d'Orsay I listened to the angry opposition of Marechal Foch. However, on the last day of the meeting, I had the satisfaction of hearing Lord Robert Cecil say, "I might sympathize with some of the points made by Marechal Foch, but we were not told to map out a policy. We were told to draw up a Convention with Germany exactly on the lines of Mr. Noyes' letter. Now let's get busy and finish it."

The result was a Civilian Occupation governed by and under the rules of the Rhineland Commission; with troops in each of the four areas, to be called in by the Rhineland Commission if events seemed to demand it but not to be called in by any other authority than the Commission.

I enjoyed my work in Coblenz tremendously, but most of the fourteen months I spent there were fighting months. The fights were often bitter, and I did not win all of them. One reward for my efforts, which I particularly valued, came from my friend, Bernard Baruch, which, at the risk of seeming egotistical, I should like to quote. "His work was outstanding. The Rhineland occupation became the center of European scheming and struggling for national advantage, and Mr. Noyes fought for American ideals skillfully and as successfully as was possible in the face of the fact that the United States was steadily retreating toward national isolation."

Perhaps this quotation is sufficient as a resumé of my Rhineland experience, but one incident may suggest the kind of tactics I was forced to employ.

Our Commission was empowered to nullify any German-made law that threatened "the safety or comfort of allied troops." At one of our meetings M. Tirard, Chairman of the Commission, announced that a recently passed German law authorizing "shop committees" was regarded by his superiors in Paris as dangerous. He was "instructed to have it nullified."

I objected; I insisted that our franchise gave us no power to nullify such a law, and assured M. Tirard that the American people would certainly object to any interference with local labor affairs. Tirard's answer was that he had no option; that his superiors insisted on nullification, fearing that the shop committee idea would spread through Alsace into France.

I knew that a nullification vote could be carried in spite of me, since Sir Harold, who would have voted with me, was temporarily in London, and since the Belgian conferee agreed with M. Tirard.

I had early discovered that the French were far superior to us Anglo-Saxons in defeating a move by tying up their opponents with silken cords, as Gulliver was tied by the Lilliputians. But I also discovered they could not cope with unorthodox methods, so I decided to ignore conventional diplomatic procedure. I sent word to M. Tirard that, if the nullification were voted, I should call the twenty-five or thirty international newspaper correspondents who haunted our offices and give them an interview. I should tell them that the American Commissioner did not believe that the Commission's charter gave it any power to interfere with local labor laws which did not threaten the "safety" or "comfort" of the troops. Furthermore, that I knew the American people would be shocked by such interference.

After much argument, M. Roussillier, the French Deputy Commissioner, went to M. Tirard, "to report my threat." Later he revisited me and, with truly French graciousness, told me that Mr. Tirard gave so much weight to my opinion, that he was taking the night train to Paris, where he would tell the Premier of the situation.

The next morning M. Roussillier entered my office with a very friendly smile on his face. He said, "M. Tirard was able to persuade his superiors in Paris to drop the nullification."

That was not the only struggle in which I was forced to use (I hope for good ends) somewhat drastic methods. One other interesting incident in Sir Harold Stuart's and my struggle to carry out the policy laid down for the Rhineland

Commission by the Peace Conference will perhaps show the kind of work I was engaged in for a year and a half.

General de Goutte, international head of all the Allied armies, suddenly announced to us that the French authorities in Paris had instructed him to mobilize his troops for an invasion of Trans-Rhine Germany through Darmstadt and Frankfort. Since, under the Treaty of Occupation, Allied troops could not be mobilized without authorization by our Commission, the general asked M. Tirard to have such permission voted by us. Such an invasion was directly contrary to the provisions of the Peace Treaty, except in case of provocative military action by Germany, which had not occurred. It was, however an expression of France's well-known ambition for a complete military occupation of German territory.

I was very much opposed to the move, and I believe that Sir Harold would have stood with me. Unfortunately, he was again in London at the time, and his Deputy, Mr. Arnold Robertson, who was strongly pro-French in his sympathies, voted with M. Tirard. I had expected the Belgian Commissioner, M. Rolin-Jaequemyns, also would vote affirmatively, but, to the great surprise of everyone, he voted with me against the move. However, at a meeting the following morning he reversed himself and voted affirmatively as we had first expected.

The whole incident was so inexplicable that the next time I went to London I traveled by the way of Brussels to see what our American Minister to Belgium, Brand Whitlock, could tell me about Rolin-Jaequemyns' vote. I had stopped over in Brussels often during the previous year so that Brand Whitlock and I had become good friends.

He was greatly interested and said, "I keep a diary. Let's

see what my diary can tell us." The diary gave us a curious explanation. "On the day when the Belgian Commissioner voted no, King Albert had attended the Council Meeting. The next day the King was absent; the commissioner, that day, voted yes." In addition, Whitlock had noted that the night before this final meeting, special agents had arrived from Paris who, he thought, were offering Belgium some favorable modifications of their agreement regarding the "border railways," possibly in return for his co-operation in the invasion of Trans-Rhine Germany.

The French invasion was a failure. A few civilians were killed through accidental machine-gun fire on curious onlookers in Frankfort, and the troops returned to occupied territory. It seemed to me that the French were somewhat embarrassed.

Only a few moments after the shooting occurred I had word of this regrettable incident by telephone from Floyd Gibbons, one of the leading American newspaper correspondents. He had been present during the incident and got into a drugstore just in time, but his automobile had several bullet holes in it.

It happened that Coblenz, where the Rhineland High Commission established itself, was in the American area. As a result of this I had charge of billeting the Commission's personnel and technical control of the city's houses. Under this arrangement I had to allocate houses for the "Top Brass" of the Commission and the Army. General Allen and Sir Harold Stuart were billeted in what were practically palaces on the Rhine Anlagen, looking down upon the river.

My wife and younger daughter Barbara and son Peter (Pierrepont T.) had joined me in August, 1919, and I chose for our quarters a large and comfortable house in Mainzer

Strasse. This house, while perhaps lacking the prestige of the mansions on the Rhine Anlagen, was beautiful without and within and, what was very essential, it was spacious enough to give Wallace Day, my deputy, and his family a fine apartment and still leave a wing for the German family who, until our coming, had occupied the whole house.

The chance for us to live in a house with the naturally hostile owners was a valuable experience and gave me a practical insight into one of the constant causes of friction which can attend the billeting of an occupying force upon a conquered people. One of the causes was the ruling against fraternization. It was against orders by both Army and Commission for the occupying forces to fraternize with the Germans. This might have been necessary, but it helped keep the humiliating issue alive and was disobeyed, of course, by many of the rank and file of the Army, though it was strictly observed by the officers and the entire staff of the Commission.

For us, it was gratifying to know that the original owners were still allowed to live in a part of their own house and were free to enjoy the beautiful gardens when they wished.

During the week between Christmas and New Year's Day, the Rhine and the Mosel Rivers, owing to recent heavy rains, began to rise to flood stage, causing much inundation of cellars and even ground floors of buildings, especially along the Rhine Anlagen. Damage and general inconvenience were widespread, of course, but one resulting incident caused me great concern, perhaps because my civilian conditioning as a business man rather than as a soldier made the rigid adherence to army regulations instead of plain common sense seem both outrageous and unrealistic.

It happened that the army had recently sold some ten

thousand no-longer-needed army trucks to Great Britain, for the price, as I remember it, of something like fifteen million dollars. These trucks had been parked temporarily on the low land bordering the Mosel River and with a flood warning out, it was obvious that they were in danger. Since muddy flood water would certainly damage them, if not ruin them altogether, I went to General Allen, the Commander of the U.S. troops in the area, and suggested that they be moved to higher ground.

The general was not interested. This was not official army business; if the British wanted to attend to the matter, that was their affair, and in any case, since, in those days we had none of today's marvelous moving equipment—bulldozers, hoisting trucks and so on—he said the job was impossible. His responsibility was only for army stores and apparently, for the flooded cellars of his own and other U.S. officers' billets.

Since I could not persuade him, I gave up for the moment, although I confess I was shocked at what seemed to me a failure to live up to the spirit of an honest bargain. Later that week, the waters which in the first stage had only covered the wheels of the parked trucks, rose to the highest level since 1882, and this time the whole fleet of trucks was completely inundated. Before the worst happened, I approached General Allen again and urged that if machinery was not available and the new owners were too far away, at Bonn and Cologne, to rescue the property, it would certainly be possible for us, with our own idle troops actually in the city, to move the trucks by sheer man power. I suppose this suggestion was shocking to the tradition-bound West Point mind, of which General Allen was a prime example. I can only say that it was at least equally shocking to me. When the flood had abated, damage to the trucks was estimated at five million dollars, which was necessarily deducted from the agreed price.

As I have said, many of the imposing houses along the Rhine Anlagen were partially flooded so that the general and Sir Harold were obliged to move temporarily to the Coblenzer Hof. I lunched with them the day they moved and kidded them by telling of a famous motto painted behind the bar of the old Knickerbocker Hotel in New York City. It read, "Ye canna' be baith graund an' comfortable." I said, "You and Sir Harold are very grand living on the Rhine Anlagen, but I am thoroughly comfortable back on Mainzer Strasse without a drop of water in my cellar."

There was one French officer, General Payot, a huge man, who is worth mentioning, partly because of the savage battles we fought with him over the carrying out of definite instructions by the Peace Commission in Paris, but also for the wonderful part he played during the war. When the Austrians were chasing the beaten and fleeing Italians at Caporetto, General Payot is said to have organized and sent a solid trainload of French troops from Paris to Italy every twenty minutes for twenty-four hours. I enjoyed him particularly because he spoke French so slowly and plainly that I could understand him. I am also, possibly, influenced by the fact that later Sir Harold and I beat him after a three-hour struggle over an important "Instruction" of the Peace Commission in Paris, which he had refused to obey. He fought us singlehanded, without help from M. Tirard and before the assembled staffs of all the Commissions. One cannot help respecting a bold adversary.

As long as the Peace Conference remained in Paris, I was obliged to be there almost every week. Afterwards I

visited London at intervals, on stated occasions calling at
the Foreign Office with Sir Harold Stuart. On one of these
London visits I spent an enjoyable weekend with H. G. Wells
at his country home in Essex.

I especially recall this visit because, as we strolled in a
neighboring park one morning, I asked him whether he still
thought that I had no "sense of State," as he had said of me
in his book, *The Future in America,* written after his visit to
Oneida in 1903. In it he drew a picture of me as one kind of
typical American. He wrote, "I never met a man before so
firmly gripped by the romantic, constructive and adventur-
ous element of business, so little concerned about personal
riches or the accumulation of wealth. He illuminated much
that had been dark to me in the American character. I think
better of business by reason of him. And time after time I
tried him upon politics. It came to nothing. Making a new
world was, he thought a rhetorical flourish about futile and
troublesome activities, and politicians merely a disreputable
sort of parasite upon honorable people who made chains
and plated spoons. All his constructive instincts, all his devotion, were for Oneida and its enterprises. America was
just the impartial space, the large liberty, in which Oneida
grew, the Stars and Stripes a wide sanction akin to the impartial, irresponsible, harboring sky overhead. Sense of the
State had never grown in him—can now, I felt convinced,
never grow. . . . But someday, I like to imagine, the World
State, and not Oneida corporations, and a nobler trade than
traps, will command such services as his."

When I reminded him of this dictum, at first he looked
puzzled. Then his face broke into a broad smile. He exclaimed
in his high-pitched voice, "Did I say that?" I must confess
that it was a pleasure to discredit this one of his prophecies.

Because of the delay in signing the Peace Treaty with Germany the Allies were still technically at war with that country and, though officially the Interallied Rhineland Commission was not yet a High Commission and did not have full power, there were still endless matters concerning the occupation to be discussed and arranged daily at the Secretariat.

The social life, however, was in no way restrained by the lagging political affairs. Army officers' wives were being allowed to join their husbands. The Casino Club, the very exclusive German Officers' Club, had been taken over by our army and once a week a grand ball was given there for the officers, their wives, the Commissioners and their wives, the ranking members of the secretariats and a score or more of girls working for the Y.M.C.A. Soon we had a wide acquaintance with the army personnel.

M. Tirard's sister came to act as hostess for him. He had moved into the Oberpraesidium Palace which he had had hung with many of the rare tapestries from the French Museum at Compeigne. After Lady Stuart arrived, she and Sir Harold established themselves in the beautiful house on the Rhine Anlagen I have mentioned before. Baron Rolin-Jaequemyns and his family were soon settled in another fine house on the Rhine. With their coming our official family was complete and social functions became part of the Order of the Day.

From the first there was a constant stream of important persons both from home and abroad visiting Coblenz for business or pleasure, as well as many commanding officers of the French and British armies, whose entertainment I shared with General Allen. Since most of the entertaining was done in our homes, our wives and families had an important part to play.

Fortunately for us, our daughter Constance, on her way home from a year's trip to Australia and the Orient with her husband, Miles E. Robertson ("Dunc" to everyone who knows him), at that time our Export Manager, was glad to stop over with us for several months while Dunc went home to report on the conditions of foreign trade. She found our Coblenz life delightful and I need not say was a great social asset.

Before I arrived in Coblenz, General Liggett, then in command of the American Army on the Rhine, had taken over the magnificent Festhalle for an entertainment center for the soldiers, and it comprised everything the most home-sick doughboy could ask for in the way of distraction. It contained a gymnasium, bowling alleys, rooms for billiards, pool and cards, baths, a cafeteria, a dance hall, a P.X. store, writing rooms, library and a splendid auditorium which was used for movies, lectures and, on Sundays, for the Germans' superb Symphony Orchestra whose concerts the citizens of the town were allowed to attend. The Commissioners' families were welcome to attend any program they might choose. A great asset, also, to music lovers was the Grand Opera at the Stadt Theatre three times a week.

So much for the social side of our life in Coblenz, but we never lost sight of the underlying reason for our being there. There was a burning question being asked continually: When will the United States ratify the treaty? France, Britain and Belgium had delayed signing, in the hope that all the Allies could sign at the same time, but still our Senate argued and debated. Why? our Allies asked. It was unthinkable that our Senate should not support a President who had been so joyfully acclaimed as the Great Deliverer by all but the enemy countries. Now it could only be construed by France and Britain as the unwillingness of America to share the responsibility for postwar reconstruction.

Some thought that the United States was waiting till Armistice Day, November eleventh, to make the grand gesture, but that day came and went without the long-hoped-for word. Then, a crushing blow, a message came through that President Wilson had suffered a cerebral hemorrhage and was in a very critical condition. That settled it. Italy had already signed on October 8, 1919. On January 10, 1920, Great Britain, France and Belgium ratified the Treaty of Peace with Germany. Only the United States abstained. Up to the last few days, still anticipating that the United States Senate would vote favorably, M. Tirard had invited all the Commissioners, Deputies and their wives to a grand jubilation dinner at the Palace. We went, the Noyeses and Days, but not as Commissioner and Deputy. Protocol decreed that Day and I and General Allen as well, be seated "below the salt," as it were, though our wives were honored as formerly.

I felt no personal humiliation. The Commissioners knew all along that I had been a sincere and ardent advocate of American ratification. Now they were still friendly, but I felt positive shame for my country that in a time of great world distress they would let party prejudice influence so gravely portentous a decision.

At this point I would have been glad to go home, but the State Department urged me to stay on "for the present" as an "official observer." The British, French and Belgians also pressed me to stay and insisted I take part in all discussions even though I had no vote. This I agreed to do, but by June all special representatives of our country were being withdrawn and I was only too willing to go. Therefore, with my family and the Days, we left the Rhineland.

After a pleasant two weeks' stay in England where Constance and my son-in-law were living, and an interesting motor trip through Wales, we returned to Oneida. It had been an intensely interesting experience, but I was glad to get back to America and resume my responsibilities as President of Oneida Community, Ltd.

As a footnote to the Coblenz chapter, there was one last curious incident. When my duties at the Commission were over, I spent a week in Berlin with the object of learning more about the whole situation. I had a most interesting time. I met the heads of government and discussed the country's economic situation with leading manufacturers and bankers.

M. Tirard had made an appointment with me before I went to Berlin, but without stating its object. In order to meet my Berlin engagements, I had been obliged to postpone this appointment. When I got back to Coblenz I learned from Sir Harold that the visit had undoubtedly cost me the French *Légion d'honneur*. During my absence, Tirard had with great ceremony presented this famous decoration to Sir Harold. It was Sir Harold's opinion—and probably the truth—that the fact I had allowed the German chancellor to entertain me had evidently displeased the French. I got no *Légion d'honneur*. I did not seriously mind the loss, since I had taken this job strictly on a business basis and in any case, decorations were out of my line. As I told Sir Harold, quite truthfully, "Where I come from, the Legion of Honor wouldn't do me a bit of good."

CHAPTER XIX

It HAPPENED THAT before leaving Coblenz I had written a long letter to Albert and the Board of Directors of the Oneida Community, Ltd. telling of my fears, aroused by the business boom reported in American newspapers. I suggested that our Company play safe, get its finances into a thoroughly liquid position. On my return to Oneida in the summer of 1920, I found the boom still on, but when the management showed me orders for more Community Plate than we could possibly manufacture, I apologized for my conservatism. I remember saying, "Perhaps I'm getting old and cautious."

A month later the boom exploded and panic conditions ensued. Throughout the fall and winter months, the mails brought few orders but there were floods of telegrams of cancellation in which were expressed, or evident, customers' hopes that they were in time to head off deliveries. The panic continued all through 1921 and although this was a short panic, as panics go, it was a real one, as businessmen who went through it will testify. Our own Company loss, during those two years, reached a figure of one and a half million dollars, and our balance sheet, as of January, 1922, showed bank loans of nearly two million dollars.

Our stockholders' loss was not the only tragedy. In the ensuing readjustment we eventually lost Albert as General Manager. After a period of acting as co-manager with me, to please the banks, and after a protracted leave of absence with pay, he asked to be relieved of all managerial responsibility in January, 1925, though he later took brilliant charge of certain new departments which needed intensive development.

It is simple justice to one of the finest and most idealistic men I ever knew to note that during the five years when Albert was acting head of the Company, the Board did much to improve the working and living conditions of employees. This was his great enthusiasm. One of Albert's outstanding accomplishments was a formula which provided that after deducting 7 per cent on the Company's capital investment, half the balance should be paid in cash to the employees and the other half added to the surplus.

As everyone knows, general business quickly recovered from the 1921 panic and soon developed into another boom which lasted until 1929. The extent of this boom and the liberality of Albert's formula is shown by the fact that at the end of 1922 more than three hundred thousand dollars were distributed as a wage bonus, and nearly five hundred thousand in 1923.

Another of Albert's achievements was the consolidation of several small employee associations (health, recreation and some others) into one large group called the Community Associated Clubs—the familiar "C.A.C." of our day—for which an ample clubhouse was provided. Our representative on the Village School Board was backed by contribution of half the cost of the grade-school and high-school buildings, and we entered into an agreement to pay one half the salaries of teachers; this to ensure a grade of teachers better than the "district" could at that time afford. Albert pushed forward house bonuses for employees building in Sherrill and persuaded the Company to contribute $110,000 to an Oneida water project which would assure good water for the village.

It would require pages to tell of all that Albert did to

develop the human side of the Company's ambitions but, since I have promised to make this part of my story sketchy, I shall content myself with the statement that Albert earned the admiration and affection of every man and woman in our Company.

At that Directors' Meeting in 1925 when Ab resigned, I announced that I would act as manager for one year more; that in January, 1926, the Directors would be called upon to elect a new General Manager. As I mentioned before, Miles E. Robertson (Dunc) was elected to that position. I retained the Presidency.

From 1926 to the present day, the story of Oneida Ltd. is chiefly Dunc's story. I hope that at some later time he will write it. Unfortunately, he is a very modest man and little inclined to personal publicity, but his account of the growth of the Company during the last thirty-one years could be as stimulating to ambitious young men as the "success stories" so popular with certain magazines.

I shall, at least, suggest the quality and results of his management during those years. He is a man of courage, but his natural aggressiveness is always balanced by an instinct which insists upon a careful study of the pertinent facts and possibilities of each situation. With him, negative facts do not necessarily forbid action, but they are always given thorough consideration. He took this Company through the perilous years of 1930 to 1933 with both courage and wisdom. In 1933, when the clouds had lifted a little and before any of our competitors got into action, Dunc "picked up the ball" (he was a football star in college) and Oneida Ltd. was the only silverware manufacturer that made a profit that year.

Later, in 1941–45, when our output was shifted from commercial business to war matériel of various kinds, from engine-bearings to bomb-cases, his efficient and farsighted management won for the Company the coveted Navy "E" for excellence. After the war, reconversion to civilian business, a job almost as difficult, was successfully accomplished.

Figures will, perhaps, best tell of the quality of his management. By 1950, Oneida Ltd.'s annual sales were nearly three times the sales made in any year before 1927. Starting in 1933 with no "operating surplus," he had by 1950 built up a surplus of nearly $11,000,000 in addition to wage bonuses, during the period, of nearly $9,000,000. He had made additions to the Pension Fund of $4,400,000 and appropriation of many millions for the furthering of factory, home and recreational improvements, as well as uninterrupted payments of liberal dividends to the stockholders.

Having declared that this is his story, I shall say no more except that today Dunc Robertson enjoys the confidence and affection of everyone connected with the Company and the respect of the very wide circle of outside businessmen with whom he has come in contact.

On August 18, 1950—my eightieth birthday—I resigned the Presidency of Oneida Ltd. and Dunc was elected to that office. Two years later, together with two of my earliest associates, Stephen Leonard and Grosvenor Allen, I resigned from the Board of Directors to make room for younger executives. For us three Directors Emeritus, the curtain falls—never on our interest in the Company's progress—but on any interference with a management in which we have perfect confidence.

After Dunc took over the position of General Manager, in 1926, my own duties were lightened and I found time for a number of new and interesting outside activities. The first of these was related to my Coblenz experience. After my departure from Germany, it had been decided to place both the civil and military governments of the Occupied Area under the army. From what I, myself, had observed, it was my considered judgment that even with the best will in the world, any purely military rule of a civilian population is bound to work hardships. General Henry Allen, commander of our forces in the Rhineland, was an able officer, but he was a man of rigid and legalistic mind, who must be expected to deal with civil problems in a military way. My friend Sir Harold Stuart had retired in favor of his deputy commissioner, Mr. Arnold Robertson, a confessed Francophile. And, as I knew too well, the attitude of the French and Belgians would, left to themselves, result in a permanent stranglehold on German economy.

It was with this thought in mind that, after my return to America, I began to speak and write in an attempt to convince my fellow citizens that, although the Treaty of Versailles had been signed, the world had not and could not hope for any lasting peace along the path we were treading. My first little book, *While Europe Waits for Peace*, was published in 1921, and from that time, for many years, I published articles and traveled widely speaking on this subject, urging that the United States join the League of Nations.

Shortly before President Wilson's death I had visited him at his home in Washington. Contrary to the stories of his mental failure, I found him surprisingly wide-awake and interested in the war settlement. Referring to the League of Nations and my speeches urging America to join the League he said—and without the personal bitterness I had been led to expect—"They'll have to come to it. It's absolutely necessary for the peace of the world."

I will simply add that after the terrible years of the Second World War, they did "come to it," merely substituting "United Nations" for Wilson's "League."

Mrs. Wilson, writing me after my visit, said, "My husband sends you his best regards and says it's fine to know that one man is keeping the torch burning."

But it was hard to make anyone listen. Those were boom years; business in the country was incredibly prosperous; the Germans had been soundly beaten—what was to be feared? My own view certainly saw appalling dangers ahead, and I suppose it was this unescapable conviction, conscious or subconscious, that brought into being my second book. Its conception was rather curious. I remember that one day in 1927 I had been slightly feverish with a cold and had taken a short nap. When I awoke, the whole framework of a story was in my head, and I knew I must write it.

I had always intended to write someday and it is amusing to recall that when H. G. Wells was visiting us in Kenwood, twenty years before, I had mentioned the fact. Wells's reply— "Yes. Everyone thinks he'll write a book when his brains are old and stiff"—came to my mind now, but did not deter me. I had something which must be said, something which obsessed me like a flash of terrifying prophecy, and although I had never considered writing fiction, this message, I knew, must be in the form of a novel. What I foresaw was the doom of mankind if it allowed its ability to destroy to grow beyond control to such a degree that we might be living in a world haunted by our own fear of another's fear. My story envisaged the development of an atomic weapon and showed what might be the logical end of a world-wide competition in such armament.

I called it *The Pallid Giant*—fear. It went through

several editions, but, Cassandra-like, its warning was little heard. Eighteen years later, in 1945, after the actual bombing of Hiroshima, a publisher remembered my story, and, after a slight revision, republished and sold many thousand copies under the title, *Gentlemen, You Are Mad*. This second version, of course, reached a wider audience, but I still wish I could shout its message from the housetops. The whole message of my book is contained in a little verse I wrote for the heading of its first chapter:

> If man unsheathe too far that flaming sword—
> The power of life and death—
> The pallid giant, Fear, will seize
> And plunge its blade into man's breast.

Another literary effort and one which gave me much pleasure to write was a story of my own childhood in the old Oneida Community, entitled, *My Father's House*. It is, I confess, an odd sort of biography in that it ends with me, at the age of sixteen, on the threshold of the strange and rather terrifying "Outside" World. This book, published in 1936, was most kindly received by the critics and I have real satisfaction in knowing that it is still in demand and that it has, I am told, pleased my readers.

At the time of its publication I had no thought of continuing the story of my life, but so many letters from readers, known and unknown to me, urged it that, just as the story of the original Oneida Community has been told, so the story of its child, The Oneida Community Limited and, one might say, its grandchild, Oneida Ltd., should also be told. On the personal side, it has been interesting to retrace, for myself as well as for others, the unpredictable course of my own life.

As I have said before, so many of the extraordinary experiences of my career have been totally unexpected: my return to Kenwood, when I thought I had left it forever and was on the highroad to worldly success; the interesting and important assignment I was given in Washington, during World War I; the almost fantastic happenstance of my appointment to the Rhineland Commission. All these were dropped in my lap, unsought and unimagined, by a kindly fate to which I shall always be grateful. I would not have missed any of them for the world.

I supposed I had had my share of adventures, but during the summer of 1930 there came to me another of those opportunities that have made my life more than ordinarily interesting.

Oneida Ltd. had recently bought the Wm. A. Rogers silverware manufacturing business and on a day in July were holding an Agents' Meeting in Niagara Falls when a telephone call came to me from Governor Roosevelt in Albany.

The Governor told me that Bernard Baruch had persuaded the State Legislature to build a really modern spa at Saratoga at a cost, it was roughly estimated, of about six million dollars. One million had been appropriated to start the work and a second million was promised for the next year.

Responsibility for building and operating the modernized spa was to be in the hands of a commission of six men to be appointed by the Governor, and, the Governor added, Mr. Baruch wished me to be one of the commissioners. With my present duties I told him that I could not find time to do justice to such an enterprise, but the Governor was quite insistent. He assured me that it would mean only a day at Saratoga once in two or three months. In the end my friendship for Baruch led me to accept the appointment.

Two weeks later the Governor called me again on the telephone. He said that Baruch was in Paris and wanted me to join him there so that he and I and an architect could visit some of the principal spas of Europe. At first I said it couldn't be done. Then a happy thought came to me. My older daughter, Constance, and I had often talked of a trip to Europe together. It was now midsummer, the dull season of our business; why not see if she could go with me? . . . She could and would. So, to make a long story short, Constance and I met Baruch in Paris, ready for the tour. We spent a pleasant two days discussing the itinerary with him but, as it happened, Baruch, himself, could not leave Paris immediately, so he suggested that we use his car and chauffeur for the drive to Germany where he and the architect would meet us at Bad Nauheim. This we did, going by way of Saarbrucken, Worms and Frankfort, and it was a delightful trip. At Nauheim our party made the first of its inspections of the method and equipment of notable European spas. From there, with Baruch and Mr. Joseph Friedlander, the architect, we went to Bad Kissingen and Bad Brucknauer, spas specializing in treatment for heart ailments. Mr. Baruch could go no farther, but wanted Connie, Friedlander and me to see Montecatini and Salso Maggiore in Italy and on the way back to visit Royat, Vichy and Vitel in France and Harrogate and Bath in England.

What astonished and shocked me was the fact that Baruch's name was not scheduled as chairman of the commission. Upon my return to America, I discussed the matter fully with the Governor and decided that I must talk with Baruch, person to person, so called him by telephone from the Governor's Mansion in Albany. My purpose was to remind him that undoubtedly the legislature, in appropriating the money for the development of the spa, had expected that he would head the commission. Both Mr. Roosevelt and I urged that he take the chairmanship for at least the first year. However, not even a half hour's telephone argument could move him, and I went home to Oneida, promising that I would call him again. In the end my associates at Oneida urged me to accept the appointment which I did.

As had happened in all the other extracurricular activities I undertook, the directing of the spa's development and management was not only more arduous but more interesting than I had foreseen. From that day on for more than twenty-two years, at least once a month I drove the hundred and ten miles from Oneida to Saratoga to meet with the commission or to confer with the officials of the institution. Saratoga came to seem almost as homelike as Oneida and I shall always hold it and the many friends I made there in warm affection. One commissioner I could always count on to be present at our meetings with his much-valued advice was Frederick H. Ecker, President of the Metropolitan Life Insurance Company.

Our architect, Mr. Friedlander, did an inspired job in the planning of the new spa and construction on the first buildings was begun in 1932. Every prospect, apparently, was favorable—and then came the blow. The increasing financial depression of the early 'thirties led the New York State Legislature to announce that there would be no more money appropriated for Saratoga. Our only recourse was to issue bonds to finance the completion of our work.

We had spent the first two million appropriated and now, with the beautiful Hall of Springs not yet completed and other buildings well started, we were suddenly without funds. We felt like a boy whose clothes had been stolen while he was in swimming. Fortunately, my six associates on the commission were Dr. Carl Comstock of Saratoga, Mr. Morton Schwartz of New York City, Mr. Frederick H. Ecker of New York City, Mr. Jerome Barnum of Syracuse, Dr. Whittington Gorham of Albany and Mr. Edward Butler of Buffalo. In this connection I must also mention Mr. Spencer Eddy, Counsel for the Commission, in whose hands we put all the financial transactions connected with the bond issue, a job requiring all his legal skill and one which he carried out most satisfactorily. They were all important men in the business or political world, so that with Baruch's help they were able to arrange, through Jesse Jones of the Reconstruction Finance Corporation, that our bonds would be bought by the State of New York. For this purpose the commission was created an Authority. This was what my father would have called a "special providence." It saved our bacon, as the saying goes, and I feel a deep satisfaction not only in the job well done but in the fact that, before I resigned from the commission, every cent of those bonds was paid in full.

During the next few years we built two handsome and perfectly equipped modern bath houses, The Roosevelt Baths, an up-to-date bottling plant for the Saratoga Spring Waters which are widely sold, a fine Administration Building with a theatre and stage for medical conventions or to be used in the season as a summer theatre for the entertainment of our guests. We built also a Recreation Center with swimming pool, gymnasium and what we called a Cardiac Golf Course —no grades over four per cent—also a golf house and archery butts. What was even more important, our new hotel, The Gideon Putnam, was so luxurious and so attractive that year after year its handsome profits enabled us to pay off our entire bonded indebtedness.

In this whole undertaking I recognized that a large part of our success was owing to the unusual ability of Cyrus Elmore, Superintendent of the Spa, who, like Wallace Day in the Rhineland, gave to the enterprise his wholehearted service and devotion. He had been trained by the Spa's former Superintendent Jones and was thoroughly familiar with the management of the older Lincoln and Washington Baths, the Mineral Springs, the old bottling plant and grounds, and so was able to fit into this larger position with ease. From the second-growth pine forest that covered our Reservation about two miles from town, he was able to clear land for the building sites, always keeping pace with the needs of the building and landscape architects, so that when each building was finished and equipped the surroundings were completed also and ready to be opened to the public.

It was in the year 1950, on my eightieth birthday, that I resigned my position on the Saratoga Authority.

Here, I think, is the place to say what is in my heart about Bernard Baruch. Simply to know of him as a world figure and a great statesman is to admire him deeply. To know him as a friend is to add to admiration a sincere affection, and that has been my rare privilege.

His idealism and ever-present interest in world welfare have always stimulated me, and my life has been richer not only for the interesting experiences he has put in my way but for his example as a man who gladly places his material means, his time and thought at the service of mankind whenever they are needed.

One other curious quirk of fate placed me as a trustee of Colgate University—my own alma mater—from 1927 to 1950. I say curious because, when I first entered the college in 1888 —it was then Madison University—I could not but be aware that my very name was under the cloud of public disapproval that then shadowed every mention of the Oneida Community. As I have related, this shadow could not black out, even at that tender age, my own natural optimism and enthusiasm for life, so that my two years as a student at Colgate were happy ones. As an older man, my twenty-three years as trustee gave me not only a deeper affection for the college, but a deeper understanding of its problems. It was an interesting and rewarding experience. Before I finally retired in 1950, I was deeply touched at receiving from the University the award of the honorary degree of L.H.D. My children are wondering now what to do with the handsome gown and hood, which I shall never wear again.

At the same time as my retirement from these other offices, I also severed my connection with a Syracuse bank, of which I had been a director for thirty-eight years. The time had come to withdraw from such activities. They are the rightful prerogative of younger men, and I wish for them in their turn, all the satisfactions they once brought me.

Before I bring my story to a close I want to express my deep thankfulness for the way Providence has cared for our Company's future. Many of the important positions in the management of the factories, the offices and the selling force have been taken over by the very able sons of my generation in Kenwood, Sherrill and from "outside," who are giving to their work a high degree of ability and the same enthusiasm and loyalty as did my own generation.

Only one interest—and that unofficial—will remain with me for the rest of my life—Oneida Limited. Its welfare, its problems, its disappointments or rejoicings will be a part of my life always. As Honorary President I am still invited to attend its directors' meetings or any others that interest me.

My son Peter, now General Manager, my son-in-law, Dunc, and my other young friends know, I'm sure, that they have not only my interest but my deep affection and my confidence in their dedication to the dream that has been the center of my life. More power to them, and I shall be on the side lines applauding every goal they make.

A PERSONAL POSTSCRIPT:

When, at my final meeting of the Board of Directors, I resigned the Presidency, I added a few words—personal words—the result of an idea which surprised me, I think, as much as it did my friends. It was this: that while writing the story of my life, upon which I am now engaged, it dawned upon me that nature never intended me for a businessman. It intended me for a preacher. I have always enjoyed selling ideas more than selling spoons, but in my youth I had to learn to sell spoons in order to sell my ideas.

My father was a preacher, descendant of a long line of preachers which reaches back into English history as well as our own. Although I never suspected it before, it occurs to me now that I, the black sheep, perhaps, of my father's flock, did, after all, inherit the old persistent passion. Looking back, I cannot honestly say now that I regret my choice of life work. If I had not chosen it, perhaps the present Oneida Limited, child of the old Oneida Community, would never have come into being. But I do see, to my own astonishment, that the impulse that motivated it was not really commercial, not really worldly in the accepted sense. It was, like my father's, an unconscious need to demonstrate the power of an idea. Insofar as I have accomplished this aim, I can say that I am satisfied. Life has been very good to me.